WILDFLOWERS
of the INDIANA DUNES NATIONAL PARK

QUARRY BOOKS

an imprint of
INDIANA UNIVERSITY PRESS

WILDFLOWERS

of the INDIANA DUNES NATIONAL PARK

**NATHANAEL PILLA &
SCOTT NAMESTNIK**

This book is a publication of

Quarry Books

an imprint of
Indiana University Press
Office of Scholarly Publishing
Herman B Wells Library 350
1320 East 10th Street
Bloomington, Indiana 47405 USA

iupress.org

© 2022 by Indiana University Press

Printed in Korea

First printing 2022

Library of Congress Cataloging-in-Publication Data

Names: Pilla, Nathanael, author. | Namestnik, Scott, author.
Title: Wildflowers of the Indiana Dunes National Park /
    Nathanael Pilla and Scott Namestnik.
Description: Bloomington : Indiana University Press, 2022. |
    Includes bibliographical references and index.
Identifiers: LCCN 2021040950 (print) | LCCN 2021040951 (ebook) |
    ISBN 9780253060419 (paperback) | ISBN 9780253060426 (ebook)
Subjects: LCSH: Wild flowers—Indiana—Identification. |
    Indiana Dunes National Park (Ind.). | Field guides.
Classification: LCC QK159 .P55 2022 (print) | LCC
    QK159 (ebook) | DDC 582.1309772/9—dc23
LC record available at https://lccn.loc.gov/2021040950
LC ebook record available at https://lccn.loc.gov/2021040951

CONTENTS

Acknowledgments　*vii*

1. Introduction　1
2. Brief History of the Indiana Dunes National Park　3
3. Using This Guide　7
4. Plant Communities of the Indiana Dunes　19
5. White, Cream, and Green Flowers　29
6. Yellow Flowers　189
7. Orange Flowers　277
8. Red Flowers　291
9. Pink, Lavender, and Magenta Flowers　313
10. Violet and Blue Flowers　381

Glossary　*427*

Recommended Reading and References　*437*

Index　*439*

ACKNOWLEDGMENTS

There are many people who have made the writing and publication of this book possible, either through direct assistance or indirectly through their guidance, instruction, encouragement, and support over the years. We apologize to any of those we've inadvertently failed to acknowledge.

First, we dedicate this book to Keith Board and David Hamilla, two dunes region botanists with huge and lasting impacts on us and the region as a whole, who both left us too soon.

We graciously thank those who have come before us in the study of the plants of the Indiana Dunes region. Keith Board, Marlin Bowles, Henry Chandler Cowles, Charles Deam, Ken Dritz, David Hamilla, Peter Hebert, E. J. Hill, Lois Howes, Ken Klick, Marcus Lyon, Dan Mason, Dan McDowell, Myrna Newgent, Julius Nieuwland, Sandy O'Brien, Noel Pavlovic, Donald Peattie, Herman Pepoon, Emma Pitcher, Barbara Plampin, Laura Rericha, Floyd Swink, Levi M. Umbach, and Gerould Wilhelm have laid the groundwork that we have built on to prepare this book.

A number of botanists and ecologists have accompanied us in the field and on botanical forays in the dunes region and beyond, and their influences are forever imprinted on us. We thank the following for their insight, guidance, and companionship in the field and for helping us to become better botanists: Mitch Alix, Karen Armina, Adam Balzer, Steve Barker, Tyler Bassett, Scott T. Bates, Matt Beatty, Christopher Benda, Eric Bird, Andrew Blackburn, Keith Board, Terry Bonace, Doug Botka, Laura Brennan, Lee Casebere, Young Choi, Noah Dell, Kevin Doyle, John Henry Drake, Jim Erdelac, Samantha Erdelac, Eric Fairlee, Mary Ann Feist, Sarah Felicelli, Mary Fisher-Dunham, Stephanie Frischie, Kathy Garness, Peter Grube, Charlotte Gyllenhaal, Molly

Hacker, David Hamilla, Drew Hart, Rich Hawksworth, Roger Hedge, Laura Henderson, Barbara Hellenthal, Andrew Hipp, Michael Homoya, Michael Huft, Jan Hunter, Samantha Kinsman, Paul Labus, Doug Ladd, Derek Luchik, Joy Marburger, Paul Marcum, Dan Mason, Dennis McKenna, Lydia Miramontes-Loyd, Derek Nimetz, Myrna Newgent, Sandy O'Brien, Noel Pavlovic, Abby Perrino, Barbara Plampin, Tom Post, Paul Quinlan, Tony Reznicek, Marge Riemenschneider, Victor Riemenschneider, Paul Rothrock, Don Ruch, Steve Sass, Carrie Satkoski, Brian Schlottman, Robin Scribailo, Bryn Scriver, Bradford Slaughter, John Smith, Nicole Staskowski, Emily Stork, Brock Struecker, Dana Thomas, Justin Thomas, Gayle Tonkovich, Tony Troche, Kevin Tungesvick, Michael Vincent, Vanessa Voelker, Mark Widrlechner, Gerould Wilhelm, Charlotte Wolfe, Robert Wolfe, George Yatskievych, and Kay Yatskievych.

We also want to acknowledge the leadership of the late Dale Engquist, former superintendent of the Indiana Dunes National Lakeshore, and Paul Labovitz, current superintendent of Indiana Dunes National Park, without whom there would be no *Wildflowers of the Indiana Dunes National Park*.

We are extremely grateful for the generosity of botanist and editor of the journal *The Great Lakes Botanist*, Michael Huft, for allowing us to use some of his gorgeous photographs in this book. Brandon Board also generously allowed us to use a photograph taken by his late father, Keith Board.

Finally, and most importantly, we thank our families for their trips with us in the field, their compassion and understanding as we spent nights and weekends writing and looking at plant photographs, and their patience when we asked them stupid questions like "Is this flower pink or blue?" or "Tell me the story of the lightning bolt hitting the clock tower in *Back to the Future*." Barbie Pilla, Dominick Pilla, Matteo Pilla, and Lindsay Namestnik, we offer our sincerest love and gratitude.

WILDFLOWERS
of the INDIANA DUNES NATIONAL PARK

1. INTRODUCTION

In 2019, the Indiana Dunes National Lakeshore received a facelift from Congress and became the sixty-first national park, Indiana Dunes National Park. This unique region at the southern tip of Lake Michigan gives rise to one of the most biologically diverse parks in the National Park system, yet, unlike many of our national parks, a basic field guide for wildflowers has not previously been compiled. With approximately 1,600 taxa of vascular plants in the roughly 15,000 acres of the park, and adoring all plants as we do, it was incredibly difficult to pick out a select group of wildflowers to showcase in this book. Even after weeding out ferns, grasses, sedges, rushes, and most woody species (trees, shrubs, and woody vines), we still spent countless hours determining which taxa to keep and which taxa could be omitted. The selected species were chosen through a combination of their frequency, abundance, charisma, and relationship to the trails through the Indiana Dunes National Park. Other than a small self-published book by Dianne Chaddock that highlighted some wildflowers from the dunes region in Indiana and Michigan, no book since Donald Peattie's 1930 technical *Flora of the Indiana Dunes* has been published to showcase the incredible floristic diversity specific to the Indiana Dunes. We decided that this needed to change. The Indiana Dunes National Park is the seventh-most-visited park in the nation, with more than 3.6 million visitors per year. This book was not written as a technical flora or as a scientific treatise but rather as a general field guide to some of the common and charismatic wildflowers of the Indiana Dunes National Park that you will see along the trails. It was our intention to not only make a wildflower book for the casual hiker but also to offer some useful information for the experienced botanist. Some of the species accounts may include faunal associates or lore, while many will passively mention look-alikes or similar species. We believe that it is the stories and faces that will be remembered, rather than the length of the petal or the hairiness of the inner sepal of a flower.

The Indiana Dunes has a rich botanical history with a collection of rare habitats that each has special plant communities. It was in the Indiana Dunes where Henry Chandler Cowles developed the idea of ecological succession through his studies of the plants and their relationships with one another. It is our hope that this book sparks an interest beyond the species we highlight here, that as you find plants not in this book, as you undoubtedly will, you decide to look through Marion Jackson's *101 Trees of Indiana* or the exhaustive *Flora of the Chicago Region* by Gerould Wilhelm and Laura Rericha. The great thing about being a botanist, whether professional or amateur, is that there is always something new to discover and experience. We hope our enthusiasm is transparent to you as you read the narratives about the plants. The images chosen for each species are not just for aesthetic eye candy but also to help you identify the plant and similar species.

We hope you enjoy this book as much as we enjoyed sharing it with you.

2. BRIEF HISTORY OF THE INDIANA DUNES NATIONAL PARK

The Indiana Dunes are a geological relic of the Wisconsin glaciation retreat of some 15,000 to 20,000 years ago. Over the millennia, shorelines turned to marshes, sand deposits stabilized through succession, and new shorelines were exposed. According to Pavlovic et al. (2021), there are seven major factors that have a role in the biodiversity of the dunes: (1) geomorphic position at the southern tip of Lake Michigan; (2) variety of substrates; (3) fire regimes; (4) physiographic location as the eastern extent of the Prairie Province, the western limit of the Eastern Deciduous Forest, and the southern terminus of the postglacial boreal and subboreal forests; (5) water levels; (6) succession and disturbance regimes; and (7) light availability. This cocktail of forces caught the attention of many scientists, nature enthusiasts, and industry in the early twentieth century.

As the industrial community was draining the "wastelands" (which we now know as important wetlands) and leveling dunes in the early twentieth century, conservation movements were brewing. In 1911, the Prairie Club pushed to save the Indiana dunes, which led to the National Park Service evaluating the region in 1916, only for the idea to be shelved due to the start of World War I. The largest sand dune on the Indiana lakeshore, called the "Hoosier slide," was turned into glass jars by the Ball Brothers around this time. In 1919, US Steel donated 116 acres to the city of Gary, which is now the area we know as Marquette Park. Conservationists still fought hard to protect the diminishing dunes. Through their efforts and those specifically of Richard Lieber, in 1926, the Indiana Dunes State Park was created, protecting approximately 1,500 acres of duneland habitat. The fight for a national park didn't stop there.

In the 1950s, the passionate Dorothy Buell took up the fight, starting the Save the Dunes Council. It was through this group of women that the purchase of the Cowles Tamarack Bog took place, which really got the ball rolling. The Save the Dunes Council became the catalyst that was needed, attracting the likes of the artist Frank Dudley, naturalist Edwin Teale, and botanist Donald Peattie, to name a few. Illinois senator Paul Douglas joined the fight to protect the Indiana Dunes, finding himself front and center to a massive political attack from those whose interest was solely in the development of industry in the dunes. It was the perseverance of Douglas and environmental activists that allowed for the "Kennedy compromise" in 1966. This compromise granted protection of the dunes, but only with the creation of the Port of Indiana, removing the large central dunes. The loss of those central dunes created an irreplaceable gap in the

In the dune and swale complex, wild lupine (*Lupinus perennis*) puts on a display in the spring in places such as Miller Woods.

connectivity of the dunes system. Notwithstanding, a large part of the Indiana Dunes were now federally protected as a National Lakeshore.

Over the decades, the Indiana Dunes National Lakeshore expanded its boundaries away from the Indiana Dunes, acquiring acreage in the city of Hobart in 1992, the Heron Rookery in Chesterton in 1980, and the Pinhook Bog unit near Michigan City in 1976. Finally, in 2019, through the congressional efforts from Indiana congressman Pete Visclosky and the leadership of Indiana Dunes superintendent Paul Labovitz, the Indiana Dunes National Lakeshore was redesignated as Indiana Dunes National Park.

3. USING THIS GUIDE

The purpose of this book is to offer you, the reader, an opportunity to experience the Indiana Dunes in a personal and exciting way. Although we expect that many will carry this resource with them while walking trails in the Indiana Dunes, we hope that you also find the material included in each species account interesting and entertaining enough to read through on a rainy or winter day.

One can use many different methods to identify plants. As professional botanists, we would be remiss if we did not say that using a technical manual (such as *Flora of the Chicago Region: An Ecological Synthesis* by Gerould Wilhelm and Laura Rericha) is the most effective way to accurately identify an unknown plant. Admittedly, technical manuals can be cumbersome to carry in the field and difficult to use for beginners, as they contain dichotomous keys and plenty of botanical terminology to pair contrasting characteristics, eventually leading you to your plant. Here, however, we use photographs and a brief description to help you identify the plants you are seeing, while also highlighting some look-alikes (you can't really *know* a plant unless you know what it isn't, right?). With that in mind, however, because the plant diversity of the Indiana Dunes is so great, it is impossible in a book of this size and scope to capture all of the species, so don't be discouraged if the plant you are trying to identify is not in this guide. In fact, finding a wildflower not in this guide could be viewed as a badge of honor. If you find a plant that we did not include, or at least mention as a look-alike, then you've found a plant that is somewhat less common than what most people will see when walking the trails through the region.

The species in this book are organized first by their typical flower color, and within each flower color section they are arranged alphabetically by botanical name.

Flower color sections used in this book are: (1) white, cream, and green (this includes flowers that are nearly white but slightly tinged with pink, lavender, or blue); (2) yellow; (3) orange; (4) red; (5) pink, lavender, and magenta; and (6) violet and blue. Even using this seemingly straightforward approach, some difficulties may be encountered. For example, we don't always use the color of the true flower but rather the color in the flowering portion of the plant that the user is most likely to see. An example of this is found in a species such as skunk cabbage (*Symplocarpus foetidus*), which has a large hoodlike spathe surrounding an ovoid spadix on which the yellowish true flowers (lacking petals) are located. Because the spathe is what most users of this guide will notice (at least at first glance), we placed it within the violet and blue flowers section, as the spathe is often purplish brown mottled with various amounts of yellowish green. A similar situation arises with some plants in the sunflower family (Asteraceae), where composite flowerheads are made up of petallike ray flowers, tubular disc flowers, or ray flowers surrounding disc flowers; in all of these cases, the flowerhead very much resembles a single flower. When the head is made up of both ray and disc flowers, and they are different colors, the plant is placed in the color section of the ray flowers. An example of this is black-eyed Susan (*Rudbeckia hirta*), which has daisylike flowerheads made up of yellow ray flowers surrounding a conical conglomeration of brownish disc flowers. Black-eyed Susan, then, can be found in the yellow flower color section of this book. Flower color can also sometimes be difficult to determine, with factors such as lighting, age, and personal opinion influencing what we see (if you don't remember the hotly contested debate about the colors in "the dress" in 2015, do a quick internet search for it). We have tried to alleviate this issue by including colors such as pink and lavender in the same section, but a flower that one observer considers pale blue may be considered lavender or even pink by another. Another issue arises with species that can have flowers of various different colors, such as dame's rocket (*Hesperis matronalis*) which can have white, pink, lavender, or violet flowers. We've placed this species in the pink, lavender, and magenta flowers section. When trying to identify an unknown plant, this book is intended to be used by flipping through the section with flower color matching your unknown plant until you find a match. We encourage you to do additional research with other resources once you've found a good match. If you don't find the plant you're looking for in one color section, and the color is debatable or you see a range of flower colors in the population, check in another section.

On the first page of each color section is a list of the species included in that section. This provides an option for a quick check if you know the plant you are wanting to read about and want to find out if it is treated in that section.

For each species treated in this guide, we include the following information: botanical name, common name, family name (technical and common), at least one photograph, a brief description of the plant, bloom time, plant communities where the plant can be found in the Indiana Dunes, something fun or special about the plant (because every plant has its own special story!), etymology, and information on any look-alike species in the Indiana Dunes.

Botanical Name, Common Name, and Family

The botanical name, made up of two parts (the genus followed by the specific epithet) is the best way to refer to a plant, and for each species account this is the first piece of information you will see at the top of the page. In a few instances, we have included a subspecies (subsp.) or variety (var.) in the botanical name. Both of these are further classifications below the species level. Although continuing research on the relationships between plant species has resulted in many plants "changing names," referring to a plant by its botanical name is still much more reliable than referring to a plant by its common name, as there are countless situations where two very different plants have the same common name. Common names still have a place in our culture, so immediately after the botanical name is the common name that we think is most frequently used, at least locally. Other common names are sometimes mentioned in the notes section.

Family is the classification one level above genus (just as related species are grouped into genera [singular = genus], related genera are grouped into families). The family name always ends in *-aceae*. The technical family name and the common name for the family are on the line following the botanical and common names.

PHOTOGRAPHS

We expect that most readers and users of this guide will focus heavily on the photographs and ignore most of the text; in fact, if you're reading this now, we commend you! For every species account, we have included at least one photograph of the plant with an emphasis on the flower(s); in some accounts there are two photographs of the same plant showing different characteristics. For instance, plants in the mustard family (Brassicaceae) often have either yellow or white 4-petaled flowers that are otherwise quite similar, so a photograph of only flowers won't be very helpful for identification. If our photograph of the flowers doesn't show more of the plant, we've included a second photograph of that species showing other characteristics of the plant useful for identification. In other species accounts, we have included a photograph of a look-alike to help you distinguish between similar species. Most of the photographs in this book were taken by the authors, but botanist and photographer Michael Huft has generously given permission to use some of his outstanding photographs in the guide as well, and Brandon Board provided a photograph taken by Keith Board. Photographs taken by Michael Huft or Keith Board are marked as such with their names.

Description

The species description is a brief narrative about the plant, starting with whether it is native or introduced in the Indiana Dunes, followed by its life history and typical height. Characteristics of the stem are sometimes provided, followed by a discussion about the leaves. The flowers and flower arrangement are discussed next, followed sometimes by fruit characteristics. Although many technical manuals use metric measurements (millimeters, centimeters, and decimeters) when describing plants, we have decided to use English measurements (inches and feet) to make this easier on the expected user.

Bloom Period

The bloom period reported in this guide includes the typical time (in months) that you might find the species in question with open flowers in the Indiana Dunes. With this said, finding a plant in bloom outside of the typical period happens (and is often exciting). In some cases, spring comes early, and you might find a plant that normally begins blooming in April in flower in March. In other cases, remontant blooms of typically spring-flowering plants can be found when temperatures cool in the fall; this is common with violets (*Viola* spp.) as well as garlic mustard (*Alliaria petiolata*) and several other plants. For situations such as this, only the main bloom period is reported.

Plant Communities

Plants have evolved to tolerate specific habitats where they may have the best chance of survival. There are many factors that influence a plant's reproductive success, including moisture availability, temperature, soil structure and type, soil reaction, and biotic influences. A species like pickerelweed (*Pontederia cordata*) may occur only in wet habitats, or bloodroot (*Sanguinaria canadensis*) may occur only in moist, closed-canopy mesophytic forest, so knowing the habitat or plant communities in which a species occurs can help you narrow down your identification. To make it easier, the next chapter in this book, "Plant Communities of the Indiana Dunes," will give you a better understanding of the plants and where to find them.

NOTES

The notes section of each species account may provide the most interest for casual reading of this guide. This section includes lore, history, notes on medicinal uses, whether or not the plant is safe to eat (everything is edible, once!), and other interesting tidbits.

ETYMOLOGY

Etymology is the study of the history of words and where and how they were derived. We have used this section to explain how the botanical names for each of the species treated in this book originated. Although the information provided in this section may not help you identify the plant, it may be useful in helping you to remember the botanical name, as many times the botanical name describes some characteristic of the plant itself. In other cases, the botanical name describes where the plant was first discovered, or it was used to honor a person. This section may prove enlightening and entertaining.

LOOK-ALIKES

As much as possible, we have provided at least one look-alike for the species treated in the guide. This is sometimes a plant in the same genus that could differ very minimally. In other cases, this could be a completely unrelated species, but one that we have seen people mistake for the plant in question. Sometimes a photograph of the look-alike is included for comparison.

It is impossible to avoid using basic botanical terminology when clearly and accurately describing certain plant features. With that said, we have tried to keep botanical jargon to a minimum, but terms that may be new to the common vocabulary are found in the glossary that follows the section on plant species accounts. As a quick reference, here are some basics regarding terminology for general plant morphology.

From bottom to top, the most basic parts of a plant are the **roots** (the underground portion of the plant that lacks leaves and provides stability), the **stem** (the portion of the plant with leaves; note that stems can be belowground, in which case they are referred to as **rhizomes**, or they can creep along the ground, be ascending, erect, or vining), the **leaves** (the often flattened and expanded photosynthetic part of the plant), and the **flower** (the reproductive part of the plant).

As with most wildflower guides, the flower is the main focus of the species accounts in this book. A flower is composed of various parts, but in the most typical sense it has a **perianth** (the protective structure that is not directly involved in reproduction but that often is involved in attracting pollinators) often surrounding **stamens** (the male reproductive organs) and **pistils** (the female reproductive organs). The perianth often is separated into two parts: the **calyx** (often green, when separate to the base called **sepals**, attached lowermost), and the **corolla** (often colorful, when separate to the base called **petals**, attached just above the calyx). When the sepals and petals are indistinguishable, they are referred to collectively as **tepals**. Attached above (or inside) the perianth are the stamens, which consist of two parts: the **filament** (essentially a stalk) and the **anther** (the pollen-producing portion). Attached above (or inside) the stamens are the pistils, which consist of three parts: the **ovary** (which is where reproduction takes place; a mature ovary is a **fruit**, containing seeds), the **style** (a tubelike stalk atop the ovary), and the **stigma** (the often sticky portion that receives pollen, attached to the top of the style). There is great variation among flowers of plants in our flora, as they can have some of these parts absent, but at a minimum an individual flower must have at least a stamen or a pistil. Flowers that have both stamens and pistils are referred to as **bisexual** or **perfect**, whereas those with only stamens or only pistils are said to be **unisexual** or **imperfect** (when only stamens are present, the flower is said to be **staminate**, and when only pistils are present, the flower is said to be **pistillate**). In plants with unisexual flowers, staminate and pistillate flowers can be present on the same plant (**monoecious**) or on separate plants (**dioecious**). A flower is said to be **regular**, **radially symmetrical**, or **actinomorphic** when it can be bisected in more than one plane and result in mirror images from each of those bisections. In contrast, a flower is said to be **irregular**, **bilaterally symmetrical**, or **zygomorphic** when it can only be bisected in one plane and still result in mirror images.

Although there is great diversity in the shapes of flowers seen on plants in the Indiana Dunes, nearly all of the plants covered in this guide have flowers that can easily be seen to follow the forms described above. Two exceptions are plants in the sunflower family (Asteraceae, such as those in the genera *Achillea*, *Ageratina*, *Antennaria*, *Bidens*, *Centaurea*, *Cichorium*, *Cirsium*, *Coreopsis*, *Doellingeria*, *Erigeron*, *Eupatorium*, *Eurybia*, *Euthamia*, *Eutrochium*, *Helianthus*, *Hieracium*, *Ionactis*, *Lactuca*, *Liatris*, *Packera*, *Parthenium*, *Prenanthes*, *Rudbeckia*, *Silphium*, *Solidago*, *Symphyotrichum*, *Tragopogon*, *Verbesina*, and *Vernonia*) and plants in the arum family (Araceae, such as those in the genera *Arisaema* and *Symplocarpus*). Each of these families has flowers in specialized structures or arrangements, as discussed below.

In the sunflower family, flowers are arranged in **composite heads** that themselves resemble individual flowers. There are two types of flowers in plants in the sunflower family: ray flowers and disc flowers. **Ray flowers** (sometimes called **ligulate flowers**) are irregular with a very small tube topped by a flattened, spreading, or ascending strap-like ray. **Disc flowers** are regular and tubular with 4 or 5 often small lobes at the top. The composite heads can be made up of all ray flowers (as in *Hieracium*), all disc flowers (as in *Liatris*), or ray flowers surrounding disc flowers (as in *Coreopsis*). Each composite head is subtended by **phyllaries** (also called **involucral bracts**) in one to several series that comprise an **involucre** (this is often similar-looking to the calyx of a flower in other families).

In the arum family, flowers are inconspicuous, often hidden, and lacking petals (or with a nearly unnoticeable perianth). The flowers are arranged in a spikelike inflorescence on a fleshy structure called a **spadix**. The spadix is usually surrounded by a hoodlike, often showy leaflike structure called a **spathe**.

Following the glossary is a section on recommended reading and references. We strongly encourage you, as your interest in plants grows, to check out as many of these as possible. Each of these resources can be beneficial to obtaining a greater understanding of what makes the flora of the Indiana Dunes so special.

Finally, in the back of the book, the index includes both common and botanical names. In addition to using the book to identify an unknown plant, you can use the index and find the page on which a plant is discussed if you're looking for more information about it.

A certain mindset is needed to correctly identify a plant. Haste is not a trait that should be employed in this endeavor . . . expect it to take some time, and be as observant as possible. When you find a plant you would like to identify, spend some time studying the plant. Look at its form and pubescence (or lack thereof), note if the leaves are opposite, alternate, or in a whorled arrangement, or if they are all basal; determine the leaf shape and whether the leaves are toothed or not, look at the flower color and number of petals, and how the petals are arranged. It helps some people to sketch the plant, as this causes them to slow down and really observe. Once you feel like you could walk away and describe the plant to someone else, try using this guide to find your plant and put a name on it. Once you think you have a match, believe it or not, the process still isn't over! Read the species account in this guide . . . especially the section on look-alikes . . . and make sure the description matches what you've found. Check other references (including those mentioned in the recommended reading and references section) to compare with what you've found. If characteristics don't match, it's possible that you've found a species not included in this guide, or that you've found an aberrant individual.

Even with all of the shortcomings inherent in a wildflower guide that by necessity must be limited in scope, it is our intention to give you, the reader, a seed of curiosity that grows beyond this book. We hope you find this book both useful and entertaining, and that it provides you with a greater appreciation for the fantastic flora of the Indiana Dunes. We also hope that this book provides a spark that makes you want to learn more and more about the plants of the Indiana Dunes and beyond. We suggest that you join and participate in your local native plant society. These organizations often hold field trips to natural areas . . . a great way for you to continue to learn about plants and natural communities. You can also improve your understanding and recognition of plant species through photographing them or, better yet, sketching them. Another way to continue to learn about native plants is to plant them in your home gardens (but don't collect them from the wild without permission!). This allows you to study these plants year-round, so that you will truly know the species when you see them in a natural area. Planting native plants is also beneficial to native insects, which feed native birds . . . so by planting native plants, you are doing your part to help restore a balance in nature. Finally, once you've progressed to the point that many of the plants you are seeing in the Indiana Dunes are not in this wildflower guide, we suggest that you up your game and begin using technical manuals, such as *Flora of the Chicago Region: A Floristic and Ecological Synthesis*. Guides such as this provide dichotomous keys that allow you to compare characteristics and whittle down the possibilities until you finally arrive at the identity of the plant you are "keying out." These guides often lack images or line drawings, so they require patience and at least a basic understanding of plant morphology terminology, but the feeling of accomplishment when you correctly identify a plant using a dichotomous key is amazing and leaves you yearning for more. We hope that many of you using this guide eventually get to this point and can fully discover the flora of the Indiana Dunes.

4. PLANT COMMUNITIES OF THE INDIANA DUNES

With habitat modification and fragmentation, many of the plants in the Indiana Dunes have, by necessity, adapted to **disturbed areas** (such as roadsides, lawns, mowed ground, edge habitat, trails, second-growth woodlots, old fields, vacant lots, etc.) that do not function as natural communities. However, remnant natural communities do remain in the Indiana Dunes. The following natural communities, broken into wetland and terrestrial communities, are based on work by Pavlovic et al. (2021).

WETLAND COMMUNITIES

Submerged aquatic communities are dominated by submerged and floating plants within bodies of water

Watershield (*Brasenia schreberi*, the smaller leaves) and American white waterlily (*Nymphaea odorata* subsp. *tuberosa*, the Pac-Man-like leaves) in a submergent marsh.

19

that are usually 2' or more deep. Often this community grades into a marsh system dominated by emergent plants. Common plants include water lilies (*Nymphaea odorata*, *Nuphar advena*), hornworts (*Ceratophyllum* spp.), common waterweed (*Elodea canadensis*), milfoils (*Myriophyllum* spp.), naiads (*Najas* spp.), pondweeds (*Potamogeton* spp.), and bladderworts (*Utricularia* spp.).

Bog is a community that occurs on a peat mat that is low in nutrients and acidic in reaction. Sphagnum moss (*Sphagnum* spp.) beds and mounds are indicative of this community. Other common plants include three-seeded sedge (*Carex trisperma*), leatherleaf (*Chamaedaphne calyculata*), northern purple pitcher plant (*Sarracenia purpurea*), tamarack (*Larix laricina*), highbush blueberry (*Vaccinium corymbosum*), and large cranberry (*Vaccinium macrocarpon*).

Marsh is an herbaceous community that is usually saturated or with surface water throughout the growing season and that is dominated by emergent vegetation,

The bog community at the end of the boardwalk at Pinhook Bog. Note the presence of the boreal-relict conifers eastern white pine (*Pinus strobus*) and tamarack (*Larix laricina*).

usually graminoids. Common plants include sedges (*Carex* spp.), bulrushes (*Schoenoplectus* spp.), and cattails (*Typha* spp.).

Prairie fen is an herbaceous community that is created by calcareous, groundwater-fed springs, where water flows through an organic soil layer close to the surface; there is often an impermeable layer beneath the organic layer. Available nutrients are high, and the soil is neutral to basic in reaction. This community is dominated by graminoids and perennial forbs, and it often occurs within more substantial wetland systems. Plants indicative of prairie fen include tussock sedge (*Carex stricta*), Ohio goldenrod (*Solidago ohioensis*), swamp betony (*Pedicularis lanceolata*), bristly aster (*Symphyotrichum puniceum*), and marsh fern (*Thelypteris palustris*).

Sedge meadow / wet prairie is an herbaceous community that is dominated by graminoids and saturated most of the year. Sedge meadows and wet prairies are often adjacent to streams or on lake plains. Dominant

Prairie fens (such as the one pictured here) are often juxtaposed at the base of oak kames (as seen in the background). Marsh blazingstar (*Liatris spicata*) is in the foreground.

species are often tussock sedge (*Carex stricta*), water sedge (*Carex aquatilis*), prairie cordgrass (*Spartina pectinata*), and blue-joint grass (*Calamagrostis canadensis*), but there is often similarity in the dominant species in this community and the prairie fen.

Panne (also called an interdunal wetland) is an herbaceous, graminoid-dominated wetland community that is positioned between old beach ridges. Water levels are often linked to the changing levels of Lake Michigan; however, in the Miller unit, the interdunal wetlands beyond the secondary dunes are not contingent on lake levels. Plants indicative of this community include slender bog arrow-grass (*Triglochin palustris*), variegated horsetail (*Equisetum variegatum*), Baltic rush (*Juncus balticus*), Kalm's St. John's-wort (*Hypericum kalmianum*), twig rush (*Cladium mariscoides*), and Kalm's lobelia (*Lobelia kalmii*).

Bottomland communities are forested wetlands that occur along rivers and streams, serving as floodplains with fluctuating seasonal water levels. Common species include red maple (*Acer rubrum*), green ash (*Fraxinus pennsylvanica*), sweet gum (*Nyssa sylvatica*), and oaks (*Quercus* spp.).

Swamp is a forested wetland type that is saturated throughout most of the year. It is represented in the dunes region as a complex made up of the following:

Hydromesophytic forest is a wooded community often characterized by moss-covered hummocks and pockets of water resulting from tree tip-ups. Dominant tree species include red maple (*Acer rubrum*), yellow birch (*Betula alleghaniensis*), pin oak (*Quercus palustris*), and musclewood (*Carpinus caroliniana*). The understory is diverse with skunk cabbage (*Symplocarpus foetidus*) and marsh marigold (*Caltha palustris*) in the seepage zones, and Canada mayflower (*Maianthemum canadense*), club-spurred orchid (*Platanthera clavellata*), greater bladder sedge (*Carex intumescens*), and northern long sedge (*Carex folliculata*) in saturated and drier areas.

The hydromesophytic forest often has an understory dominated by skunk cabbage (*Symplocarpus foetidus*).

Conifer swamp is nearly extirpated from the Indiana Dunes with a small remnant in Cowles Bog. Indicative species include tamarack (*Larix laricina*), northern white cedar (*Thuja occidentalis*), and yellow birch (*Betula alleghaniensis*). This community may not survive climate change, as it appears to be transitioning to a red maple swamp.

Pin oak flatwoods is similar to the hydromesophytic forest community but is positioned within wet depressions within oak savannas; pin oak (*Quercus palustris*) is the dominant tree species.

TERRESTRIAL COMMUNITIES

Pavlovic et al. (2021) arranged the terrestrial communities by their role in succession, which is described here.

Beach is a plant community consisting of a narrow sandy strip along the shoreline of Lake Michigan. Few plant species can survive the harsh conditions created by nutrient-poor and ever-moving substrate, wave action and intermittent inundation, and persistent wind;

Foredunes along Lake Michigan are characterized by American beach grass (*Ammophila breviligulata*).

those include American sea rocket (*Cakile edentula* var. *lacustris*) and seaside spurge (*Euphorbia polygonifolia*).

Foredune is the first succession of usually smaller dunes that faces Lake Michigan. Species indicative of this community include American beach grass (*Ammophila breviligulata*) and eastern cottonwood (*Populus deltoides*).

Secondary dune is situated behind the foredunes with less persistent disturbance, increased nutrients, and a higher biodiversity of sand prairie species, such as little bluestem (*Schizachyrium scoparium*), gray goldenrod (*Solidago nemoralis*), sand reed grass (*Calamovilfa longifolia* var. *magna*), and common milkweed (*Asclepias syriaca*).

Blowout communities are dynamic in that they are created by strong lake winds that deposit and erode sand, burying vegetation. This buried vegetation reroots and grows through the sand. A species that relies on this

Within this secondary dune, the blowout in the foreground sits above a panne surrounded by jack pine (*Pinus banksiana*).

disturbance is the federally threatened Pitcher's thistle (*Cirsium pitcheri*).

Prairie complex is a compilation of treeless, fire-dependent, grass-dominated communities consisting of a mosaic of rich, tallgrass-dominated landscapes and shorter-stature sand prairies. Plant species that typify this complex include Indian grass (*Sorghastrum nutans*), big bluestem (*Andropogon gerardii*), butterflyweed (*Asclepias tuberosa*), and sunflowers (*Helianthus* spp.).

Savanna complex is a group of transitional communities with mostly prairie understory but that have 20–50 percent tree canopy throughout. The savannas in the Indiana Dunes are dominated by sassafras (*Sassafras albidum*), black oak (*Quercus velutina*) or white oak (*Quercus alba*), and hickory (*Carya* spp.). A few species indicative of this complex include June grass (*Koeleria macrantha*), bird's foot violet (*Viola pedata*), round-headed bushclover (*Lespedeza capitata*), wild lupine (*Lupinus*

Sand prairies of the prairie complex are quite showy in the late summer, when gray goldenrod (*Solidago nemoralis*) and rough blazingstar (*Liatris aspera*) are dominant.

The savanna complex is characterized by widely spaced black oak (*Quercus velutina*) with a sand prairie understory (note the Indian grass, *Sorghastrum nutans*, in the foreground).

Mesophytic forests are most showy in the spring, when species such as great white trillium (*Trillium grandiflorum*) are in flower.

perennis), goat's-rue (*Tephrosia virginiana*), and Indian grass (*Sorghastrum nutans*). Bracken fern (*Pteridium aquilinum*) is also typical of the complex. Due to restoration activity in the park, some of the complex has less than 20 percent canopy cover. On the other end of the spectrum, due to fire suppression, some of the complex has more than 50 percent canopy cover. In latter situations, the understory has more of a woodland herbaceous composition.

Mesophytic forest is a woodland community dominated by sugar maple (*Acer saccharum*), basswood (*Tilia americana*), and American beech (*Fagus grandifolia*). This community type is not fire or drought tolerant. Spring ephemerals are abundant in this community and include bloodroot (*Sanguinaria canadensis*), spring beauty (*Claytonia virginica*), trout-lilies (*Erythronium* spp.), and trilliums (*Trillium* spp.), to name a few.

5. WHITE, CREAM, AND GREEN FLOWERS

Achillea millefolium, common yarrow
Actaea pachypoda, doll's eyes
Ageratina altissima, white snakeroot
Alliaria petiolata, garlic mustard
Allium tricoccum, ramps
Anemone cylindrica, thimbleweed
Angelica atropurpurea, great Angelica
Antennaria parlinii, Parlin's pussytoes
Apocynum cannabinum, dogbane
Arabidopsis lyrata, sandcress
Aralia nudicaulis, wild sarsaparilla
Arisaema triphyllum, Jack-in-the-pulpit
Baptisia alba, white wild indigo
Cardamine concatenata, cutleaf toothwort
Chelone glabra, white turtlehead
Cicuta maculata, water-hemlock
Clematis virginiana, virgin's bower
Comandra umbellata, bastard toadflax
Conopholis americana, bear corn
Daucus carota, Queen Anne's lace
Dicentra cucullaria, Dutchman's breeches
Doellingeria umbellata, flat-topped aster
Drosera intermedia, spoonleaf sundew
Enemion biternatum, false rue anemone
Epipactis helleborine, helleborine
Erigenia bulbosa, harbinger-of-spring
Erigeron annuus, annual fleabane
Eryngium yuccifolium, rattlesnake-master
Eupatorium perfoliatum, common boneset
Eupatorium serotinum, late boneset
Euphorbia corollata, flowering spurge
Eurybia macrophylla, bigleaf aster
Fragaria virginiana, Virginia strawberry

Geum canadense, white avens
Hydrophyllum virginianum, Virginia waterleaf
Lactuca biennis, tall blue lettuce
Laportea canadensis, wood nettle
Lespedeza capitata, round-headed bushclover
Maianthemum canadense, Canada mayflower
Maianthemum racemosum, feathery false Solomon's seal
Melilotus albus, white sweet clover
Mitchella repens, partridge berry
Mitella diphylla, bishop's cap
Monotropa uniflora, ghostpipe
Nymphaea odorata subsp. *tuberosa*,
    American white waterlily
Panax trifolius, dwarf ginseng
Parthenium integrifolium, wild quinine
Penstemon digitalis, foxglove beard-tongue
Persicaria lapathifolia, pale smartweed
Persicaria punctata, dotted smartweed
Persicaria virginiana, jumpseed
Phytolacca americana, American pokeweed
Podophyllum peltatum, mayapple
Polygonatum biflorum, smooth Solomon's seal
Pycnanthemum virginianum, Virginia mountain-mint
Rumex verticillatus, swamp dock
Sagittaria latifolia, duck-potato
Sanguinaria canadensis, bloodroot
Sanicula marilandica, Maryland black snakeroot
Saururus cernuus, lizard's tail
Silene latifolia, white campion
Solanum carolinense, Carolina horsenettle
Spiraea alba, white meadowsweet
Spiranthes incurva, sphinx ladies' tresses
Symphyotrichum ericoides, white heath aster
Symphyotrichum lanceolatum, panicled aster
Trillium grandiflorum, great white trillium
Vaccinium macrocarpon, large cranberry
Veronicastrum virginicum, culver's root

Achillea millefolium (COMMON YARROW)

ASTERACEAE—sunflower family

Description A native or introduced perennial growing to 3' tall. The fernlike leaves are alternately arranged along the stem. Stems are covered with white, cob-webby hairs of variable density. The leaves and stem have a delightful spicy sage-like smell when crushed. Individual flowerheads are made up of a few small white petallike ray flowers (rarely pink) and a few yellowish-to-white disc flowers; these are arranged in showy flat-topped arrays. Plants can spread via rhizomes and wind-dispersed seeds.

Bloom Period June–September

Plant Communities Disturbed areas, prairie complex, savanna complex

Notes Common yarrow has a deep history in lore and ancient medicine. It was thought to treat almost any ailment. Beyond the magical medicinal usage of the plant, many cultivars with a large palette of colors have been bred for our gardens, including the "Tutti Frutti" series.

This attractive plant is cosmopolitan in its range and has been moved around over time, making our native populations nearly impossible to identify from the European imports.

Etymology The genus name comes from the Greek demigod Achilles, who used the plant to mend the wounds of his soldiers. The specific epithet comes from the finely dissected leaves that appear to be made up of a thousand little leaves (*millefolium*, meaning "thousand leaves").

Look-alikes Its leaves may be confused for Queen Anne's lace (*Daucus carota*), but the leaves of the latter are not as finely dissected, and its 5-parted flowers are unlike the composite flowerheads of common yarrow.

ACTAEA PACHYPODA (DOLL'S EYES)

RANUNCULACEAE—buttercup family

Description A native perennial that grows up to 3' tall. The stems are hairless, often with purplish blotches on the nodes. Leaves are compound 2–3 times with sharp-pointed lobes and teeth. Small white flowers are in a densely clustered terminal raceme. The fruit are white berries with the black remnant style on the

Doll's eyes fruit.

top, making each berry look like an eyeball. It can also spread by rhizomes.

Bloom Period April–June

Plant Communities Mesophytic forest, savanna complex

Notes The common name comes from the white (very rarely red) berries that look eerily like a display of eyes that have been extracted from dolls' heads. Any part of the plant can be toxic to humans if consumed, leading to another common name for this showy plant: white baneberry.

Etymology The genus name comes from the Greek word for "elder," due to its supposed similarity to elderberry (*Sambucus*) leaves. The specific epithet *pachypoda* is derived from *pachy-*, meaning "thick," and *-poda*, meaning "having feet," thus "having thick feet." This is thought to be a reference to the thick flower/fruit stalks.

Look-alikes Red baneberry (*Actaea rubra*) has a more northern distribution and is rare in Indiana, with the most recent Indiana Dunes region collection coming from Cowles Bog in 1982. It differs from doll's eyes by its slender flower/fruit stalks (not more than 0.02" thick). Red baneberry has red fruit (very rarely white).

Red baneberry fruit.

AGERATINA ALTISSIMA (**WHITE SNAKEROOT**)

ASTERACEAE—sunflower family

Description A native perennial that can grow to 4' tall
(usually shorter). The oppositely arranged leaves are
generally ovate to deltoid in shape, toothed, and tapering to a pointed tip. Look for distinctive lighter-colored
"mining trails" on the leaves in the late summer (these
created by the larvae of the leaf-mining fly *Liriomyza
eupatoriella*). Flowerheads are made up of tiny white
5-parted disc flowers; heads form showy flattish to
dome-shaped arrays in the upper part of the plant. It
spreads by rhizomes and wind-dispersed seeds.

Bloom Period June–October

Plant Communities Disturbed areas, mesophytic forest, savanna complex

Notes White snakeroot is the reason that Illinois, not Indiana, is known as "the Land of Lincoln." While the Lincoln family was living in southern Indiana, Nancy, Honest Abe's mother, died of milk sickness. White snakeroot contains a toxin, and when it is eaten by cows, their milk becomes poisonous. Because of Nancy's passing, the Lincoln family moved to Illinois, the Prairie State, where this common woodland plant was less frequent.

Etymology *Ageratina* translates to "little Ageratum," meaning "small age-less," a reference to its flower size and long blooming period. *Altissima* means "tall."

Look-alikes Although commonly used in landscaping, the similar blue mistflower (*Conoclinium coelestinum*) was not collected from the wild in the Indiana Dunes until recently. It is native south of our region and is often used in "native" plantings, spreading from there. Like white snakeroot, blue mistflower has opposite, toothed leaves, but its disc flowers are pale blue to lavender.

Blue mistflower.

Alliaria petiolata (Garlic Mustard)

BRASSICACEAE—mustard family

Description A nonnative, invasive biennial that usually grows up to 3' tall (rarely taller). It produces basal leaves that are kidney-shaped with scalloped margins the first year; second-year leaves are more triangular-shaped, growing alternately along the stem. The flowers are 4-parted and white. It spreads profusely from seeds after second-year plants produce long, skinny fruit (siliques).

Bloom Period May–June (sometimes again in fall)

Plant Communities Disturbed areas, hydromesophytic forest, savanna complex, mesophytic forest

Notes Known for its tendency to invade woodlands and forests, garlic mustard is also a wonderful edible; this is thought to be the reason it was introduced to North America. Garlic mustard's flavor is quite peppery, and it smells like garlic. The tendency to invade natural areas is thought to be in part due to its allelopathy and the lack of coevolved predators.

Etymology The genus *Alliaria* means "onion" or "garlic," in reference to the genus *Allium*, due to its onion-like taste (despite being in an entirely unrelated family). *Petiolata* means "having petioles."

Look-alikes There are many plants in the mustard family that have small white 4-parted flowers; however, garlic mustard differs from these in that it has large coarsely toothed leaves, a peppery taste, and a garlic odor.

Allium tricoccum (RAMPS)

AMARYLLIDACEAE—amaryllis family

Description A native perennial that grows 0.75–1.5' tall. It begins the year in the spring with 2–3 basal leaves with red leaf stalks. The leaves die back by the time the plant produces flowers. The solitary flower stalk stands erect and holds at its apex an umbel of

Courtesy Michael Huft.

15–50 small white bell-shaped flowers. The fruit is a 3-chambered capsule with a single shiny bluish-black seed in each chamber. It can spread asexually through the budding of new bulbs.

Bloom Period June–August

Plant Communities Mesophytic forest

Notes Also called wild leek, the leaves are a delicacy for many chefs. Ramps' smooth leaves provide a dynamic texture to the forest landscape in the spring during the ephemeral extravaganza of blooming wildflowers.

Etymology *Allium* means "garlic." *Tricoccum* is from the Latin for "three" (*tri-*) and "seed" (*-coccum*), a reference to its 3-lobed fruit.

Look-alikes Narrow-leaved wild leek (*Allium burdickii*) is taxonomically lumped with *A. tricoccum* or treated only at the varietal level by some botanists, but we feel the two are quite distinct in our area. The leaves of narrow-leaved wild leek are green (or white) at the base all the way into the ground (lacking red on the stalks), and they are narrower (usually under 1.5" wide); also, plants typically have fewer than 20 flowers per umbel.

Ramps (*left*) vs. narrow-leaved wild leek (*right*).

Anemone cylindrica (**Thimbleweed**)

RANUNCULACEAE—buttercup family

Courtesy Michael Huft.

Description A sand- and gravel-loving native perennial that grows up to 3' tall. The basal leaves are on long stalks and are deeply lobed or palmately compound. Along the hairy stem, a single whorl of three or more palmately compound leaves with lobed leaflets, each with a wedge-shaped base, set the stage for the flowering stalks. Erect flowering stalks 1–8" long emerge from the whorled leaves with a 5-parted white flower sitting alone at the end of each stalk. The fruit are tiny achenes attached to a woolly or cottony fluff collectively in a fruiting head that is 2–4 times as long as it is wide.

Courtesy Michael Huft.

The fruiting head often persists into winter as a messy, cottony terminal cluster.

Bloom Period June–August

Plant Communities Secondary dune, prairie complex, savanna complex

Notes A Greek creation myth of the anemone tells of Aphrodite's mortal lover, Adonis, who was mutilated by a wild boar. It is of some debate over what god sent the boar. Nevertheless, Adonis bled to death in the arms of Aphrodite, whose tears flowed with his blood. When hitting the ground, the blood and tears grew into a gorgeous little plant . . . an anemone. Other common names include candle anemone and cottonweed.

Etymology *Anemone* translates to "wind" in Greek (some *Anemone* species are known as "windflower" because the flowers are said to be blown around by the slightest breezes), and *cylindrica* means "cylinder-shaped," a reference to the fruiting head shape.

Look-alikes Tall thimbleweed (*Anemone virginiana*) differs in having fruiting heads usually less than 2–2.5 times as long as wide, stem hair sparse and spreading (abundant and appressed in thimbleweed), and leaves toothed over halfway down the lobes (lobes of thimbleweed leaves toothed only apically). The more wedge-shaped leaflets of thimbleweed are also more leathery in texture.

Angelica atropurpurea (Great Angelica)

APIACEAE—carrot family

Description A native perennial that can grow over 8' tall. The pinnately compound leaves are large, measuring up to 2.5' long with stalks that sheath the stout purple hollow stem. Greenish-white 5-parted small flowers are in clusters of umbellets, making up a larger spherical umbel. Five stamens protrude wildly beyond the petals. The fruit are dry, thin, winged schizocarps.

Bloom Period May–June

Plant Communities Marsh, prairie fen, sedge meadow / wet prairie, bottomland

Notes There are few wildflowers as tall as great Angelica, which is also known as purplestem Angelica. In a 1991 *New York Times* article, Anne River described the genus as "a kind of six-armed Indian goddess, holding aloft melon-size umbels of flowers that look like huge green sparklers."

In a 1687 letter, John Clayton wrote that a Native American dug up part of the root of a great Angelica plant and rubbed it on his hand upwind of a deer. The deer sniffed the air and walked toward him, curious about the smell. Once the deer was close enough, the Native American shot it.

There is so much lore and myth that surrounds this plant that an entire chapter could be written simply on its ethnobotanical history.

Great Angelica would be a fitting complement in the world of Malacandra.

Etymology The genus has a history rooted in myth and folklore. Legend has it that an angel shared with a monk that species of *Angelica* have a magical property to heal

Cow parsnip.

the plague, thus Linnaeus chose this name for the genus, due to the many medicinal uses of the plant. Or, *Angelica* was so named because it was in bloom during the feast of Saint Michael the Archangel. In 1884, Robert Folkard wrote that in Germany they commonly called this genus the "Root of the Holy Spirit." The specific epithet of our species is less exciting, meaning "dark purple," a reference to the stem color.

Look-alikes Not much looks like great Angelica. The most similar-looking species is probably cow parsnip (*Heracleum maximum*), which is large and can grow in the same habitat (but it is often found in shaded bottomlands). Cow parsnip has palmately compound leaves, green stems, white petals, and flat-topped umbels.

ANTENNARIA PARLINII (PARLIN'S PUSSYTOES)

ASTERACEAE—sunflower family

Female flowerheads.

Description A native perennial that grows to 15" tall. The basal leaves are ovate and stalked, with undersides covered in woolly, white, dense matted hairs, and upper surfaces dull green with hair (subsp. *fallax*) or not (subsp. *parlinii*). The stem leaves are scalelike and alternately arranged. Male and female flowerheads are usually on separate plants with the females looking like the end of a Q-tip and the males looking more like a scrub brush.

Male flowerheads.

All of the flowers in the flowerheads are disc flowers. Plants spread by seed and from stolons, which often produce mats of basal leaves.

Bloom Period April–May

Plant Communities Disturbed areas, savanna complex

Notes The common name pussytoes is a reference to the flowerheads, which are said to resemble the toes of a cat. The male flowerheads have been referred to as dog's-toes, and the female flowerheads have been referred to as pussytoes.

Etymology *Antennaria* comes from the Latin word *antenna*, a reference to the bristles of the pappus (in the flowerheads) looking like an insect's antennae. *Parlinii* is a nod to botanist John Crawford Parlin, who discovered this species.

Look-alikes There are four native pussytoe species in the Indiana Dunes. Howell's and field pussytoes (*Antennaria howellii* and *A. neglecta*) both have no apparent veins other than the midvein on the undersides of the basal leaves. Plantain-leaved pussytoes (*A. plantaginifolia*), like Parlin's pussytoes, has more than one vein on basal leaves but has the larger involucral bracts of female flowers up to 0.3" long (up to 0.5" long in *A. parlinii*).

Apocynum cannabinum (DOGBANE)

APOCYNACEAE—dogbane family

Description A native, clonal perennial that can grow up to 4' tall from a thick taproot. The leaves and reddish stems contain a milky latex. The oppositely arranged leaves are short-stalked or stalkless, turning a lovely yellow in the fall. The small 5-parted flowers are bell-shaped and clustered. The fruit is a follicle similar to that of milkweeds (*Asclepias*), with the seeds attached to tufts of silky hair, which allows them to be dispersed by wind.

Bloom Period June–August

Plant Communities Disturbed areas, prairie fen, sedge meadow / wet prairie, prairie complex, savanna complex

Notes Also called Indian hemp, the fibers from the stems were used by Native Americans to make ropes and sacks in the same way that hemp was used by colonists. There is a bit of controversy on the separation of taxa within the genus *Apocynum*. Some botanists separate numerous varieties, while others break them into species. The dogbane beetle (*Chrysochus auratus*), which relies on dogbanes and sometimes milkweeds as its sole food source, is one of the most beautiful insects in North America; it exhibits metallic hues that change as sunlight hits it. Dogbane is also an important host plant for many other species, such as dogbane tiger moth (*Cycnia tenera*) and dogbane saucrobotys moth (*Saucrobotys futilalis*).

Etymology In Greek, *apo-* means "away," and *-cynum* means "dog." So, why "away dog"? Lore has it that dogs were poisoned by this plant, thus the common name dogbane. *Cannabinum* refers to the hemp-like (*Cannabis*) quality of the plant.

Look-alikes Here we take a broad species approach, but some botanists split *A. sibiricum* from *A. cannabinum*, with the former having stalkless (or nearly so) leaves that are somewhat heart-shaped at the base, and the latter having leaf bases rounded to a definite stalk. The native spreading dogbane (*Apocynum androsaemifolium*) can be confused with dogbane, but it has branches that are more spreading, flowers that are a bit larger with pink candy cane stripes on the inside, and corolla lobes that are spreading to recurved.

Spreading dogbane.

Apocynum cannabinum (DOGBANE)

APOCYNACEAE—dogbane family

Description A native, clonal perennial that can grow up to 4' tall from a thick taproot. The leaves and reddish stems contain a milky latex. The oppositely arranged leaves are short-stalked or stalkless, turning a lovely yellow in the fall. The small 5-parted flowers are bell-shaped and clustered. The fruit is a follicle similar to that of milkweeds (*Asclepias*), with the seeds attached to tufts of silky hair, which allows them to be dispersed by wind.

Bloom Period June–August

Plant Communities Disturbed areas, prairie fen, sedge meadow / wet prairie, prairie complex, savanna complex

Notes Also called Indian hemp, the fibers from the stems were used by Native Americans to make ropes and sacks in the same way that hemp was used by colonists. There is a bit of controversy on the separation of taxa within the genus *Apocynum*. Some botanists separate numerous varieties, while others break them into species. The dogbane beetle (*Chrysochus auratus*), which relies on dogbanes and sometimes milkweeds as its sole food source, is one of the most beautiful insects in North America; it exhibits metallic hues that change as sunlight hits it. Dogbane is also an important host plant for many other species, such as dogbane tiger moth (*Cycnia tenera*) and dogbane saucrobotys moth (*Saucrobotys futilalis*).

Etymology In Greek, *apo-* means "away," and *-cynum* means "dog." So, why "away dog"? Lore has it that dogs were poisoned by this plant, thus the common name dogbane. *Cannabinum* refers to the hemp-like (*Cannabis*) quality of the plant.

Look-alikes Here we take a broad species approach, but some botanists split *A. sibiricum* from *A. cannabinum*, with the former having stalkless (or nearly so) leaves that are somewhat heart-shaped at the base, and the latter having leaf bases rounded to a definite stalk. The native spreading dogbane (*Apocynum androsaemifolium*) can be confused with dogbane, but it has branches that are more spreading, flowers that are a bit larger with pink candy cane stripes on the inside, and corolla lobes that are spreading to recurved.

Spreading dogbane.

Arabidopsis lyrata (SANDCRESS)

BRASSICACEAE—mustard family

Description A small native biennial or perennial that grows up to 18" tall. The leaves are mostly basal with a large terminal lobe and a couple of smaller lateral lobes (lobes sometimes reduced to coarse teeth), covered with stiff hairs; these are usually gone when the plant is in flower. The stem leaves are few, small, narrow, often unlobed, and alternately arranged. Basal leaves are sparse

Basal leaves. Courtesy Keith Board.

to absent at flowering. Flowers are white and 4-parted, maturing into an upright, slender seed pod (silique).

Bloom Period April–September

Plant Communities Foredune, secondary dune, blow-out, savanna complex

Notes The Olympia marble (*Euchloe olympia*), a threatened butterfly in Indiana, relies on sandcress as one of its most important larval host plants.

Etymology *Arabidopsis* means "looks like an *Arabis*," and *Arabis* means "Arabian," apparently a reference to the sandy or rocky soil (similar to that in Arabia) in which plants in this genus tend to grow. The specific epithet *lyrata* is from the resemblance of the leaves to the shape of the lyre, a musical instrument.

Look-alikes The dainty little whitlow-grass (*Draba verna*), primarily found in disturbed areas, looks a bit like sandcress in that they both have hair on the stems or leaves and the petals are white. They differ in that the fruit pod is slender and long (usually at least ten times longer than wide; a silique) in sandcress while being somewhat short and round (a silicle) in whitlow-grass. Whitlow-grass also never has stem leaves.

Whitlow-grass.

ARALIA NUDICAULIS (WILD SARSAPARILLA)

ARALIACEAE—ginseng family

Description A native, rhizomatous perennial that grows to 1–1.5' tall. A single double-compound leaf emerges with a glorious bronze color (usually becoming green) from its rhizome. Each of the three divisions of the leaf has 3–5 (rarely 7) ultimate leaflets that umbrella over a spherical, umbellate flowerhead that looks like a firework in mid-explosion. The flowerhead is on a naked stem arising from the rhizome. Individual flowers are white to greenish and 5-parted with petals that bend back, showcasing the long erect and protruding stamens and styles. Each plant is functionally either male or female (rarely both), yet their nonfunctional reproductive parts remain on the flower. The fruit is a dark-purple berry.

Bloom Period May–July

Plant Communities Hydromesophytic forest, savanna complex

Notes As the common name implies, the roots were once used as a substitute for sarsaparilla (which is a greenbrier [*Smilax ornata*] from Mexico and Central

America) to make root beer. The root is still used to brew teas.

Etymology It is unknown where the name *Aralia* came from, but it is thought that it was an Iroquois name that the French-Canadians used for the plant. *Nudi-caulis* means "naked stem," a reference to the leafless flowering stalks.

Look-alikes Although wild sarsaparilla is a distinctive plant, it looks superficially similar to American ginseng (*Panax quinquefolius*), at least vegetatively. The latter has a whorl typically made up of 3 leaves, each palmately compound with 5 leaflets (pinnate arrangement in wild sarsaparilla), and the small cluster of flowers arises from the middle of the whorl of leaves.

Arisaema triphyllum (Jack-in-the-pulpit)

ARACEAE—arum family

Description A native, clonal perennial that grows from 0.5' to 2' tall. Jack-in-the-pulpit produces one trifoliate compound leaf on sterile or male plants and two trifoliate compound leaves on female or hermaphroditic plants. The small flowers are produced on a fleshy fingerlike structure called a spadix. Surrounding the spadix is a leafy pitcher-like structure called a spathe. The spathe is green to greenish purple and often has stripes that are yellowish white, white, or purple. A hood on the spathe hangs over the spadix. In late summer, when the leaves and spathe die back, a cluster of berries remains, starting green and maturing to bright red.

Bloom Period April–July

Plant Communities Bottomland, hydromesophytic forest, conifer swamp, mesophytic forest

Notes Jack-in-the-pulpit is unique in that an individual plant can change its sex annually. To the time of the writing of this book, there is still some disagreement among scientists as to what triggers this gender change and why this group of species has developed this adaptation. A small number of individuals can be bisexual; however, it is more often than not that a plant is functionally male or female, not both. Larger individual plants are female, and smaller plants are male. The flowers are pollinated mostly by flies and fungus gnats attracted to the slightly rotten odor of the flowers. In plants with male flowers, there is a tiny hole in the bottom of the spathe so that after the insect enters, it can easily find a way out. In female plants, however, there is no exit from the spathe!

Etymology *Arisaema* is from *aris-*, meaning "arum" and *-heama*, meaning "blood," named by German seventeenth-century botanist C. F. P. von Martius after

three Himalayan species that had deep red edging on the leaves. *Triphyllum* means "three leaves," referencing the 3-parted leaves.

Look-alikes Jack-in-the-pulpit's sister species, green dragon (*Arisaema dracontium*), looks somewhat similar. It differs in having a single compound leaf that has 5–15 leaflets in a circular fanlike form, with the spathe often rising within the circle like a dragon head. The spathe has a pointed tip, with the spadix long exserted.

Baptisia alba (WHITE WILD INDIGO)

FABACEAE—legume family

Description A robust native perennial that grows to 3–6' tall with a somewhat bushy form. The stem is smooth, glaucous, and purplish green to grayish green. Its compound leaves are trifoliate. Flowers are white with a typical legume shape, approximately 0.5–1" long, in an upright terminal raceme. The fruit is a cylindrical legume that starts green and turns nearly black.

Bloom Period June–August

Plant Communities Sedge meadow / wet prairie, prairie complex, savanna complex

Notes This handsome species, an important part of the prairie systems that were once more common in

northwest Indiana, attracts bumblebees and is poisonous to most mammals. Ours is var. *macrophylla*, with
var. *alba* occurring in the southeastern United States.

Etymology *Baptisia* is from the Greek word *baptizein*,
which means "to dye," as many of the species in this genus were used in dyes. *Alba* means "white," in reference
to the flower color.

Look-alikes Blue wild indigo (*Baptisia australis*) did not
occur naturally in the Indiana Dunes, but it has been
introduced through recent prairie plantings adjacent to
the Indiana Dunes Visitor Center. It differs from white
wild indigo by its blue-violet flowers.

Cardamine concatenata (CUTLEAF TOOTHWORT)

BRASSICACEAE—mustard family

Description An erect native perennial spring ephemeral that grows from 6" to 15" tall. The leaves are variable, usually whorled or opposite (sometimes alternate), trifoliate (with lateral leaflets very deeply lobed and thus appearing palmately 5-foliate), and with leaflets and lobes toothed or sometimes entire. Flowers are 4-parted and white, sometimes turning a light pink to pinkish purple, often nodding in a loose, ascending-to-erect terminal cluster. The fruit is a slender silique.

Bloom Period March–May

Plant Communities Disturbed areas, bottomland, hydromesophytic forest, mesophytic forest

Notes The common name toothwort doesn't refer to a wart on a tooth, as it may seem to imply. *Wort*, like in St. John's-wort, spleenwort, mugwort, and so forth, comes from the Old English word *wyrt*, which was another name for a plant. Because the flowers somewhat resemble a tooth, it was once believed that cutleaf toothwort helped with toothaches due to the archaic belief in the Doctrine of Signatures. The leaves are edible, as with most plants in the mustard family.

Purple cress.

Etymology *Cardamine* was thought to be coined by Dioscorides, referring to the cress plants. *Concatenata* is derived from the Greek word *concatenatus*, which means "joined together." This is a reference to the jointed rhizomes.

Look-alikes There are many cress species (*Cardamine* spp.) that occur in the Indiana Dunes. Two that are common and that bloom about the same time as cutleaf toothwort are spring cress (*C. bulbosa*) and purple cress (*C. douglassii*). In these two species, the stem leaves are all simple and unlobed, often with a few teeth, whereas cutleaf toothwort's leaves are compound and deeply lobed.

Spring cress and purple cress differ from each other in that, as the name implies, the latter usually has pinkish-lavender petals. Another difference between the two is that spring cress is hairless on the upper part of the stem, whereas purple cress is hairy on the stem beneath the flowers. Spring cress blooms slightly later than purple cress.

Chelone glabra (White Turtlehead)

PLANTAGINACEAE—plantain family

Description A native perennial that grows up to 2–4' tall. Leaves are oppositely arranged, up to 6–8" long, sharply toothed, usually hairless, and tapering to a point. The top of the leaf is a rich dark green with a light midvein, contrasting with the pale-green underside. Individual flowers are white (rarely with a pink blush), shaped like a turtle's head; they are oriented in a terminal cluster.

Bloom Period August–September

Plant Communities Marsh, prairie fen, sedge meadow / wet prairie, bottomland, hydromesophytic forest, conifer swamp

Notes White turtlehead is the host plant for the Baltimore checkerspot butterfly (*Euphydryas phaeton*). The flowers are commonly visited by bumblebees.

Etymology Legend has it that a mythological mountain nymph named Chelone was invited to Zeus and Hera's wedding at Hermes's place but thought it a waste of her time. In response, Hermes took Chelone, threw her house on her back, and chucked both into the river where they turned into a tortoise. As a result, *chelone* is Greek for "tortoise," a reference to the flowers that look like turtle heads. *Glabra* means "smooth, hairless," referencing the hairless stems and leaves of this species.

Look-alikes Although white turtlehead is a fairly distinctive plant in the Indiana Dunes, the most similar-looking species in our region is swamp betony (*Pedicularis lanceolata*), which has opposite leaves and whitish flowers in a terminal raceme; the shape of both is different, however (see treatment for wood betony, *P. canadensis*, in the yellow flowers section).

Cicuta maculata (water-hemlock)

APIACEAE—carrot family

Description A native biennial to perennial that grows up to 6' tall. The stems are usually branched and green, green with purple splotches, or purple. The leaves are alternately arranged on the stem and are 2–3 times compound. The leaflets are toothed with the leaf veins ending in the sinuses of the teeth (not the teeth tips). The tiny white 5-parted flowers are in umbellets in umbels to 6" across.

Bloom Period June–August

Plant Communities Marsh, prairie fen, sedge meadow / wet prairie, bottomland, hydromesophytic forest, pin oak flatwoods

Notes Water-hemlock is legendary for being one of the most poisonous plants in North America. Eating any part of this plant, especially the roots, could cause vomiting, seizures, convulsions, delirium, and death. The Iroquois commonly called it the suicide root. Good thing it isn't on the menu!

Etymology *Cicuta* is Latin for "hemlock," and *maculata* means "spotted," a reference to the stems.

Look-alikes Bulblet water-hemlock (*Cicuta bulbifera*) looks somewhat similar, but its leaflets are much narrower (less than 0.12" wide; those of water-hemlock are over 0.2" wide). Bulblet water-hemlock also produces bulblets in the upper leaf axils and is consistently under 4' tall. The highly invasive poison hemlock (*Conium maculatum*), also deadly poisonous (just ask Socrates), has more numerous and smaller umbels and more dissected fernlike leaves. Hemlock water parsnip (*Sium suave*) looks enough like water-hemlock that their common names bump shoulders. Hemlock water parsnip has compound leaves, not double-compound, with over 7 leaflets that are regularly sharply toothed. Cowbane (*Oxypolis rigidior*) also has compound leaves, but leaflets are entire or irregularly sparsely toothed, with whitened undersides.

CLEMATIS VIRGINIANA (VIRGIN'S BOWER)

RANUNCULACEAE—buttercup family

Courtesy Michael Huft.

Description A climbing, twining native perennial vine that grows up to 10–15' tall. The leaves are trifoliate and coarsely toothed with pointed tips. Flowers are white and 4-parted on a branched inflorescence. The fruit is a small achene with a long beak that is covered in whitish to rusty hairs; collectively, the fruiting head resembles the mane of Doc Brown in *Back to the Future*

as he was plugging the wire into the DeLorean when lightning struck the clock tower.

Bloom Period July–August

Plant Communities Disturbed areas, prairie fen, sedge meadow / wet prairie, bottomland, savanna complex

Notes The common name virgin's bower is up for some good debate. One story has it that Mary and Joseph, on their way to Bethlehem, were sheltered by a *Clematis*. Another story has it that *Clematis* was first introduced in Britain during Queen Elizabeth's reign; she was often referred to as the "virgin queen," leading to the name of the plant.

Also called devil's darning needles and old man's beard.

Etymology *Clematis* is derived from the Greek words meaning "branches with vines," and *virginiana* means "from Virginia," as the species was described based on a specimen from colonial Virginia.

Look-alikes The nonnative, invasive, ornamental sister species autumn clematis (*Clematis terniflora*) is sometimes planted within landscapes surrounding the dunes. Autumn clematis blooms later than virgin's bower, and the five pinnately compound leaflets are not toothed.

Comandra umbellata (Bastard Toadflax)

SANTALACEAE—sandalwood family

Description A native, hemiparasitic perennial that grows up to 1' tall. The alternately arranged leaves are entire, glabrous, and stalkless. The flowers are white, 5-parted, and shaped like a small funnel. The fruit is a somewhat globe-shaped drupe that contains a single seed.

Bloom Period May–July

Plant Communities Prairie fen, prairie complex, savanna complex

Notes In the common name, the word *bastard* is not referring to the plant being fatherless but rather means "false." Bastard toadflax is not actually a toadflax, but its foliage was thought to resemble a true toadflax, so the name stuck. As a hemiparasitic plant, bastard toadflax creates its own food through photosynthesis, but it can double-dip by parasitizing neighboring plants through rootlike structures called haustoria that attach to roots of the host and suck out nutrients. Because it produces extensive rhizomes, it can capture nutrients from many species underground. In fact, bastard toadflax can parasitize over 200 species of plants just in the Great Lakes region, ranging from grasses to ferns to trees. It has even been found with its haustoria attached to its own roots! Is this truly parasitism or rather masochism?

Etymology *Comandra* comes from the Greek words meaning "hair" and "a male." This refers to the hairy base of the male reproductive parts, the anthers. *Umbellata* simply means "having umbels," even though the inflorescence is technically a cyme (though it can resemble an umbel).

Look-alikes Flowering spurge (*Euphorbia corollata*) looks similar to bastard toadflax, but the foliage of the former contains a white latex.

Conopholis americana (BEAR CORN)

OROBANCHACEAE—broomrape family

Description A native, parasitic perennial that grows up to 9" tall. The stem is unbranched and stout, covered with overlapping, alternately arranged scalelike leaves. Little tubular 5-parted creamy-white flowers are arranged in a raceme that makes up nearly the entire aboveground portion. Each flower sits atop a small tan to brown bract. Flowers are replaced by egg-shaped capsules that start white then turn dark brown to black.

Bloom Period May–June

Plant Communities Savanna complex, mesophytic forest.

Notes Bear corn is often confused with a fungus, due to its lack of chlorophyll, parasitizing oaks (*Quercus* spp.). A bear corn seed germinates near an oak root, parasitizing it! The oak tree forms a gall, which fills up with tissue from the parasite. It takes around 4 to 5 years before the bear corn is ready to flower as it breaks through the thick wall of the gall.

The common name comes from black bears often foraging on the flowering stalks. It is thought that bears spread the seed through their feces. Another common name is the derogatory but still commonly used *squaw-root*, which comes from its historical use by Native Americans for menopause symptoms. Another commonly used name is *cancer-root*, due to the tumor-like gall growing off the oak root.

Etymology *Conopholis* comes from the Greek words *co-nos* and *pholis*, meaning "cone" and "scale." *Americana* means "from America."

Look-alikes None in the Indiana Dunes.

Daucus carota (Queen Anne's lace)

APIACEAE—carrot family

Description A weedy, nonnative biennial that grows from 2' to 3.5' tall. The first-year growth is a vegetative basal rosette. In the second year, fernlike compound leaves divided into narrow segments are alternately arranged on the stem. The lower leaves can be twice compound. Stalks of stem leaves are sheathed. Flowers are 5-parted in flat umbrella-shaped umbellets, forming umbels. The flowers on the outer edge of the umbel have larger petals than those in the center. The center flower of the entire umbel is often red to reddish purple. As it goes to fruit, the umbel folds upward like a cup. When the fruit matures, it opens back outward, dumping the mature seeds.

Bloom Period June–October

Plant Communities Disturbed areas, prairie complex, savanna complex

Notes The grocery store carrot was cultivated from Queen Anne's lace. There are many folk origin tales about the common name. Queen Anne of England was a legit lace maker, but one day she pricked her finger with a needle, and a drop of blood dripped on the center

of the lace (like the dark central flower of the umbel). Curiously, however, in England *Daucus carota* is referred to as "wild carrot." Another explanation is that it wasn't named after Queen Anne of England but rather Saint Anne, the patron of lace. Bottom line here is that you can make up your own Queen Anne origin tale, and it may be better than the dozen or so floating around.

Etymology *Daucus* is the Greek name for this plant, and *carota* means "carrot."

Look-alikes Vegetative plants may be confused for common yarrow (*Achillea millefolium*), but the leaves of the latter are more finely dissected, and its arrays are made up of composite flowerheads.

Dicentra cucullaria (Dutchman's breeches)

PAPAVERACEAE—poppy family

Description A native spring ephemeral that grows up to 8" tall. The leaves are basal, yellowish to grayish green and divided, with 4 orders of leaflets and lobes, appearing fernlike. The underside of the leaf is lighter green. Flowers are in the shape of an eighteenth-century Dutchman's breeches hanging upside down to dry. The flowers are white (sometimes with a pink blush) with two of the petals spreading and yellow to orange. The "pantaloons" are actually nectar spurs of the corolla; flowers are pollinated by long-tongued insects and bumblebees.

Bloom Period March–May

Plant Communities Mesophytic forest

Notes Dutchman's breeches is also known as "little blue staggers." When cattle eat this plant, they stagger as if drunk, due to the cocktail of chemicals (isoquinoline alkaloids) produced by the plant. This is probably why the plant was once considered a "love charm," as young Native Americans would chew a portion of the plant and breathe on their intended mate, expecting

that they then would be irresistible. Of all the bleeding hearts (*Dicentra* spp.), Dutchman's breeches is the most toxic, with a higher concentration in the roots.

Attached to the seeds is a fleshy structure (called an elaiosome) that is full of lipids and protein, which ants love. Ants take the seeds underground, where they partake in the delicious elaiosomes. Ants are thought to excrete secretions with antifungal and antibiotic properties. In a potential evolutionary win-win, the ant gets food and the seed gets planted in a safe place to grow, where it won't get decimated by fungal or bacterial agents.

Etymology *Dicentra* comes from the Greek *di-* and *kentron*, meaning "two spurs," and *cucullaria* means "hooded." This pretty accurately describes the flowers!

Look-alikes Overlapping with the blooming period of Dutchman's breeches is squirrel corn (*Dicentra canadensis*). The flowers of the latter have short, rounded nectar spurs, and flowers often start blooming a week or two later than Dutchman's breeches. Squirrel corn also has subterranean bulblets that are round and yellow (they look like corn kernels), whereas Dutchman's breeches has clusters of pink teardrop-shaped subterranean bulblets.

Squirrel corn.

DOELLINGERIA UMBELLATA (FLAT-TOPPED ASTER)

ASTERACEAE—sunflower family

Description A native perennial that can reach 6' tall or more (but often is around 3–4' tall). The leaves are alternately arranged along an often linearly furrowed stem. Each leaf has rugose venation with a prominent midvein with two divergent veins that parallel the leaf margins. Flowerheads are made up of 5–15 white petal-like ray flowers and 11–50 light-yellow disc flowers, and are arranged in a terminal flat-topped array.

Bloom Period July–October

Plant Communities Prairie fen, sedge meadow / wet prairie, bottomland, hydromesophytic forest, pin oak flatwoods, savanna complex

Notes Previously called *Aster umbellatus*, this is a host plant for the larvae of Harris's checkerspot butterfly (*Chlosyne harrisii*) and can serve as a food source for the adult pearl crescent butterfly (*Phyciodes tharos*). The petallike ray flowers are arranged irregularly, making it appear as though one or more is missing.

Etymology *Doellingeria* is in honor of German botanist, professor, and physician Ignatz Doellinger, and *umbellata* means "umbrella," due to the flat-topped shape of the floral arrays.

Look-alikes Many plants in the sunflower family with white ray flowers surrounding yellow discs (such as some *Symphyotrichum*, *Eurybia*, *Boltonia*, and *Erigeron* species) can look superficially like flat-topped aster, but the flat-topped floral array and leaves that are widest near the middle, tapering to the tips and bases, should provide an accurate identification.

Drosera intermedia (SPOONLEAF SUNDEW)

DROSERACEAE—sundew family

Description A native, carnivorous perennial that grows up to 8" tall. The leaves are paddle-shaped with red or green hairless stalks in a basal rosette, and are covered by red glandular sticky hairs. Flowers are white and 5-parted, borne on a single side of the upright stem that arises from the middle of the rosette. The fruit is a capsule containing many tiny, warty seeds.

Bloom Period July–September

Plant Communities Disturbed areas (scraped wet sand), bog, sedge meadow / wet prairie

Notes Spoonleaf sundew, an acidophile, forms a hibernaculum in the form of a leafy bud to protect it from the cold midwestern winters. What makes them the talk of the town, however, is their ability to eat animals. Because they grow in low-nutrient areas, they supplement not with over-the-counter vitamins but with good ol' animal protein. Sundews have two levels of sticky glandular multicelled hairs. The first level consists of longer hairs with a sticky substance that glues the passing insect to the leaf. The hairs then respond to

the catch by pulling it down to the lower level of hairs, which have an enzyme that begins to digest the prey alive. The leaves then absorb the "bug soup."

Etymology *Drosera* means "dewy" in Greek, a reference to the sticky droplets at the ends of hairs that cover the leaves. *Intermedia* means "intermediate," a reference to the leaf shape, which is neither round nor linear.

Look-alikes Round-leaf sundew (*Drosera rotundifolia*) looks very much like spoonleaf sundew but with round leaf blades and white pollen (pollen is yellow in spoon-leaf sundew).

Round-leaf sundew.

ENEMION BITERNATUM (FALSE RUE ANEMONE)

RANUNCULACEAE—buttercup family

Description A native, perennial, colony-forming spring ephemeral that can reach 15.5" tall (usually shorter) in moist, rich forests. The leaves are hairless, 3-parted 2–3 times, and alternately arranged along the stem. Each leaflet lobe has a tiny point at the tip. Basal leaves have long stalks; stem leaves have short stalks with a semi-circular papery stipule at the base. The flowers have 5 white petallike sepals. The fruit are follicles arranged like a star on a Christmas tree.

Rue anemone.

Bloom Period March–June

Plant Communities Disturbed areas (second-growth woodlots), bottomland, mesophytic forest

Notes After spring, false rue anemone goes dormant, returning in the fall with lovely purplish-colored leaves that last throughout the winter. Plants occasionally bloom again in the fall.

Wood anemone.

Etymology *Enemion*, synonymous with *anemone*, means "wind" in Greek, a reference to similar species that have flowers that are blown around by the slightest of breezes. *Biternatum* is derived from the Latin for "twice in three," referring to the leaves.

Look-alikes False rue anemone is often confused with rue anemone (*Thalictrum thalictroides*). The latter does not form dense colonies and often has more than 5 white (sometimes pinkish) petallike sepals. It also has basal leaves and opposite leaves (that appear whorled) beneath the flowers, rather than alternate stem leaves. Its leaflets are less deeply lobed and lack tiny points on their tips. Another similar species often confused with false rue anemone is wood anemone (*Anemone quinque-folia*), a colony-forming species that has fine hairs on the more sharply toothed, whorled leaves.

Epipactis helleborine (HELLEBORINE)

ORCHIDACEAE—orchid family

Description A nonnative perennial orchid that grows up to 3' tall but that is usually much shorter. The alternately arranged, toothless stem leaves range from 3 to over 10 on large individuals with the lower to middle leaves usually more orbicular and upper leaves often more lanceolate. Leaves are sparsely to densely rough hairy and clasp the stem. Flowers are borne on a terminal raceme that is often one-sided with flowers subtended by leaflike bracts. Flowers range from greenish white to pinkish purple. The lower petal (lip) is cup-shaped with a tip that curls back. Two lateral upper petals are like ears protruding behind the column, with three greenish sepals between the petals. The fruit is a capsule.

Bloom Period June–August

Plant Communities Disturbed areas, savanna complex

Notes This European weedy orchid was purposefully introduced as an ornamental and has naturalized throughout the Midwest. It is common along the trails of the Indiana Dunes savanna complexes. Because it spreads by rhizomes, pulling the plant is fruitless in removing it from a site. It is the only naturalized non-native orchid in the Indiana Dunes.

Within the nectar of helleborine is a chemical mixture that entices insects to not only visit but also to stay a while, ensuring pollination. Pollinators have been seen becoming disoriented and sluggish after taking their nectar reward. This is due to the chemical mixture of the nectar, which potentially has narcotic or hallucinogenic compounds. The same insects often return to the flowers to get another hit.

Etymology *Epipactis* is of Greek origin as a name for hellebore and was given to the plant by Theophrastus for "a plant that curdles milk." *Helleborine* means "like a hellebore."

Look-alikes The leaves of feathery false Solomon's seal (*Maianthemum racemosum*) are somewhat similar to those of helleborine but are stalkless, not clasping.

Erigenia bulbosa (HARBINGER-OF-SPRING)

APIACEAE—carrot family

Description An inconspicuous spring ephemeral that barely reaches 8" tall, usually shorter, and somewhat sprawling. The leaves are compound and 3-parted. The tiny, white, 5-parted flowers are in a compound umbel that is easy to overlook. Color composition of the flowers is similar to the Good & Plenty candy.

Bloom Period March–April

Plant Communities Mesophytic forest

Notes Harbinger-of-spring is one of the earliest-blooming wildflowers in the Indiana Dunes, thus the common name; this little plant is a glorious sign of winter's end and springtime's entrance. Another common

name for this plant is pepper-and-salt, a reference to the purplish or black anthers (pepper) and white petals (salt).

Etymology *Erigenia* is derived from the Greek for "early" (*eri-*) and "born" (*genitus*). This is in reference to the early-spring blooming of the flowers. The specific epithet, *bulbosa*, means "bearing bulbs," as the plant grows from a subterranean bulb.

Look-alikes Due to the early bloom time, compound leaves, and tiny flowers, there is nothing that this could be confused with in the Indiana Dunes.

Erigeron annuus (ANNUAL FLEABANE)

ASTERACEAE—sunflower family

Description A native annual or biennial that grows up to 3' tall with spreading hairs on the stem. The leaves are alternately arranged and often have a few large teeth predominantly in the apical half. Leaves higher on the stem are often toothless. The leaf stalk is winged; upper leaves are stalkless. Flowerheads are made up of white (rarely with pinkish blush) petallike ray flowers and yellow disc flowers. Each flowerhead is approximately ¾" diameter. It spreads by windblown seeds.

Bloom Period May–October

Plant Communities Disturbed areas, prairie complex, savanna complex

Notes This weedy daisylike plant is probably in your backyard or garden, as it thrives in full sun and disturbance. It is said that the common name, fleabane, comes from the smell of the flowers, which supposedly repels flies.

Etymology *Eri-* is Greek for "early," a reference to the early-season bloom time for many members of the genus; *-geron* means "old-man," as the seed heads supposedly look like the head of hair on an old man. *Annuus* simply describes the (sometimes) annual growth of the plant.

Philadelphia fleabane.

Look-alikes Not including plants in the genus *Conyza*, which is sometimes taxonomically lumped into *Erigeron*, there are four species of fleabane (*Erigeron* spp.) in the Indiana Dunes. Annual fleabane looks most similar to Philadelphia fleabane (*E. strigosus*). The latter has fewer and narrower leaves that are entire and appressed stem hairs. The other two species are Robin's plantain (*E. philadelphicus*) and Robin's plantain (*E. pulchellus*), both of which have clasping leaves; the former tends to grow in moist areas and has numerous flowerheads, sometimes with pink ray flowers, whereas the latter grows in drier conditions and has at most four flowerheads. Also compare with white-flowered *Symphyotrichum* spp.

Robin's plantain.

Eryngium yuccifolium (rattlesnake-master)

APIACEAE—carrot family

Description A native perennial that looks like it was taken from the desert with its yucca-like leaves growing up to 3–5' tall. The alternately arranged leaves, clustered toward the base of the plant, are stiff, gray-green, and sharp tipped, and have scattered bristles on the margins. There can be more than 50 flowerheads on one plant, each with over 100 tiny white, 5-parted flowers densely packed in the nearly spherical head. Each flower sits comfortably in a sharp floral bractlet.

Bloom Period July–September

Plant Communities Sedge meadow / wet prairie, prairie complex

Notes There are at least six known North American tribes that historically used rattlesnake-master medicinally to treat snake envenomations. This is more than likely where the common name is derived from. The rattlesnake-master borer moth (*Papaipema eryngii*) is a rare species of moth that is completely reliant on rattlesnake-master for its survival. This moth is a

candidate for federal listing and has been recorded in the Chicago region but is currently thought to be extirpated from Indiana.

Etymology The genus name is the ancient Greco-Latin word for the sea-holly plant, and *yuccifolium* unsurprisingly means "yucca-like leaves."

Weak-leaf yucca.

Look-alikes The only species in the Indiana Dunes that could be mistaken for rattlesnake-master is weak-leaf yucca (*Yucca flaccida*). The latter has all of its swordlike leaves in basal rosettes and a panicle of large, drooping, bell-shaped, 6-parted flowers; it is found in disturbed areas and ornamental plantings.

Eupatorium perfoliatum (COMMON BONESET)

ASTERACEAE—sunflower family

Description A common, native perennial that grows to 4'+ tall that is quite hairy, from the leaves to the stem to the flower bracts. The opposite leaves clasp the stem and are joined to one another (perfoliate), as if it is one leaf with the stem poking through. The flowerhead is a composite of white disc flowers, these arranged in flat-topped arrays at the top of the plant.

Bloom Period July–October

Plant Communities Disturbed areas, marsh, prairie fen, sedge meadow / wet prairie, bottomland, pin oak flatwoods

Notes Common boneset has a deep medicinal history. The Doctrine of Signatures expressed a prescientific belief that if a plant part looked like a part of the human body, it could potentially be used to heal ailments to that part of the body. Because the leaves at their connection point look like two bones fusing together, the Doctrine of Signatures assigned it to be wrapped around a splinted broken bone to heal the break. With the same logic, it was used to treat dengue fever, also known as "bone break fever," which caused intense bone aches; it was also used more broadly to treat fevers.

Eupatorium was derived from the great Mithridates IV Eupator Dionysus, king of Pontus, who created a Black Sea empire that challenged the power of Rome. Legendarily, his paranoia of being poisoned led him to seek elixirs that he would regularly drink. One of these was supposedly from a species in this genus that was named by Pliny the Elder as *Eupatorium*. The specific epithet *perfoliatum* is derived from the words *per* and *folia*, meaning "through the leaves," referring to the perfoliate leaves that encircle the stem.

Look-alikes Upland boneset (*Eupatorium sessilifolium*) also has sessile, opposite leaves with flowerheads similar to common boneset, but it grows in drier areas such as within the savanna complex. The leaves of the former, however, do not clasp around the stem, and the stem is mostly hairless.

Upland boneset.

Eupatorium serotinum (LATE BONESET)

ASTERACEAE—sunflower family

Description An often weedy native perennial growing to 5' tall. The stem is covered in soft, downy hair. The leaves are oppositely arranged (some of the upper leaves can be alternate) and coarsely toothed along the entirety of the leaf margin; they have three veins running from the base of the leaf to the tip. Leaf stalks are up to 1" long. The flowerhead is a composite of fragrant white disc flowers; these are arranged in flat-topped arrays.

Bloom Period July–October.

Plant Communities Disturbed areas, sedge meadow / wet prairie, secondary dune, prairie complex, savanna complex

Notes Late boneset is quite common throughout the Indiana Dunes, as deer and livestock avoid it. In fact, the mammalian herbivores avoid all bonesets. However, insects find this plant incredibly desirable, from caterpillars munching the leaves to wasps, flies, bees, moths, and beetles visiting the flowers for nectar and pollen.

Etymology See *Eupatorium perfoliatum* for genus etymology. *Serotinum* means "late-coming," describing the late blooming period.

Look-alikes Tall boneset (*Eupatorium altissimum*) is easily confused with late boneset; its leaves taper to sessile or subsessile bases, and its leaf margins are only toothed in the apical half. The two commonly hybridize. False boneset (*Brickellia eupatorioides*) is similar but has alternate irregularly toothed leaves and cream-colored disc flowers.

Tall boneset.

Euphorbia corollata (FLOWERING SPURGE)

EUPHORBIACEAE—spurge family

Description An erect perennial 1–3' tall. Several shoots can arise from a single rootstock. The leaves are stalkless or short stalked; the lower are alternate along the stem, becoming opposite to whorled at the top of the plant. Flowers are highly modified; tiny greenish male or female flowers are surrounded by five white petal-like appendages, causing the flowers to appear white; these are arranged in a flat-topped inflorescence. Female flowers mature into a globular 3-lobed capsule that looks awkwardly positioned on a stalk above the white appendages.

Bloom Period June–September

Plant Communities Secondary dune, blowout, prairie complex, savanna complex

Notes Flowering spurge (and other plants in the genus *Euphorbia*) has a unique flower structure. The specialized false-flower is called the cyathium. Flowering spurge's cyathium usually has five white petallike appendages, each with a green nectar-producing gland at the base. The staminate (male) and pistillate (female) flowers are tucked in the center, surrounded by these glands. Flowering spurge cannot self-pollinate; it takes a genetically separate individual's pollen to reproduce. It also exudes a milky sap when damaged; the sap is poisonous if ingested and can irritate skin in some people.

Etymology *Euphorbia* was named after the Greek physician Euphorbus, presumably due to the medicinal qualities of some members of the genus; it is derived from *Eu-* and *phoebe*, meaning "good fodder" or "well fed." *Corollata* means that it has corollas. Don't tell the plant, though, that its name is a lie!

Look-alikes Bastard toadflax (*Comandra umbellata*) looks somewhat like flowering spurge, especially when not in flower, but the former, which has more gray-green foliage, lacks milky sap when a leaf is pulled from the stem.

Eurybia macrophylla (BIGLEAF ASTER)

ASTERACEAE—sunflower family

Description A native perennial 1–3.5' tall. The basal leaves are large (up to 6" across), heart-shaped, and on a long, often winged stalk. Stem leaves are alternately arranged and stalked, becoming smaller and stalkless up the stem, and glandular hairy on the veins on the undersides. All of the leaves are coarsely toothed. The flowerheads have over 9 petallike ray flowers that are whitish to pale blue lavender surrounding creamy-yellow disc flowers that turn brownish purple with age. Few to numerous flowerheads are arranged in a flat-topped array at the top of the plant. The fruit is a seedlike achene with a fluff of hair (pappus) attached to the top. It often occurs in large colonies, due to extensive rhizomatous asexual reproduction.

Bloom Period July–October

Plant Communities Hydromesophytic forest, savanna complex, mesophytic forest

Notes *Eurybia macrophylla* was previously called *Aster macrophyllus*. Our *Eurybia* species differ from other former *Aster* species in having both flat-topped arrays and heart-shaped leaves.

Etymology *Eurybia* is named after the Greek goddess of the seas, with the name literally translated to "wide force," representing her power over the seas. In mythology, she married the titan Krios, giving birth to Astraeus, who then gave birth to all of the stars in the heavens. *Macrophylla* means "big-leaf," a clear reference to the basal leaves.

Look-alikes Forked aster (*Eurybia furcata*) and white wood aster (*E. divaricata*) are both very rare in the Indiana Dunes. Both lack the glandular hairs in the inflorescence that are present in big-leaved aster. The former has rough-textured leaves, whereas those of the latter are smooth or sparsely soft hairy. White wood aster is native in the eastern United States but has been introduced in our area.

Fragaria virginiana (Virginia strawberry)

ROSACEAE—rose family

Description A short native perennial that stands 3–6" tall and spreads by stolons. The 3-parted toothed leaves grow basally. The flowers are 5-parted and about ¾" wide. The 5 round petals surround approximately 20 yellow stamens. The fruit are small and dry seedlike achenes, positioned in the sunken pits of the swollen and fleshy red receptacle, which can reach up to approximately ½" in length. The fruit and receptacle are edible, with a tart and sweet taste.

Bloom Period April–June

Plant Communities Disturbed areas, sedge meadow / wet prairie, secondary dune, prairie complex, savanna complex

Notes It is often thought that strawberries are called such because straw was used around the plants; however, the name *strawberry* precedes the cultivation of the plant, so this is a myth. Other theories exist, but it seems the true origin of the word is unknown. As with the garden strawberry, *Fragaria × ananassa*, Virginia strawberry is quite delicious, though smaller. The garden strawberry came about when Virginia strawberry and sand strawberry (*F. chiloensis*) hybridized in a French garden in the eighteenth century (a perfect love story). The resulting plant had the sweetness of Virginia strawberry and the size of sand strawberry. Botanist Antoine Nicolas Duchesne took note of this, describing and providing a botanical name for garden strawberry. Hybridization does naturally occur between these two species in northwestern North America.

Indian-strawberry. Courtesy Michael Huft.

Etymology *Fragaria* is Latin for "strawberry," and *virginiana* refers to it being "of Virginia," referencing the location of early collections.

Look-alikes The nonnative and weedy Indian-strawberry (*Potentilla indica*, also known as *Duchesnea indica* [where have we seen that genus name?]) is often confused with Virginia strawberry but has yellow flowers. It also has a single trifoliate leaf rising from the stolons and fruit that tastes like your grandma's bland coffee water.

Geum canadense (White Avens)

ROSACEAE—rose family

Courtesy Michael Huft.

Description A widespread native perennial that grows to 1–3' tall, sometimes with variegated foliage. Basal leaves are simple or compound with 3–5 leaflets, with the terminal leaflet being the largest. The stem leaves are alternately arranged, toothed, usually trifoliate with some unlobed leaves above. Flowers are 5-parted with round white petals and triangular green sepals with numerous white-tipped stamens crowded in the middle. The fruit are in a nearly spherical cluster, each with a hooked tip allowing it to latch onto an animal's fur or human clothing for dispersal. The receptacle, visible after fruit have dispersed, is conical and hairy.

Bloom Period May–July

Plant Communities Disturbed areas, sedge meadow / wet prairie, bottomland, hydromesophytic forest, conifer swamp, pin oak flatwoods, prairie complex, savanna complex, mesophytic forest

Notes The Iroquois used a brew from white avens to make a love potion. Scattered flowers can be seen on plants after the typical bloom period, sometimes into October.

Courtesy Michael Huft.

Rough avens.

Etymology *Geum*, meaning "blessed herb," was a name that Pliny the Elder gave to another plant in the genus, referencing its medicinal properties. *Canadense* means "of Canada," presumably giving insight into where this species was first collected.

Look-alikes Rough avens (*Geum laciniatum*) differs from white avens in that it has green sepals that are longer than its white petals and a flowering stalk with spreading, long, glistening hairs. Its fruiting cluster is perfectly round, and the receptacle is smooth or with very short (nearly unnoticeable) hairs.

HYDROPHYLLUM VIRGINIANUM
(VIRGINIA WATERLEAF)

HYDROPHYLLACEAE—waterleaf family

Courtesy Michael Huft.

Description A rhizomatous native perennial that reaches 0.5–2' tall. The basal and alternate leaves are stalked and pinnately divided nearly to the midvein into 3–7 lobes, with coarse teeth on the lobes. The leaves are sometimes mottled with whitish gray, as if they were stained by water (see etymology). Eight to 15+ flowers are borne on a hairy cyme in a dense, rounded cluster. The 5-parted tubular flower is usually white to pinkish or lavender, set within 5 fringed sepals. The 5 hairy

stamen filaments protrude beyond the corolla lobes. The fruit is a rounded capsule with few seeds.

Bloom Period May–June

Plant Communities Disturbed areas, bottomland, mesophytic forest

Notes Young leaves were once harvested by Native Americans and early European pioneers, giving it other common names such as Shawnee salad and John's cabbage.

Great waterleaf.

Etymology *Hydrophyllum* is derived from Greek, meaning "water-leaf," often thought to be in reference to the mottling on the leaves that looks like water stains. A more accepted theory, however, is that Linnaeus named the genus based on a specimen of Canada waterleaf (*Hydrophyllum canadense*) (which, at the time, he considered the Canadian form of Virginia waterleaf). The overwintering leaves of Canada waterleaf look different from the leaves it sends up in the spring. Remember that Linnaeus was naming North American plants from the other side of the ocean as they were shipped to him by American collectors. Having not seen the plants in situ, he made the assumption that the sole species of *Hydrophyllum* of which he was aware was an aquatic plant with submerged leaves different from the emergent ones. As such, he used the Greek form of "water-leaf" to name the genus. *Virginianum* is more simple, meaning "from Virginia."

Look-alikes Both great waterleaf (*Hydrophyllum appendiculatum*) and Canada waterleaf (*H. canadense*) have stem leaves that are more palmately lobed and somewhat maplelike.

Lactuca biennis (TALL BLUE LETTUCE)

ASTERACEAE—sunflower family

Description A common native annual or biennial that grows to over 10' tall. The variably shaped, alternately arranged leaves are often deeply pinnately lobed lower on the stem, becoming unlobed higher up, sometimes with arrow-shaped bases. The midvein on the underside of the leaf is usually lined with hairs. When the leaf or stem is broken, it exudes a white milky sap. Flower-heads are composed of numerous cream to whitish or pale-blue ray flowers. The beak of the seedlike achene

is less than half as long as the body (or absent), with a grayish-brown hairlike pappus at the top.

Bloom Period August–September

Plant Communities Disturbed areas, sedge meadow / wet prairie, prairie complex, savanna complex, mesophytic forest

Notes Although we do not recommend eating the leaves of this plant, its close relative butterhead lettuce (*Lactuca sativa*) is delicious fresh out of the garden, drizzled with balsamic vinegar and olive oil.

Etymology *Lactuca* is derived from the Latin word meaning "milk" (think lactating), due to the milky sap. *Biennis* means "biennial," describing the life history of this species.

Look-alikes Wild lettuce (*Lactuca canadensis*) looks similar but has yellow flowerheads (sometimes reddish orange) and lighter green, smoother-looking leaves; it also exudes a salmon-colored sap. Prickly lettuce (*L. serriola*) differs from tall blue lettuce in that it has stiff prickles on the midvein of the leaf underside, yellow flowerheads, and a smooth, glaucous stem. Both wild lettuce and prickly lettuce also have the beak of the achene about half as long as the body but topped with a white pappus.

Wild lettuce.

Laportea canadensis (WOOD NETTLE)

URTICACEAE—nettle family

Description A native perennial growing to 5' tall, covered in tiny translucent stinging hairs as well as smaller non-stinging hairs. The alternately arranged toothed leaves are egg-shaped, ending in a pointed tip. Leaf stalks can be as long as 6–12". Flowers are at the top of the plant and are either male or female, both occurring on the same plant. Male flowers are tiny, 5-parted, and green to white, scattered on a panicle. Female flowers are even less showy than the male flowers but are oddly shaped, with a feathery style and 2–4 appressed green tepals.

Bloom Period July–September

Plant Communities Bottomland, hydromesophytic forest, mesophytic forest

Notes Meeting wood nettle is usually not so much discovering the beauty and complexity of the flowers or morphology of the plant as it is an agonizing exclamation of "What the hell was that?!" You've just been stung. And you'll feel a sting or itch for a while. The sting is caused by a concoction of chemicals, including formic acid. When you or an unsuspecting animal rubs against the hairs that cover the leaves and stems, the tips of the hairs break off, exposing a needlelike structure that contains the irritating, burning chemical cocktail. Anecdotal evidence by both authors notes that there is a differing sensation between wood nettle (sometimes called stinging nettle) and tall nettle (*Urtica dioica* subsp. *gracilis*) (also sometimes called stinging nettle), with the former being much more painful. If wood nettle gets whacked and loses a leaf or stem, the regrowth will have denser stinging hairs. Regardless of the discomfort it can cause, wood nettle was an important food (prepared the right way) for Native Americans. Bon appetit.

Etymology *Laportea* is named after French naturalist François Laporte. The specific epithet, *canadensis*, means "from Canada."

Clearweed.

Look-alikes There are six species within the family Urticaceae in the Indiana Dunes, all with some similar structures that may confuse the passerby. False nettle (*Boehmeria cylindrica*) and clearweeds (*Pilea* spp.) have opposite leaves and no stinging hairs. Pennsylvania pellitory (*Parietaria pensylvanica*) has alternate, entire leaves and also lacks stinging hairs. Tall nettle, which has stinging hairs, can quickly be distinguished in that it has narrower, opposite leaves, and axillary inflorescences.

Tall nettle.

Lespedeza capitata
(ROUND-HEADED BUSHCLOVER)
FABACEAE—legume family

Description A native perennial growing to 2–5' tall. The alternately arranged leaves are trifoliate, sessile to subsessile, and often covered with hairs on at least the underside. The leaflets are over twice as long as wide. The flowers are small and creamy white with a reddish-purple splotch on the large banner petal; they are clustered in short-stalked, packed heads in axils of

leaves near the top of the plant. As the flower matures to fruit, the calyx turns a brown color, making it a striking plant within the winter landscape.

Bloom Period July–September

Plant Communities Secondary dune, prairie complex, savanna complex

Notes Mammals often eat round-headed bushclover as it is growing, and many birds enjoy feasting on the seeds. This gorgeous plant serves as a host plant for many butterfly and moth species, as well as being an attractive nectar source for butterflies and long- and short-tongued bees.

Etymology *Lespedeza* was named to honor a politician, a Spanish governing official of East Florida named Vicente Manuel de Céspedes. André Michaux, in honor of

Silky bushclover.

Céspedes's generosity in allowing him to botanize the region, made the genus his namesake in Michaux's book *Flora Boreali-Americana*. Unfortunately, in the book, someone goofed and put an *L* instead of a *C* (most of the botanists that we know have pretty poor handwriting!). So instead of *Cespedeza*, we have *Lespedeza*. Moral of the story: don't name a plant after a politician. The specific epithet *capitata* isn't as exciting; it just means "head," referring to the dense flower and fruit clusters.

Look-alikes The native hairy bushclover (*Lespedeza hirta*) looks very similar to round-headed bushclover and often occupies the same habitat; however, hairy bushclover has rounder leaflets that are less than twice as long as wide. Also, the flowerhead stalks of hairy bushclover are longer than the leaves directly beneath them, whereas the stalk is shorter in round-headed bushclover. Sounds easy enough, right? But these two species hybridize, forming *Lespedeza* × *longifolia*. The nonnative and invasive silky bushclover (*L. cuneata*), also called sericea lespedeza, similarly has creamy flowers but with narrower leaflets and one to few flowers in each head.

Maianthemum canadense (Canada mayflower)

ASPARAGACEAE—asparagus family

Courtesy Michael Huft.

Description A colony-forming native perennial that typically grows to 4–9" tall. The sterile plants have a single leaf; fertile plants have 2 (rarely 3) alternately arranged leaves. The leaves are egg-shaped with a heart-shaped base and pointed tip. The upper surface of the leaf is glossy and hairless; the underside is hairless in var. *canadense* and hairy in var. *interius*. Flowers are 4-parted and clustered in a raceme that resembles a constellation of stars. The fruit is a round red berry that has green spots when young that fade away at maturity.

Bloom Period May–June

Plant Communities Bog, hydromesophytic forest, conifer swamp, pin oak flatwoods, savanna complex, mesophytic forest

Notes Also called wild lily-of-the-valley.

Etymology *Maianthemum* means "May flower," and *canadense* means "from Canada." This is one of the few plants whose common name aligns perfectly with its scientific name.

Look-alikes The nonnative and invasive lily-of-the-valley (*Convallaria majalis*), often found near old homesites, is similar but has more upright leaves (similar to those of ramps [*Allium tricoccum*]) and a raceme of dangling bell-shaped flowers, each with 6 recurved lobes.

Maianthemum racemosum
(feathery false Solomon's seal)

ASPARAGACEAE—asparagus family

Description An ascending native perennial that grows up to 1–3' tall. There is typically some reddish coloration toward the base of the green, arching stem. The toothless, sessile, or very short-stalked leaves are alternately arranged in a subtle zigzag up the stem. The 6-parted flowers are arranged in a feathery terminal panicle, with each inflorescence having 70–250 flowers. The fruit are berries that start green with goldish-copper or purple spots and mature to a brilliant red.

Bloom Period April–June

Plant Communities Bottomland, hydromesophytic forest, savanna complex, mesophytic forest

Notes Ironically, the flowers are not in fact in a raceme, as the botanical name suggests, but in a panicle. However, its sister species, starry false Solomon's seal (*Maianthemum stellatum*), does have its flowers in a true raceme. The fruit of feathery false Solomon's seal are said to be edible, raw or cooked. If eaten raw, they could cause a little rumble in your tummy, as they have laxative properties that are lost when cooked. A common synonym is *Smilacina racemosa*.

Etymology *Maianthemum* means "May flower," and *racemosum* means "having a raceme" (technically speaking, a panicle could be described as smaller racemes off of the main inflorescence axis).

Look-alikes Starry false Solomon's seal looks similar to feathery false Solomon's seal; however, it has fewer, larger flowers that are in a terminal raceme. Its leaves are also typically longer and narrower than those of feathery false Solomon's seal.

Starry false Solomon's seal.

Melilotus albus (White Sweet Clover)

FABACEAE—legume family

Description An aggressive nonnative biennial that grows to around 3–6' tall but in perfect conditions can reach 10' tall. The stem is coarse, erect, hairless, and branched with a bushy form. The leaflets of the alternately arranged, stalked, trifoliate leaves are elliptic-oblong or oblong. The tiny pealike, sweet-smelling flowers are set in slender racemes in leaf axils and at the ends of branches. Fruit are small, round, veiny legumes, each with only one seed.

Bloom Period June–November

Plant Communities Disturbed areas, secondary dune, prairie complex, savanna complex

Notes Sweet clover has been used as a forage crop, bee nectar source, and soil stabilizer. It threatens native flora by releasing chemicals that prevent the growth of other plants. Even though it was introduced as a forage crop, at certain times of the year sweet clover produces a chemical compound called coumarin, which can poison livestock. Rubbing the foliage emits a faint sweet scent.

Etymology *Melilotus* is derived from *meli-*, meaning "honey" (either because of the sweet-scented foliage or because it is a valuable plant for producing honey), and *lotus*, which refers to a leguminous plant. The specific epithet *albus* means "white," referencing the color of the flowers.

Look-alikes White sweet clover is sometimes taxonomically placed as a subspecies within its sister species, yellow sweet clover (*Melilotus officinalis*). The two differ in flower color as the common names imply. Although there certainly is overlap in bloom period, yellow sweet clover begins flowering about 2 weeks before white sweet clover at the same site. White sweet clover also has racemes that are usually longer than those of yellow sweet clover.

Yellow sweet clover.

MITCHELLA REPENS (PARTRIDGE BERRY)

RUBIACEAE—madder family

Description A native creeping perennial that grows from 4" to 12" long and roots at the nodes. The oppositely arranged, broadly egg-shaped evergreen leaves are dark green contrasted with a cream-colored midrib. The small flowers are paired, 4-parted, funnel-shaped, and hairy within the throat and inner lobes; it is good luck if you find a flower with 3 or 6 lobes . . . but it is bad luck if you find one with 5 lobes. Although the flowers are paired, both need to be pollinated to produce the red berry. If you look closely at the berry, you'll see the

two scars representing the fusion of the ovaries of the two flowers.

Bloom Period May–August

Plant Communities Hydromesophytic forest, conifer swamp, pin oak flatwoods, mesophytic forest

Notes John Mitchell was a physician who was, as were many physicians of the time, interested in botany. In 1741, he had described 30 genera. Carl Linnaeus was impressed with Mitchell's work and thus changed Mitchell's genus *Chamaedaphne* to *Mitchella* to honor his friend. *Chamaedaphne* was later used for another North American genus, named in 1794.

Etymology The genus name *Mitchella* honors Dr. John Mitchell (see notes), and *repens* means "creeping," describing the growth form.

Look-alikes When in flower, nothing in the Indiana Dunes looks quite like partridge berry. Vegetatively, one might confuse it with moneywort (*Lysimachia nummularia*). The latter has nearly round leaves that lack a lightened midvein and that are not as dark green, thick, or leathery as those of partridge berry; it also has 5-parted yellow flowers. The two grow in different habitats, with moneywort growing in disturbed areas, bottomlands, and hydromesophytic forest. Within the latter community, moneywort grows in the saturated muck, whereas partridge berry is more restricted to the hummocks.

Mitella diphylla (bishop's cap)

SAXIFRAGACEAE—saxifrage family

Description A native spring ephemeral perennial that grows to 18" tall. The basal leaves are coarsely toothed, shallowly palmately 3- to 5-lobed, and have a heart-shaped base attached to a long leaf stalk. Many flowering stems can emerge from the basal leaves. Each flowering stem has one pair of oppositely arranged, coarsely toothed 3-lobed, stalkless leaves near the middle. Overall, the plant is covered in short hairs. Flowers are small, with 5 feather-like petals arranged

alternately in a terminal raceme. After the flower dies back, the cuplike calyx holds the small, shiny, black seeds.

Bloom Period April–June

Plant Communities Hydromesophytic forest, mesophytic forest

Notes This captivating wildflower, with flowers that look like tiny snowflakes, is also called eastern mitrewort.

Etymology *Mitella* comes from the Greek word *mitra*, which means "cap," referring to the shape of the calyx in fruit. *Diphylla* simply means "two leaves," referencing the pair of leaves on the flowering stem.

Look-alikes The basal leaves of bishop's cap can be confused with prairie alumroot (*Heuchera richardsonii*), with the latter having yellow irregular flowers that do not resemble snowflakes. Prairie alumroot also grows in drier communities, such as the prairie and savanna complexes.

Monotropa uniflora (Ghostpipe)

ERICACEAE—heath family

Description Often confused for a fungus, this parasitic native perennial grows up to 8" tall. The entire plant is usually ghost white but sometimes has a pink or reddish blush. The leaves are reduced to small, ascending scales. The flower is terminal and solitary, drooping as if it is bowing to the great forest in jest, becoming erect in fruit, with a globose capsule.

Bloom Period June–September

Plant Communities Hydromesophytic forest, pin oak flatwoods, savanna complex, mesophytic forest

Notes Also commonly called corpse flower, due to the outdated belief that it was saprophytic. It has long been known that ghostpipe tricks mycorrhizal fungi (specifically *Lactarius* spp. [milkcaps] and *Russula* spp. [russulas]) into what initially appears to be a symbiotic relationship, then turns it into a parasitic relationship by taking without giving anything back. Because it is completely parasitic, it does not need to produce any chlorophyll, which is why it is white. Another common name is Indian pipe.

Pinesap. Courtesy Michael Huft.

Etymology *Monotropa* is derived from the Greek *mono-* and *-tropa*, meaning "one" and "turned," referring to the drooping flower, and *uniflora* means "one flower."

Look-alikes Pinesap (*Hypopitys monotropa*) looks very much like ghostpipe but is somewhat hairy, has more than one flower per stem, and is creamy yellow to yellowish orange. Some pinesap with pink to reddish stems is referred to as *H. lanuginosa*.

Pinesap. Courtesy Michael Huft.

Nymphaea odorata subsp. tuberosa
(American white waterlily)

NYMPHAEACEAE—waterlily family

Description A native aquatic perennial that can grow in water up to 8' deep, rooted underwater. The round, toothless leaves to 1' in diameter are usually floating and have a slit from the base to the middle, where the stalk is attached; the leaf underside is often purple. The long leaf and flowering stalks come from a large root-stock sometimes as large as an arm (maybe not Arnold Schwarzenegger's). The fragrant flowers are quite large (to 7.5" wide) and showy, with 20–40 petals; they sit on the surface of the water and close each evening as the sun sets.

Bloom Period May–September

Plant Communities Submerged aquatic, bog, marsh, panne

Notes Henry David Thoreau wrote in his journals that the American white waterlily "bursts up so pure and fair to the eye and so sweet to the scent, as if to show us what purity and sweetness reside in and can be extracted from the slime and muck of earth."

This plant derived from one of the oldest evolutionary lineages of flowering plants! There once was, and maybe still is, a belief that eating the flowers in a jam can cause a relaxing effect and ease sexual desire (a good thing to give to your teenage child). The rootstock was used by many Native American tribes for numerous ailments.

Etymology *Nymphaea* means "water-nymph," *odorata* means "fragrant," and *tuberosa* means "with tubers," all accurately describing this wildflower.

Look-alikes There are no naturally occurring plants in the Indiana Dunes that look like American white waterlily, but it is often found growing with another plant with smaller floating leaves: watershield (*Brasenia schreberi*). The leaves of the latter are oval and lacking a slit, with the stem attached in the middle of the underside of the leaf; the leaf undersides and stems are covered in a gelatinous goo. Its flowers stick out of the water and have 3 to 4 petals and 3 to 4 sepals, ranging from cream colored to pinkish.

Watershield.

Panax trifolius (DWARF GINSENG)

ARALIACEAE—ginseng family

Description A short-stature native perennial that grows no taller than 6". The leaves are in a single whorl of three (usually) along the stem, with each leaf palmately separated into 3–5 finely toothed, stalkless leaflets. Flowers are set in a nearly spherical terminal umbel with each individual flower 5-parted. Sometimes the white flower will have a pinkish blush. The fruit are small, yellowish green, and berrylike.

Bloom Period April–May

Plant Communities Hydromesophytic forest, mesophytic forest

Notes Dwarf ginseng is diphasic, which means it can change sex. Immature plants lack flowers; as they mature, the flowers of a plant will be functionally all male, and at full maturity the flowers are hermaphroditic, having both functional male and female parts. When flowers are functionally male, they have 5 stamens and a small, nonfunctional pistil. When they are in the hermaphroditic phase, they are protandrous, meaning that the stamens are functional before the pistil is, keeping the flowers from self-pollinating.

Etymology *Panax* is derived from the word "panacea," which means "a remedy for all troubles or diseases." Linnaeus named the genus *Panax*, due to its legendary ability in Chinese medicine to heal many ailments. *Trifolius* means "three-leaved."

Look-alikes Dwarf ginseng's sister species, American ginseng (*Panax quinquefolius*), is much rarer in the Indiana Dunes. It differs in that all of its leaflets are stalked, the plant is larger, the flowers are green, and the berries are red.

American ginseng.

Parthenium integrifolium (WILD QUININE)

ASTERACEAE—sunflower family

Description A native perennial that grows to a little over 3' tall. The basal leaves can be up to 1' long, ovate to broadly lanceolate, with broad-based teeth, a white midvein, and winged stalks. The alternately arranged leaves are similar, with the upper ones often clasping the stem. The flowerheads usually have 5 cuplike ray flowers that loosely surround the 15–35+ male disc florets.

Bloom Period July–September

Plant Communities Prairie complex, savanna complex

Notes A common story found in wildflower guides mentions that when quinine, which is derived from the bark of the South American cinchona tree (*Cinchona* spp.), became less accessible during World War I, wild quinine was used in a similar way to treat malaria. We could not find any substantive evidence of this other than in a 1987 literature review for the American Herbal Products Association Standard Committee by Steven Foster entitled "Echinacea Quality Control Monograph: A Literature Review." Historically, wild quinine root was often found to be an adulterant with echinacea root in herbal supplements due to the similarity of their taproots. Another common name, American feverfew, resulted from its use to treat fevers. It has also been used to treat burns.

Etymology *Parthenium* is derived from the Greek word *parthenos*, which means "virgin," referring to the disc florets that do not produce fruit because they are functionally male. *Integrifolium* comes from the Latin *integer* and *-folium*, meaning "entire leaves," referring to the leaves of this plant, which are clearly coarsely toothed. Confused by the etymology of the specific epithet of this species? We are!

Look-alikes There isn't much in the Indiana Dunes that looks like wild quinine. Vegetatively, the basal leaves of prairie dock (*Silphium terebinthinaceum*) could be confused for wild quinine, as the two are often found in the same habitat, but the leaves of the former are broad at the flat base, rather than tapering to a winged stalk.

Penstemon digitalis (FOXGLOVE BEARD-TONGUE)

PLANTAGINACEAE—plantain family

Description A native perennial that grows up to 3–5′ tall. The stem is glabrous except in the inflorescence. Basal leaves are stalked and entire, whereas the oppositely arranged stem leaves are sessile, often slightly clasping, and toothed; leaves, especially basal, often have at least some reddish-purple coloration. Tubular 5-lobed flowers have light-purple stripes in the throat; these look black when using a UV light. The anthers possess a few short, stiff hairs.

Bloom Period May–July

Plant Communities Disturbed areas, sedge meadow / wet prairie, prairie complex

When in full bloom, the showy trumpet-shaped flowers of foxglove beard-tongue look as if Ornette Coleman was serenading you. The common name beard-tongue is visually gross but comes from the hairy sterile stamen (called a staminode). Another common name is dead-man's bells because it was known to grow on old grave sites.

Penstemon is derived from the Greek words *pente* and *stemon*, meaning "five stamen," as the genus is characterized by having four fertile stamens and one stamen that does not produce pollen (the staminode). The specific epithet *digitalis* means "fingers" (think digits) because the shape of the flower looks like a thimble.

The similar long-sepal beard-tongue (*Penstemon calycosus*) differs in that it has hairless anthers and flowers that are faintly pink to purplish-pink and usually slightly narrower.

Persicaria lapathifolia (PALE SMARTWEED)

POLYGONACEAE—buckwheat family

Description A disturbance-dependent, incredibly variable native annual that grows up to ~5' tall. The alternately arranged lanceolate leaves taper to a point and are often on petioles up to 0.5" long on unbranched or branched stems. The underside of the leaf can be slightly hairy, smooth, or gland dotted with the midvien having broad-based scale-like hairs. There is sometimes a darker crescent to-V-shaped smear on the leaf. The ocreae typically lack bristles at their summits. Flowers have 4–5 greenish-white to pink tepals and are borne in dense, mostly terminal, typically nodding spikelike racemes with stalkless glands below the inflorescences.

The fruit are seedlike achenes that are brownish black and flattish.

Bloom Period June–October

Plant Communities Disturbed areas, marsh, sedge meadow / wet prairie

Notes Pale smartweed has been found in areas that have high levels of pollution. It has recently been discovered that the seeds contain antifungal and antibacterial compounds. Pale smartweed is also a larval host plant for the bronze copper butterfly (*Lycaena hyllus*).

Etymology *Persicaria* means "peach-like," referring to the leaves that are shaped somewhat like those of peach (*Prunus persica*). *Lapathifolia* is derived from the Latin word *lapathium*, meaning "dock" or "sorrel," and *folia*, meaning "leaf." This is in reference to its dock-like (*Rumex*) leaves. So . . . are the leaves peach-like or dock-like?

Oriental lady's thumb.

Look-alikes Oriental lady's thumb (*Persicaria longiseta*), also called creeping smartweed, differs in usually being smaller, having long bristles on the ocreae, and having achenes that are 3-sided. Spotted lady's thumb (*P. maculosa*) has the darker splotch on the leaf and flattish achenes; however, it differs in also having ocreae topped by bristles. Pennsylvania smartweed (*P. pensylvanica*) is the closest in morphology to pale smartweed; it differs in that it typically has 5 tepals, has slightly larger pink (usually) flowers in thicker spikelike racemes, and has stalked glands below the inflorescences.

From left to right, Pennsylvania smartweed, spotted lady's thumb, and pale smartweed.

PERSICARIA PUNCTATA (DOTTED SMARTWEED)

POLYGONACEAE—buckwheat family

Description A common, often overlooked native annual that grows up to 2.5' tall. The undersides of the alternate leaves are covered in glandular divots (punctate), often with a few hairs on the midvein. The ocreae are topped by long bristles. Loose spikelike racemes terminate branches, with each flower having 5 tepals that are pitted with miniscule glands. The seedlike achenes are smooth and shiny.

Bloom Period July–September

Plant Communities Disturbed areas, marsh, bottomland, hydromesophytic forest

Chewing on the leaves yields a delayed spicy, peppery sensation (you've got to try it). The Iroquois made a decoction from dotted smartweed to help with mental issues. The fruit is an important food source for birds.

Etymology See *Persicaria lapathifolia* for genus etymology. *Punctata* means "spotted," referring to the glands on the tepals.

Look-alikes There are many look-alikes in the Indiana Dunes, with one of the most confused being common water-pepper (*Persicaria hydropiper*), which has pitted,

Common water-pepper.

dull achenes and self-pollinating cleistogamous flowers concealed within some of the ocreae. Another similar species that was thought to be extirpated from Indiana, stout smartweed (*P. robustior*), was rediscovered south of the Heron Rookery by the authors in 2018; it is a much larger plant with leaf blades over 1" wide (leaves of dotted smartweed are usually 0.2–0.8" wide) and a tighter inflorescence. Mild water-pepper (*P. hydropiperoides*) is also similar but is perennial; it lacks glandular dots on the tepals, and its leaves lack the peppery taste.

Mild water-pepper.

PERSICARIA VIRGINIANA (JUMPSEED)

POLYGONACEAE—buckwheat family

Description A common native perennial that grows to over 2' tall. The large alternately arranged leaves are toothless and short-stalked or sessile; there is sometimes a dark chevron in the middle of each leaf. Ocreae are green to brown to reddish, covered in hairs. The long, loose spikelike terminal raceme has scattered 4-parted, starlike flowers with small pointed tepals that are usually white but occasionally are green to pinkish. The fruit is a dry seedlike achene with a hooked tip.

Bloom Period July–September

Plant Communities Disturbed areas, bottomland, savanna complex, mesophytic forest

Notes A plant of many names, jumpseed is also called woodland knotweed and Virginia knotweed, and some botanists place it in the genus *Antenoron*, while others place it in the genus *Tovara*. Stalks of individual fruit are twisted with enough pressure built up that, when bumped, they shoot the achenes up to 10' away from the plant.

Etymology See *Persicaria lapathifolia* for genus etymology. *Virginiana* means "from Virginia," as the species was described based on a specimen from colonial Virginia.

Look-alikes None.

Phytolacca americana (American pokeweed)

PHYTOLACCACEAE—pokeweed family

Description An odd-looking native perennial that grows up to 10' tall. Stems are usually reddish or green, especially when young. The large alternately arranged leaves are up to 10" long, smelling musty when crushed. Flowers are white, sometimes pinkish, with 5 petallike sepals, no true petals, stamens slightly protruding, and a dozen or so fused pistils in the middle. The fruit is a dark purple (nearly black) berry that is accented brilliantly by the red stems and stalks.

Bloom Period June–October

Plant Communities Disturbed areas, savanna complex, mesophytic forest

Notes When a stable woodland ecosystem is disturbed (even by well-intentioned land managers), American pokeweed happily takes over, often becoming quite weedy. This is a case of a plant doing what it has evolved to do; American pokeweed is a pioneer species, a colonizer, a healer of wounds to the earth. The berries are an important food for birds. Another common name, used in the southeastern United States, is poke sallet.

The plant is used as a cooked green after being collected when young and properly prepared; all parts of the plant are poisonous if not prepared correctly. Tony Joe White's classic song, "Polk Salad Annie," is in reference to this southern dish. In fact, you should stop reading now and turn on a little Tony Joe White.

Etymology The genus name is from the two roots *phyto-* and *-lacca*, meaning "plant" and "lake," with the latter referring to the color crimson lake, also called carmine, from the dye produced by the berries. The specific epithet *americana* refers to it being from America.

Look-alikes Vegetatively, American pokeweed can be confused for poke milkweed (*Asclepias exaltata*), but the latter has opposite leaves, and, once in flower, there is no mistaking the two.

Podophyllum peltatum (mayapple)

BERBERIDACEAE—barberry family

Description A rhizomatous colony-forming native perennial that grows up to 1.5–2' tall. Sterile individual ramets produce a leaf with the stalk attached in the middle. Each leaf can grow over 1' in diameter, is somewhat round in general outline, and is 5–9 lobed. The fertile ramet produces two nearly opposite leaves with stalks attached to the base of each blade, with a relatively large solitary drooping flower emerging from the fork in the stem under the leaves. The flower is fragrant, with 6 sepals and 6–9 white petals. The fruit is a yellow berry that reaches up to 2" long.

Bloom Period May–June

Plant Communities Disturbed areas, hydromesophytic forest, savanna complex, mesophytic forest

Notes Mayapple has been praised for its edibility; however, unless the fruit is ripe, the plant is toxic. The seeds also contain toxins. Before the fruit is completely ripe, it is probably eaten by eastern box turtles, gray squirrels, and white-footed mice. One of the authors once ate an unripe fruit and ended up with extreme nausea. The other author knows better. We'll let you guess which is which.

Etymology The genus name comes from the Greek *podo-* and *phyllo*, meaning "foot" and "leaf." Originally, it was named *Anapodophyllum*, which means "duck's foot leaf," but this was shortened by Linnaeus to *Podophyllum*; in this case, the name with more syllables would have been more suitable, as the leaves have the appearance of webbed feet. The specific epithet *peltatum* means "shield-bearing," referring to the attachment of the leaf stalk into the middle of the sterile ramet leaf blade (an attachment referred to as "peltate").

Look-alikes None.

Polygonatum biflorum
(smooth Solomon's seal)

ASPARAGACEAE—asparagus family

Courtesy Michael Huft.

Description A native perennial that grows from 1' to 3' tall, typically with some bluish coloration toward the base of the stem. The hairless and somewhat clasping leaves are alternately arranged along the arching stem. Flowers are like miniature dangling bells up to 1" long hanging below each leaf axil. The flowers, each with 6 small lobes, are usually in pairs or threes. Fruits are blue berries, but not "blueberries"!

Bloom Period May–July

Plant Communities Disturbed areas, prairie complex, savanna complex

Notes The common name of this elegant plant is thought to be derived from the rhizomes that, when broken, look like a seal or Hebrew signature. It has also been conjectured that the name came from the 6 lobes on the flower, like the Star of David. In short, it is hard to say if anyone really knows.

Smooth Solomon's seal's rhizomes were consumed like potatoes by Native Americans.

Etymology The genus name comes from the Greek words *poly* and *gonu*, meaning "many knee-joints," referring to the subterranean knobby joints of the rhizomes. *Biflorum* means "two flowers," as the flowers are sometimes in pairs.

Look-alikes Hairy Solomon's seal (*Polygonatum pubescens*) looks similar but differs in having hair on the undersides of the leaves, at least along the veins; it is more frequent in mesophytic forest. False Solomon's seals (*Maianthemum* spp.) can also be confused with this species but have terminal inflorescences and usually reddish coloration near the base of the plants.

PYCNANTHEMUM VIRGINIANUM
(VIRGINIA MOUNTAIN-MINT)

LAMIACEAE—mint family

Description A native perennial that grows up to 3' tall. The stems are 4-angled with hairs on the angles. The oppositely arranged, toothless leaves are hairless, lance-linear, stalkless, and taper to a point, and when crushed yield a pleasant aroma ranging from citrus to mint to oregano. Flowers are in dense terminal clusters, making up a flattish inflorescence. Each irregular flower is 5-parted, with 2 lobes on the top and 3 on the bottom; purple spots are scattered on the lobes.

July–September

Prairie fen, sedge meadow / wet prairie, prairie complex

Notes The fragrance of the leaves of Virginia mountain-mint is breathtakingly pleasant; the leaves have been used to make tea to aid in digestion and can be eaten raw or cooked.

Etymology *Pycnanthemum* is derived from two Greek words, *pyknos* and *anthos*, which together mean "dense flowers," referencing the inflorescence. *Virginianum* means "from Virginia," as the species was described based on a specimen from colonial Virginia.

Look-alikes Slender mountain-mint (*Pycnanthemum tenuifolium*) differs in having hairless or nearly hairless stems. Although there is overlap, its leaves are narrower and usually lack the strong fragrance, and foliage is more yellow green (as compared to deeper green in Virginia mountain-mint). Intermediate hybrids are often found in prairie plantings.

Rumex verticillatus (SWAMP DOCK)

POLYGONACEAE—buckwheat family

Description A native perennial that can grow to 4–5'
tall. Stems are hairless. The alternately arranged leaves
are up to 1' long, toothless, hairless, and flat. Dangling
greenish-white flowers are clustered with about a dozen
or so in separated whorls along the terminal inflorescence. Each flower has 6 tepals that are usually green
and 6 stamens that are usually whitish and slightly
protruding beyond the tepals. The fruit is surrounded

by 3 specialized inner tepals that form the valves that wrap around the achene. A tubercle (or grain) enlarges on each of the valves.

Bloom Period June–August

Plant Communities Marsh, bottomland, hydromesophytic forest, pin oak flatwoods

Notes Swamp dock, the species of *Rumex* most likely to be found in standing water and swamps, is a larval host for the bronze copper butterfly (*Lycaena hyllus*) and the American copper (*L. phlaeas*). Because of the high concentrations of oxalic acid in the leaves, it should not be consumed.

Etymology *Rumex* is the Latin word referencing the docks, and *verticillatus* means "forming whorls," a reference to the whorls of flowers in the inflorescence.

Look-alikes Within the Indiana Dunes there are six species in the genus *Rumex*, with swamp dock differing by having all three grains of the valves present and the same size, entire leaves, and fruit stalks that are over two times longer than the fruit itself. Oftentimes curly dock (*Rumex crispus*) is mistaken for swamp dock; however, curly dock has wavy and shallowly toothed leaf margins, usually grows in drier habitats (usually in disturbed areas), and has one large grain and the other two usually less developed or absent on the valves.

SAGITTARIA LATIFOLIA (DUCK-POTATO)

ALISMATACEAE—water-plantain family

Courtesy Michael Huft.

Description An emergent perennial that grows up to 4' tall. Basal leaves are variable in size but usually look like an arrowhead (sagittate) when emergent and are linear or ribbonlike when submerged. The leaves are hairless and toothless with the sagittate lobes up to as long as the non-sagittate portion. The 3-parted flowers are arranged in a raceme in separated whorls of three. Flowers are either male or female, found on the same plant, with males above and females below. Fruiting heads are globular, tightly packed clusters of beaked achenes, with the beak at a right angle relative to the body.

Bloom Period June–September

Plant Communities Bog, marsh, sedge meadow / wet prairie, bottomland

Notes In Europe and Asia, duck-potato is often viewed as an invasive species due to its tendency to exploit disturbed wet areas such as channels and ditches, being somewhat tolerant of pollution (it's always interesting to find plants native to the United States that are invasive in the Old World, as so many of their plants are invasive here). A large suite of insects visit its flowers and foliage. Ducks and other waterfowl are often found feeding on the tubers and fruit. The tubers were also eaten raw, roasted, or dried by Native Americans. Also called common arrowhead.

Etymology *Sagittaria* is derived from the Latin word meaning "arrow," depicting the leaf shape, and *latifolia* means "broad-leaf," which is sometimes (but not always) true for this species.

Look-alikes There are three other *Sagittaria* species known from the Indiana Dunes, with another, arum-leaved arrowhead (*S. cuneata*), found in nearby counties. Duck-potato differs from similar species by having the following combination of characters: (1) no bisexual flowers; (2) emergent, sagittate leaves; (3) bracts where each flower stalk attaches to the stem are under ½" long and shaped like the bow of a canoe; and (4) achenes are not winged.

Sanguinaria canadensis (BLOODROOT)

PAPAVERACEAE—poppy family

Description A native perennial that grows to 12" tall. The shallowly palmately 5–9 lobed, and often bluntly toothed basal leaf initially wraps tightly around the emerging flowering stalk, protecting the solitary terminal flower bud from the frost. As the flower opens, the leaf unfurls like an open hand. The flower opens when the sun is out and folds in the shadows. The number of petals on a flower is variable, ranging from 5 to 10+, usually having 8. This is peculiar, as most flowers in the poppy family normally have 4 petals. The fruit is an elongated capsule that tapers at both ends.

Bloom Period March–May

Plant Communities Mesophytic forest

Notes When any part of the plant (except the flower) is broken, a blood-red sap bleeds out; this is especially true of the large root. This sap was used by Native Americans for dye, face paint, and insect repellent. Although bloodroot historically had medicinal uses, it contains many toxic chemicals and should not be consumed. The flowers start out with the stamens positioned away from the stigmas so as to not self-pollinate; however, if no pollinator visits the flowers after a couple of days, the stamens bend down to the stigma and self-pollinate before dying back.

Bloodroot seeds possess a fleshy structure (an elaiosome) that is full of lipids and sugars, which ants love. Ants take the seeds underground, where they partake in the delicious elaiosomes. Secretions from the ants have antifungal and antibiotic properties, so as the ants get a tasty treat, the seed gets dispersed in a safe place where it potentially won't get decimated by fungal or bacterial agents.

Elaiosomes on the seeds.

Etymology The genus name comes from the Latin word *sanguis*, which means "blood" (an obvious reference), and *canadensis* means "from Canada."

Look-alikes There is nothing in the Indiana Dunes that looks like bloodroot, but outside of our region, twinleaf (*Jeffersonia diphylla*) looks similar; its leaves consist of two identical broadly toothed leaflets, and the flowers drop their petals very soon after opening.

SANICULA MARILANDICA
(MARYLAND BLACK SNAKEROOT)

APIACEAE—carrot family

Courtesy Michael Huft.

Description An erect native perennial that grows up to 2–4' tall with hairless stems. Basal leaves have long stalks and are sharply toothed, hairless, and palmately compound, divided into 5–7 leaflets (or at least appearing so). The alternately arranged stem leaves are similar, reduced in size and becoming stalkless up the stem. Flowers are white to greenish white, 5-parted, either male or bisexual, with the stamens protruding far out of the flowers. The flowers are clustered in umbels, with up to 60 flowers in their small, tight umbellets; each umbellet often has far more stalked male flowers than sessile bisexual ones. Mature dry fruits have curved bristles and split into two parts.

Bloom Period June–July

Plant Communities Savanna complex

Notes Native Americans would make a cataplasm from the roots to cure snake bites, which is where the common name originated.

Etymology *Sanicula* is derived from the Latin word *sanus*, which means "to heal" or "to be healthy," referring to its history in European herbal medicine. *Marilandica* means "from Maryland."

Look-alikes Two other common snakeroot species in the Indiana Dunes are Canadian black snakeroot (*Sanicula canadensis*) and clustered black snakeroot (*S. odorata*). In Canadian black snakeroot the styles are shorter than the calyx of the bisexual flowers, and there are only a few sterile staminate flowers. Clustered black snakeroot differs in that it has smaller, yellow flowers with the calyx <1 mm in length (>1 mm in length in Maryland black snakeroot). Both Canadian and clustered black snakeroot also differ in having only 3–5 leaflets/lobes; they are also both generally smaller plants. Furthermore, Canadian black snakeroot and clustered black snakeroot both inhabit a wider range of disturbed and natural communities. Identification of these will probably require you to use some magnification until you are familiar with all three.

Clustered black snakeroot.

Saururus cernuus (Lizard's Tail)

SAURURACEAE—lizard tail family

Description A native perennial that grows up to 3' tall. The stems are erect to ascending. The alternately arranged heart-shaped leaves are dark green with impressed veins and emit a sweet aroma when crushed. The leaf stalk has a sheath around its base and the stem. Up to 350 flowers are arranged on a long, often nodding spikelike raceme that looks like a white magic wand. Each flower has 4–8 white stamens, 3–5 white carpels, and no petals or sepals. The fragrance of the flowers is citrusy and strong. The fruit is a schizocarp.

Bloom Period June–August

Plant Communities Marsh, bottomland, hydromesophytic forest, pin oak flatwoods

Notes This fantastical plant is part of a primitive lineage of flowering plants that occurred prior to the evolution of petals and sepals. Fragments of the roots can break off, float down the river, and grow in new locations.

Etymology *Saururus* is derived from the ancient Greek words meaning "lizard tail," likely referring to the shape of the inflorescence. *Cernuus* means "bowing, nodding, or arching," also referencing the inflorescence shape.

Look-alikes None.

Silene latifolia (white campion)

CARYOPHYLLACEAE—pink family

Courtesy Michael Huft.

Description A nonnative weed that grows up to 2–3' tall, sometimes as an annual but frequently as a short-lived perennial. The opposite, finely hairy, light-green, sessile to subsessile leaves get smaller in size up the hairy stem. The long-stalked basal leaves are usually gone by the time of flowering. Fragrant flowers are about 1" in diameter and either male or female. The calyx beneath the 5 spreading white corolla lobes is inflated and has prominent veins that are purplish to dark green, 10 in male flowers and 20 in female flowers. Corolla lobes are 2-lobed at the tip with an upright fringe at the base, the latter collectively forming a collar of sorts at the top of the floral tube. The fruit is a vase-shaped capsule.

Bloom Period May–October

Plant Communities Disturbed areas, secondary dune, prairie complex, savanna complex

Notes This weed was thought to have been introduced to the United States in contaminated seed crop. One of the common names for the genus *Silene* is "catchfly." It gets this name from flies that land on the glutinous

Soapwort. Courtesy Michael Huft.

Glaucous bladder campion.

stems of some species only to find themselves stuck. The common name campion is from "champion," as in the flowery crown put on a champion's head; this is a reference to the collar at the top of the corolla tube. The flowers open in the late afternoon and close by midday the following day.

Etymology It is unknown where the genus name comes from, but it may be derived from the Greek word for "saliva," due to the sticky, sometimes foamlike substance on the stems of some species, or from the Greek drunk Silenus, who was often covered in sticky alcoholic beverages. *Latifolia* means "broad-leaf," as the leaves of this species are broad relative to some others in the genus.

Look-alikes There are several pink family plants that look similar to white campion. Soapwort (*Saponaria officinalis*), glaucous bladder campion (*Silene csereii*), and bladder campion (*Silene vulgaris*) all have bisexual flowers and hairless calyces. All of these are also introduced.

Solanum carolinense (Carolina horsenettle)

SOLANACEAE—nightshade family

Description A native perennial weed that grows from 0.5' to 3' tall, usually with prickly stems. The alternately arranged leaves are somewhat oak-shaped with 2–5 shallow lobes and prickles on the undersides along the veins. Flowers to about ¾" wide are stalked in a terminal cluster and are usually white but sometimes faintly lavender. They are 5-parted, with the 5 corolla lobes united at the base and 5 banana-like stamens surrounding a slender green style. The fruit are round yellow berries that sometimes hold on through the winter.

Bloom Period June–September

Plant Communities Disturbed areas, secondary dune, prairie complex, savanna complex

Notes Once rare in northern Indiana, this species has clearly expanded its range due to disturbance and possibly climate change. It is sometimes considered introduced to our region. Don't let the tomato-like fruit fool you; all parts of the plant, including the berries, are extremely poisonous, a characteristic shared by many plants in the nightshade family.

Etymology The derivation of *Solanum* is unknown, as it was originally applied by Plinius to a nightshade. One explanation is that it comes from the Latin word *solacium*, which means "to comfort" or "solace," due to the narcotic effects of the plant. Another explanation is that it is derived from the word *sol*, meaning "sun." *Carolinense* means "from Carolina."

Look-alikes Black nightshade (*Solanum ptychanthum*) can be confused with Carolina horsenettle, with the former having no prickles on the stem, smaller white flowers, and black mature fruit.

Spiraea alba (WHITE MEADOWSWEET)

ROSACEAE—rose family

Description A shrub that grows up to 4–6.5' tall. The alternately arranged, toothed, slightly hairy to hairless leaves have short stalks and are widest above the middle. The mostly terminal, pyramidal panicles of numerous flowers are explosions of white. Each small flower has 5 showy white stamens surpassing the 5 petals; a contrasting pink to orange ring is present at the base of the petals. Fruit are shiny, small follicles that open at the top to release seeds.

Bloom Period June–September

Plant Communities Marsh, prairie fen, sedge meadow / wet prairie

Notes We decided to include white meadowsweet, although it is technically considered a shrub, because it is often confused for a large herbaceous plant. It does have a woody stem and perennial habit. The flowers have a pleasant fragrance.

Etymology *Spiraea* is Greek for "spiraled wreath," referring to some of the species' spiraled wreath–like seed heads, and *alba* means "white," referring to the color of the flowers.

Look-alikes There are many garden cultivars of *Spiraea*, especially of Japanese spiraea (*S. japonica*), which usually has pink flowers in flat-topped clusters and hairless leaves, and is planted in nearly every box store parking lot. The lovely native sister species of white meadowsweet, steeplebush (*Spiraea tomentosa*) (also called hardhack), differs in that it has pink flowers (very rarely white) and densely hairy leaf undersides, giving it an overall grayish color. It is also more of an acidophile than white meadowsweet, frequently occurring in bogs and pin oak flatwoods.

Steeplebush.

ORCHIDACEAE—*orchid family*

Description A native perennial that grows up to 15" tall. There are 1–5 narrow, lanceolate leaves at the base or sometimes on the lower part of the stem, with stem leaves being reduced to appressed scales. The glistening creamy-white flowers are slightly ascending to nodding and tubular with 3 sepals and 3 petals. Each fragrant flower is set like a step on a spiral staircase, with at least two intermingled spirals present. As with nearly all of our orchids, the flower is actually rotated upside down (resupinate). The flower's lower lip petal has wavy edges, often with a pale-yellowish blush on the tongue. The lateral sepals are straight, appressed to the rest of the flower or slightly spreading.

Bloom Period August–October

Plant Communities Prairie fen, sedge meadow / wet prairie, panne

Notes Sphinx ladies' tresses was recently taxonomically split out from the nodding ladies' tresses (*Spiranthes cernua*) complex as a distinct species. Current genetic evidence places this orchid as a speciated result of past hybridization between nodding ladies' tresses and Great Plains ladies' tresses (*S. magnicamporum*). The common name ladies' tresses refers to the resemblance of the flower arrangement to that of a woman's braided hair. The name "sphinx" is used as the common name because, as with the mythological creature, it is a hybrid with a questionable past.

Etymology *Spiranthes* is Greek for "spiraled flowers," an apt description of the inflorescence, and *incurva* means "incurved," in reference to the curved extensions of the lower lip base.

Great Plains ladies' tresses.

Great Plains ladies' tresses (*Spiranthes magnicamporum*) looks very much like sphinx ladies' tresses, but its flowers have inwardly curved spreading and ascending lateral sepals. The flowers of both species can have a vanilla aroma, but those of the latter are not nearly as strong as those of Great Plains ladies' tresses, which can often be smelled from a distance.

Symphyotrichum ericoides
(WHITE HEATH ASTER)

ASTERACEAE—sunflower family

Description A native perennial that reaches to 1–3' tall, usually with a bushy form. The alternately arranged, linear leaves are stalkless on the hairy stem, with the lower leaves usually withering by flowering time. The leaves are usually toothless and variable in their hairiness. Leaves are smaller than those of other asters in the Indiana Dunes, reaching up to 3" in length and ¼" across; on flowering branches, leaves are dense, spreading, and much shorter. Flowerheads are relatively small (to ½" wide), with a single plant being able to showcase over 200 of them in pyramidal, crowded arrays.

Each flowerhead has 10–20 white petallike ray flowers (rarely with a pink or blue blush) surrounding 6–12+ yellow (reddish with age) disc flowers. The subtending phyllaries each have a transparent, papery border around the top of the green diamond-shaped zone and are hairy. The fruit is a seedlike achene with a tuft of fluffy hair (pappus) attached to the top.

Bloom Period August–October

Plant Communities Sedge meadow / wet prairie, secondary dune, prairie complex

Notes Due to the explosive snowstorm of color that white heath aster produces, horticultural growers have taken note, developing cultivars such as "snow flurry" and "first snow," which are derived from the European lineage of white heath asters. New England aster

Rice button aster.

(*Symphyotrichum novae-angliae*) and white heath aster have been known to hybridize, creating amethyst aster (*Symphyotrichum* × *amethystinum*).

Etymology See *Symphyotrichum novae-angliae* for genus etymology. *Ericoides* refers to the fact that the plant looks like a heath plant (*Erica* sp.), with *-oides* meaning "looks like."

Look-alikes With the many aster species in the park, rice button aster (*Symphyotrichum dumosum*) and hairy frost aster (*S. pilosum*) are the easiest to confuse with white heath aster. Both of these species have hairless phyllaries and larger leaves, with the latter having a tiny needlelike projection on the tip of each phyllary. Hairy frost aster is common in disturbed areas (especially old fields) and has the largest flowerheads of the three.

Hairy frost aster.

Symphyotrichum lanceolatum
(panicled aster)

ASTERACEAE—aster family

Description One of our most abundant native perennial asters, growing to 1–5' tall, forming colonies. The alternately arranged, hairless, lance-linear leaves are stalkless, tapering to the stem. Leaves often have a few scattered teeth on the apical half. Basal leaves usually wither by flowering time but are wider and have winged, ciliate leaf stalks. Flowerheads are .5–1" wide, each with 16–50 white petallike ray flowers (rarely with a pink or blue blush) surrounding 20–40+ yellow (turning purple with age) disc flowers. The fruit is a seedlike achene with a fluffy tuft of hair (pappus) attached to the top.

Bloom Period August–November

Plant Communities Disturbed areas, marsh, prairie fen, sedge meadow / wet prairie, bottomland, hydromesophytic forest, conifer swamp, pin oak flatwoods, prairie complex, savanna complex

Notes There are many varieties of panicled aster, with at least two, var. *lanceolatum* and var. *interior*, occurring in the Indiana Dunes. In the latter, the smaller heads with involucres under 0.16" tall are crowded on the branches. In the former, which is much more common, flowerheads are less crowded and have involucres over 0.16" tall.

Etymology See *Symphyotrichum novae-angliae* for genus etymology. *Lanceolatum* means "lance-shaped," referring to the leaves.

Look-alikes Panicled aster can be confused with calico aster (*Symphyotrichum lateriflorum*) and willow aster (*S. praealtum*). Calico aster differs in having hair on the undersides of the leaves along the midvein; it is also less colony forming and has smaller flowerheads that are on lateral branches rather than in a terminal paniculate array. Willow aster differs in having pale-blue ray flowers (rarely white) and narrow (nearly linear) leaves with the margins rolled under, a pronounced reticulate pattern on the leaf undersides, and glaucous stems.

Calico aster.

Trillium grandiflorum (Great White Trillium)

MELANTHIACEAE—bunchflower family

Description A native spring ephemeral and long-lived perennial that can grow up to 16" tall. The three whorled "leaves" are actually bracts, and the aboveground "stem" is actually a lateral branch, as the main stem is a subterranean, horizontal rhizome with alternately arranged, papery, scalelike leaves. The bracts are sessile or subsessile. Flowers show off their 3 large white petals offset by 3 green sepals that are shorter than the petals. In the center of the large flower are 6 yellow stamens formed in two whorls. The petals often fade to pink as they age (though there is also a pink-flowered form of this species). The fruit is a subtly 6-angled green capsule.

Bloom Period April–June

Plant Communities Hydromesophytic forest, mesophytic forest

Notes There are few things as stunning as a forest understory white as snow from great white trilliums. Sometimes the petals may exhibit a green streak through them or, even worse, a deformity that is fitting only to Frankenstein's monster. These ungodly aberrations are due to mycoplasma infections. These parasitic infections can greatly hurt the population as they spread through the rhizomes to each ramet.

Individual with a mycoplasma infection.

Etymology *Trillium* means "triple lily," referring to the structures of the lily-like plant coming in threes. *Grandiflorum* means "big flower," an obvious reference.

Look-alikes Drooping trillium (*Trillium flexipes*) is similar to great white trillium but has smaller flowers with recurved petals, with sepals nearly the same length. The flowers are on long stalks that can be above the plane of the bracts but that are often hidden beneath them.

Drooping trillium.

Vaccinium macrocarpon (LARGE CRANBERRY)

ERICACEAE—heath family

Description A low trailing shrub that grows up to 6" tall. The alternately arranged leaves are small, evergreen, hairless, leathery, subsessile, slightly rounded-elliptical, and sometimes with a minute notch at the tip. Flowers are usually white but often have a strong pink blush. They are 4-parted, nodding, and have strongly reflexed petals that openly expose the reddish-yellow stamens and longer single style. The

flowering stalk has a pair of small, green, oppositely arranged leaflike bracts. The fruit is an edible, shiny red berry that is the size of a large marble and usually persists throughout the winter.

Bloom Period June–August

Plant Communities Bog

Notes Most are familiar with the berries of this plant, as it is often served in various forms at Christmas or Thanksgiving meals. The name *cranberry* is in reference to the flowers, which look a bit like the head of a crane. Native Americans ate the berries as well as used them for dyes. It is widely thought that drinking cranberry juice can help prevent urinary tract infections; however, the science is not conclusive.

Etymology The genus name has unknown origin other than its ancient Latin reference for bilberries, and *macrocarpon* means "large fruit."

Look-alikes Large cranberry's sister species, small cranberry (*Vaccinium oxycoccos*), is easily confused. The latter has a pair of tiny, red leaflike bracts on the flowering stalks and leaves that are more acute at the tip rather than rounded. It also tends to have flowers at the top of the plant, whereas the flowers in large cranberry are typically near the middle.

VERONICASTRUM VIRGINICUM (CULVER'S ROOT)

PLANTAGINACEAE—plantain family

Description An erect native perennial that grows up to 3–6' tall. The toothed, sessile to subsessile leaves are along the stem in several whorls of usually 3–6, up to 8. A cluster of several large, erect flowering spikes terminates the stem. Individual flowers are small, 4-parted, and tubular.

Bloom Period June–August

Plant Communities Sedge meadow / wet prairie, prairie complex, savanna complex

Notes Flowers are visited predominantly by long- and short-tongued bees. The root is toxic and has been used as an intense laxative. Culver's root is the host plant for the culver's root borer moth (*Papaipema sciata*).

Etymology The genus name means "looks like a *Veronica*," which refers to the genus *Veronica*, named after St. Veronica, who, in the Christian narrative, wiped Jesus's face with a cloth as he carried his cross to Golgotha (the site of his crucifixion). The legend has it that the cloth that she used magically imprinted Jesus's face on it. It is said to reside in the Vatican today. The specific epithet means "from Virginia."

Look-alikes None, including our numerous *Veronica* species.

6. YELLOW FLOWERS

Agrimonia parviflora, swamp agrimony
Aureolaria flava, yellow false foxglove
Bidens cernua, nodding beggartick
Caltha palustris, marsh marigold
Caulophyllum thalictroides, blue cohosh
Coreopsis tripteris, tall tickseed
Erythronium americanum, American trout-lily
Euphorbia cyparissias, cypress spurge
Euthamia graminifolia, flat-topped golden-top
Helianthus divaricatus, woodland sunflower
Helianthus grosseserratus, sawtooth sunflower
Helianthus petiolaris, prairie sunflower
Hieracium gronovii, queendevil
Hypericum perforatum, common St. John's-wort
Lithospermum caroliniense var. *croceum*, hairy puccoon
Ludwigia alternifolia, seedbox
Lysimachia ciliata, fringed loosestrife
Lysimachia terrestris, swamp candles
Monarda punctata, horsemint
Nuphar advena, yellow pond-lily
Oenothera biennis, common evening primrose
Opuntia cespitosa, eastern prickly pear
Oxalis stricta, common yellow wood sorrel
Packera aurea, golden ragwort
Pedicularis canadensis, wood betony
Ranunculus hispidus var. *nitidus*, bristly buttercup
Rudbeckia hirta, black-eyed Susan
Rudbeckia laciniata, cutleaf coneflower
Silphium integrifolium, rosinweed
Solidago altissima, tall goldenrod
Solidago caesia, blue-stemmed goldenrod
Solidago rigidiuscula, showy goldenrod
Tragopogon dubius, western goat's beard
Utricularia vulgaris, common bladderwort

Verbascum thapsus, great mullein
Verbesina alternifolia, wingstem
Viola pubescens var. *scabriuscula*, downy yellow violet
Zizia aurea, golden alexandersv

Agrimonia parviflora (swamp agrimony)

ROSACEAE—rose family

Description An erect perennial that grows to 2.5–4'
tall. The alternately arranged, pinnately compound
leaves are divided into 11–23 large leaflets with much
smaller leaflets in between. Leaflets are glandular,
sparsely hairy, and coarsely toothed with a pointed
tip. A pair of coarsely toothed leafy stipules hug the
stem. The small flowers are 5-parted on short stalks,
arranged sparsely on the upright inflorescence in a raceme that can be up to 2' tall. In fruit the hypanthium

reveals hooked bristles and a beak of persistent, closed sepals that slightly protrude beyond them.

Bloom Period July–August

Plant Communities Disturbed areas, prairie fen, sedge meadow / wet prairie, bottomland, hydromesophytic forest, prairie complex

Notes When the leaves begin unraveling from the very hairy stem, they and the stipule look as though the Vipper of Vipp is emerging from the plant. The fruit of swamp agrimony commonly sticks to animal fur, bird feathers, or human pants / shoes that brush against the plant. There are glands on the plant that make it aromatic.

Etymology *Agrimonia* could have been derived from a combination of the words *argos* and *monos*, meaning "alone in a field." Other sources claim it comes from the Greek word *argema*, referring to an eye condition. Or, it may come from a distortion of the name of the poppy-like herb *Argemone*, as mentioned by Pliny. *Parviflora* means "small flowered."

Tall agrimony.

Look-alikes Two other common species of agrimony in the Indiana Dunes are soft agrimony (*Agrimonia pubescens*) and tall agrimony (*A. gryposepala*). Both of these species usually grow in drier habitats than swamp agrimony and have fewer than 11 large leaflets (usually 5–9). In the former, the leaves are soft hairy beneath; the latter has hairs beneath on the veins only.

Aureolaria flava (YELLOW FALSE FOXGLOVE)

OROBANCHACEAE—broomrape family

Description A native perennial that grows up to 5.5' tall. The stems are often purplish blue, covered in a glaucous coat, and lacking hairs. The hairless, oppositely arranged leaves are lanceolate and pinnately divided. The basal leaves are twice-pinnately divided. Large yellow flowers look like a Muppet head; they are hairless, 5-lobed, and bell-shaped. The fruit is a dry, dark, round to pear-shaped capsule.

Bloom Period July–September

Plant Communities Savanna complex

Notes This spectacular plant is a hemiparasite that restricts its parasitism solely to white oak (*Quercus alba*) as its host. The similar species fern-leaf false foxglove (*Aureolaria pedicularia*) and downy false foxglove (*A. virginica*) parasitize black oak (*Q. velutina*).

Etymology *Aureolaria* means "golden," and *flava* means "blonde" or "yellow"; in this species both the genus and specific epithet refer to the color of the flowers.

Fern-leaf false foxglove.

Look-alikes Fern-leaf false foxglove and downy false foxglove look similar; both have a pubescent stem, calyx, and fruit. The former has fernlike, deeply lobed, bipinnatifid leaves. The latter has entire and unlobed or once-lobed leaves. Mullein false foxglove (*Dasistoma macrophylla*) can also be confused with yellow false foxglove, but it has flowers that are subsessile and much smaller, with hairy calyces.

Bidens cernua (NODDING BEGGARTICK)

ASTERACEAE—sunflower family

Description A native annual that usually grows from 1' to 4' tall but that can flower when much shorter. Stems are green but often have a purplish-red color to them. The oppositely arranged, hairless, toothed leaves are sessile to clasping. Flowerheads are usually nodding (especially with age), having usually 6–8 petallike ray flowers (these are sometimes absent). There can be up to 100 disc florets. The fruit are dark-brown achenes with 4 stiff, barbed pappus bristles at the top that attach to animals or clothes of those that pass by.

Bloom Period August–October

Plant Communities Disturbed areas, marsh, sedge meadow / wet prairie, bottomland, hydromesophytic forest, pin oak flatwoods

Notes When in bloom, nodding beggartick gives your eyes an appetizing banquet of yellow, but when in fruit it may cause you to curse, as the scores of fruit readily attach to your clothing. Naturalist and writer Henry David Thoreau once wrote of the fruit of *Bidens* in his journal, "I have found myself often covered, as it were with . . . a bristling *chevaux-de-frise* of beggar-ticks, and I had to spend a quarter of an hour or more picking them off . . . and so they got just what they want, deposited in another place." He added that they "prophesy the coming of the traveler, brute, or human, that will transport their seed on their coat!"

Etymology *Bidens* comes from the Latin *bi-* and *dens*, meaning "two teeth," referring to the 2 stiff pappus bristles of the achenes on some members of the genus (others have 3 or 4), and *cernua* means "nodding" or "drooping," referring to the flowerheads.

Look-alikes Of the 10 *Bidens* in the Indiana Dunes, several of which are common, nodding beggartick differs by having the combination of these traits: (1) fruit have 4 stiff, barbed pappus bristles; (2) leaves are sessile to clasping, simple, and unlobed; (3) usually has showy ray flowers; and (4) flowerheads nod.

Caltha palustris (Marsh Marigold)

RANUNCULACEAE—buttercup family

Description A spring-blooming, colony-forming native perennial that grows up to 2' tall. The stem is smooth and hollow. The glossy basal leaves and alternately arranged stem leaves are hairless and round, ovate, or heart-shaped. Each inflorescence has 1–7 relatively large flowers up to 1.75" in diameter. The 5 (up to 9) petallike sepals are brilliant yellow arranged around numerous stamens surrounding the pistils. The pistils develop into capsules containing many seeds.

Bloom Period April–May

Plant Communities Bottomland, hydromesophytic forest, conifer swamp, pin oak flatwoods

Notes In natural light, marsh marigold is a showstopper with its bright-yellow flowers, but under UV light, the flowers explode into a spectacular purple and blue. As with other species in the buttercup family, parts of the plant contain toxins that, if digested, could cause a suite of bad symptoms. It also contains a sap that can be a skin irritant. Even so, it has been historically used as a food source by cooking young stems to burn off

Fruit and seeds.

the toxins. The common name of marigold, as with the common marigolds of the sunflower family (Asteraceae), is said to be in reference to its flowering on Easter as a floral accent to honor Mary. Or, more realistically, it is from the Anglo-Saxon derivation of *meargealla*, meaning "horse-blister," in that the buds look like horse blisters.

Etymology *Caltha* is derived from the Greek word meaning "goblet," referring to the flower shape, and in Latin referencing marigolds. The specific epithet *palustris* is Latin for "marsh" or "swamp," referencing the habitat of this species.

Look-alikes The invasive, nonnative fig buttercup (*Ficaria verna*) can be confused for marsh marigold but differs in having 3 green sepals and 7–12 yellow true petals; it also forms a dense groundcover.

Caulophyllum thalictroides (BLUE COHOSH)

BERBERIDACEAE—barberry family

Description An early-blooming perennial that grows up to 3' tall. The stem is glaucous and grayish green often with a purple blush (especially when young). The leaves are 3-ternate (branched into 3 branches, then branched again into 3 branches, which then end in 3 more leaflets). There is 1 leaf on nonflowering plants and most often 2 leaves on fertile plants, with the first leaf sometimes 4-ternate. For those counting, this results in a lot of leaflets! Leaflets often are purplish as they emerge, becoming green when fully unfurled. Flowers are yellowish green (sometimes maroonish) with 6 petallike sepals and 6 inconspicuous petals beneath the 6 stamens. Oftentimes the flowers are open before the leaves are fully expanded. The deep-blue, glaucous, berrylike "fruit" is actually not a fruit at all but rather a fleshy seed that has busted through the ovary wall. The fleshy seed coat protects the smaller brown seed within.

Bloom Period April–May

Plant Communities Mesophytic forest

Courtesy Michael Huft.

Notes Native Americans used blue cohosh (often the rootstocks) medicinally for many ailments, including but not limited to indigestion, toothaches, epilepsy, and fever, as well as during childbirth. The seeds and leaves are toxic if eaten, containing a cocktail of glycosides.

Etymology *Caulophyllum* comes from the words *caulis* and *phyllon*, meaning "stem" and "leaf," referring to the way the leaf looks like a continuation of the stem. *Thalictroides* means "looks like a *Thalictrum*," referring to its leaves, which appear similar to those of the meadow rue (*Thalictrum* spp., in the family Ranunculaceae).

Look-alikes There are no look-alikes known to occur in the Indiana Dunes. However, giant blue cohosh (*Caulophyllum giganteum*), known from east of our region, has flowers that are more regularly deep maroon with much longer, beak-like styles.

Coreopsis tripteris (Tall Tickseed)

ASTERACEAE—sunflower family

Description A native perennial that can grow over 8' tall. The stem is hairless and often glaucous. The stalked, oppositely arranged leaves are simple on young plants. On mature plants, the leaves can be unlobed on the upper or lower part of the stem but are typically divided into 3–5 long, elliptic leaflets. Near the top of the stem, a few leaves may be alternately arranged. The lateral leaflets are sessile, and the terminal leaflet is stalked. The upper side of the leaf is a darker green than the underside. Flowerheads are about 1–2" in diameter. Petallike ray flowers are yellow and up to 1" long. The tubular disc flowers start yellow but soon turn dark purple to reddish brown. The fruit is a small achene.

Bloom Period July–September

Plant Communities Sedge meadow / wet prairie, secondary dune, prairie complex, savanna complex

Notes This elegant plant must be attractive to passersby. One of the authors once witnessed a car stop in front of his house only to have the driver quickly jump out and cut and leave with a bouquet of flowering tall

tickseed, which was surrounded by numerous other flowering plants that were left unharmed.

Etymology *Coreopsis* comes from the Greek *koris* and *-opsis*, meaning "bug-like," referring to the fruit, which looks similar to a little bug or a hideous tick. This is also where the common name *tickseed* comes from. *Tripteris* is derived from the Greek *tri-* and *pteron*, meaning "three wings," apparently in reference to the 3-parted leaves.

Sand tickseed.

Look-alikes Sand tickseed (*Coreopsis lanceolata*), a shorter plant, has unlobed leaves (rarely with a pair of lobes toward the base) restricted to the lower half to quarter of the stem and is found in drier habitats. Prairie tickseed (*C. palmata*) has 3-lobed leaves, but the leaves are stalkless; it is also shorter than tall tickseed and grows in drier soils. Gray-headed coneflower (*Ratibida pinnata*) also can look similar, but its disc is conical and taller, and its leaves are alternately arranged.

Erythronium americanum
(American trout-lily)

LILIACEAE—lily family

Description A native spring ephemeral that grows up to 5–9" tall. The flowering plants usually have 2 basal egg-shaped to lanceolate glossy leaves that taper to both ends and have dark mottling. Nonflowering plants have a single basal leaf. Each plant has a solitary nodding flower with yellow tepals that sometimes are red-spotted. The 6 tepals are reflexed, showcasing the 6 long stamens that can have deep red or yellow anthers. The fruit is an erect capsule.

Bloom Period April–May

Plant Communities Mesophytic forest

Notes When found in dense colonies, there are always more nonflowering plants than flowering ones. The common name trout-lily comes from the mottled leaves that resemble trout. Another common name is fawn lily. Sometimes you may see American trout-lily's white stolon-like structure sneaking out of the ground like a smooth white rope.

Etymology *Erythronium* comes from the Greek word for "red," referring to a red-flowered European species in this genus, and *americanum* means "from America."

Look-alikes White trout-lily (*Erythronium albidum*) differs in having white flowers; it blooms a tad earlier.

White trout-lily.

EUPHORBIA CYPARISSIAS (CYPRESS SPURGE)
EUPHORBIACEAE—spurge family

Courtesy Michael Huft.

Description A nonnative perennial that grows up to 1' tall. The narrow, sessile, hairless, alternately arranged leaves are crammed together along the stem, giving it a bushy appearance. The bluish-green leaves are often so close together that they can appear whorled. The flowers are ambiguous and tiny in cyathia, surrounded by pet-allike yellow bracts and arranged in umbrella-shaped clusters. Seed capsules explode to disperse seeds.

Bloom Period April–August

Plant Communities Disturbed areas

Notes Damaged vegetative parts of the plant emit a white milky sap that can be toxic to some animals. The Mt. Baldy parking lot is infested with this species. It has been cultivated as a low-maintenance landscape plant. Much of what we have in North America are sterile individuals that spread vegetatively; however, seed-producing plants can become quite problematic, forming large populations.

Courtesy Michael Huft.

Etymology *Euphorbia* was named after the Greek physician Euphorbus. *Cyparissias* is a reference to cypress (of various genera), as the foliage resembles them.

Look-alikes The sister species, leafy spurge (*Euphorbia virgata*), looks similar but is larger in size than cypress spurge, with leaves over 0.12" wide (narrower in cypress spurge). The two have been known to hybridize (*Euphorbia × pseudoesula*).

Euthamia graminifolia
(FLAT-TOPPED GOLDEN-TOP)

ASTERACEAE—sunflower family

Description A native perennial that can grow up to 5′ tall. The leaves are alternately arranged, linear to linear lanceolate, are reduced gradually up the stem, and at least some on a plant have 5 or more prominent parallel veins. The stem and veins on the leaf undersides are hairy (in var. *nuttallii*, which is sometimes considered a separate species [*Euthamia nuttallii*]) or not (in var. *graminifolia*). Flowerheads are arranged in a dense, flat-topped array (thus the common name) with usually 20+ tiny ray and disc flowers.

Bloom Period July–October

Plant Communities Disturbed areas, prairie fen, sedge meadow / wet prairie, prairie complex

Notes Also commonly called grass-leaved goldenrod, with var. *nuttallii* called hairy grass-leaved goldenrod. The "grasslike" linear leaves often are used by gall midges (*Asteromyia euthamiae*), which leave characteristic roundish, white-bordered black spots (the galls) on the leaves; each of these spots encloses a larva of this species. An orange, powderlike rust (*Coleosporium delicatulum*) is also common on the foliage. The crushed leaves emit a sweet, earthy, spicy odor. There have been recent taxonomic revisions that may result in future name changes to the species mentioned here.

Etymology *Euthamia* is thought to come from the Greek word meaning "crowded," referring to the crowded inflorescence, and *graminifolia* means "grass-leaf."

Look-alikes Great Plains flat-topped golden-top (*Euthamia gymnospermoides*) looks similar but has leaves 0.11–0.15" wide with 1–3 (usually 3) prominent veins and less than 20 ray and disc flowers on a flowerhead; its flowerheads are often subtly larger than those of flat-topped golden-top. Slender golden-top (*E. caroliniana*) has leaves up to 0.11" wide with 1 (sometimes 3) vein and smaller flowerheads; it also has very shiny foliage in the upper part of the plant.

Slender golden-top.

Helianthus divaricatus
(WOODLAND SUNFLOWER)

ASTERACEAE—sunflower family

Description A native perennial that typically grows to 3–4' tall. The stem is often glaucous and may have some sparse hair under the inflorescence, but not usually below the first or second set of upper leaves. The oppositely arranged leaves are sessile to very short-stalked, widest at the base and tapering to the tip, and have short stiff hairs on the top surface. Flowerheads are made up of 8–10 petallike ray flowers and over 40 disc flowers.

Bloom Period July–October

Plant Communities Secondary dune, savanna complex

Notes This is the attractive sunflower that makes up a majority of the herbaceous vegetation color in the savanna complex of the Indiana Dunes throughout the summer. The flowerheads are visited by a number of insects.

Etymology *Helianthus* is derived from two Greek words meaning "sun flower." *Divaricatus* means "spreading apart," which may be a reference to either the spreading ray flowers or the spreading leaves.

Look-alikes Although we all like to be able to taxonomically place species in pretty, tidy little boxes, without any variation or introgression with other species, this sometimes is not possible; such is notoriously the case with our shade- or partial-shade-loving sunflowers. Ten-petaled sunflower (*Helianthus decapetalus*), hairy woodland sunflower (*H. hirsutus*), and pale-leaved sunflower (*H. strumosus*) are all quite similar and can share characteristics with woodland sunflower. Both ten-petaled sunflower and pale-leaved sunflower have leaves that routinely have petioles over 0.2" long; the former tends to have more toothy, thinner-textured leaves than the latter. Hairy woodland sunflower is harder to differentiate, as it often has numerous similar, overlapping characters; however, hairy woodland sunflower should never have glaucous stems and most of the time has hairs (even if sparse) from top to bottom along the stem.

Helianthus grosseserratus
(SAWTOOTH SUNFLOWER)

ASTERACEAE—sunflower family

Description A towering native perennial that can reach to over 16' tall but usually is around 6–10' tall. The stem is mostly hairless and often glaucous with a reddish-purple color. Leaves are oppositely arranged lower on the stem and often alternately arranged higher on the stem. They are 3 veined, coarsely toothed, flat to slightly folded along the midvein, and often arching. Leaf stalks are usually over 0.2" long. The often numerous flowerheads have 8–20 petallike ray florets and over 100 disc florets.

Bloom Period July–October

Plant Communities Disturbed areas, sedge meadow / wet prairie, prairie complex

Notes Although native, sawtooth sunflower has a tendency to form dense colonies and can sometimes appear invasive.

Etymology See *Helianthus divaricatus* for genus etymology. *Grosseserratus* means "big saw tooth," a characteristic evident on the leaf margins.

Look-alikes Giant sunflower (*Helianthus giganteus*) looks quite similar but has hairy stems and leaf stalks under 0.16" long. Although it, too, has sharply toothed leaf margins, the teeth are usually not as coarse as those in sawtooth sunflower. It is typically found in prairie fen and sedge meadow / wet prairie communities.

Giant sunflower.

Helianthus petiolaris (PRAIRIE SUNFLOWER)

ASTERACEAE—sunflower family

Description A nonnative annual that grows up to 4'
tall. The leaves are usually alternately arranged, though
there can be some oppositely arranged leaves along the
lower part of the stem. Leaf shape is quite variable,
ranging from triangular to elliptic. They have 3 prominent parallel veins, are mostly toothless but sometimes
with shallow teeth on the wavy margins, and are rough
and darker green on the top surface and very hairy and
lighter green on the lower surface. The showy flowerheads are large, with 10–30 sterile, yellow petallike
ray florets and 50–100 fertile dark-reddish-brown to
purple disc flowers. The fruit, a seedlike achene, lacks

a hairy appendage present in many other species in the sunflower family.

Bloom Period June–September

Plant Communities Disturbed areas, foredune, secondary dune

Notes Although quite alluring, prairie sunflower is native to the western United States but adventive in the Indiana Dunes. When doing native landscaping, we suggest sticking to our truly native species, despite how pretty a flower or flowerhead may be.

Etymology See *Helianthus divaricatus* for genus etymology. *Petiolaris* means "having petioles," referencing the stalked leaves.

Look-alikes Prairie sunflower looks like a smaller version of the cultivated annual, common sunflower (*Helianthus annuus*). The latter is much larger overall with larger flowerheads that have over 150 disc flowers (better start counting!), more consistently toothed leaves, and flat leaf margins.

HIERACIUM GRONOVII (QUEENDEVIL)

ASTERACEAE—sunflower family

Description An overlooked native perennial that can grow to over 1.5' tall. The basal leaves have somewhat short white hairs and are up to 6" long. Stem leaves are alternately arranged, toothless, hairy, and much smaller than the basal leaves, with the upper half of the stem usually leafless. There can be up to 50 flower-heads on a single plant, with each flowerhead containing 15–25+ petallike ray florets and no disc florets. The fruit is a spindle-shaped seedlike achene that tapers to a point, where there is a fluff of hair (pappus) attached.

Bloom Period June–October

Plant Communities Savanna complex

Notes It is thought by some that the common name kingdevil refers to some of the weedy species in the genus *Hieracium* that often "spread like the devil" in agricultural fields. Using this logic, we suspect that *queendevil* was chosen as a common name for this well-behaved, regal native plant because it is much more gentle and respectful.

Etymology *Hieracium* is derived from the Greek word meaning "hawk," due to Pliny the Elder's theory that hawks ate plants in this genus to improve their eyesight. *Gronovii* honors Dutch botanist and Linnaeus's friend Jan Fredrik Gronovius, who had a spectacular herbarium containing specimens from the great American botanist John Clayton (see *Claytonia virginica*).

Look-alikes Several native species in the genus *Hieracium* are similar. Prairie hawkweed (*Hieracium longipilum*) differs in having hairs on the leaves and stem well exceeding 0.3" long (it's a hairy devil!), whereas those of queendevil are consistently under 0.35" long. Rough hawkweed (*H. scabrum*) is similar but has more rounded, truncate fruit, over 40 flowers per flowerhead, and leaves that are consistently arranged more or less along the stem instead of crowded at the base. Using a hand lens and looking at the undersides of the leaves, you will notice that queendevil has straight hairs and also very tiny clusters of stellate hairs (several hairs spreading from a common point) much shorter and covering the surface; the undersides of rough hawkweed only have the longer, straight hairs. Northern hawkweed (*H. umbellatum*) differs in that it has larger flowerheads and is leafier along the stem. Our nonnative *Hieracium*, which are common in disturbed areas, have nearly all of their leaves in a basal rosette.

Hypericum perforatum
(common St. John's-wort)

HYPERICACEAE—St. John's-wort family

Courtesy Michael Huft.

Description A weedy, nonnative perennial that grows up to 2.5' tall. The oppositely arranged leaves are sessile or on short stalks, entire margined, and covered with clear to black spots. The inflorescence is branched with each flower having 5 petals. The petals have black spots restricted to their margins. In the center of the flower there is a cluster of 50–80 stamens. The often numerous flowers are up to 1" in diameter.

Bloom Period June–September

Plant Communities Disturbed areas

Notes Although the genus had a close religious tie to ancient Greeks, it was Christianized, being dedicated to St. John the Baptist. It was an easy transition, as it was already used in pagan rituals to decorate religious images around the Midsummer's Eve, which ironically (or unironically) corresponded to the supposed birthday of St. John.

Common St. John's-wort in the medieval time was referred to as *fuga daemonum*, meaning "to make the demons flee." It appears the plant has transcended many myths. Medicinally, this species has been used to treat depression and anxiety; however, it is not recommended to take with other antidepressants, as it can cause life-threatening side effects.

Etymology The genus name *Hypericum* is derived from the Greek words "hyper" and "eikon," meaning "above" and "image," respectively. The ancient Greeks would hang the *Hypericum* above their religious figurines, believing it would scare off the evil spirits. *Perforatum* references the "perforated" (often by clear spots) leaves.

Look-alikes There are 7 native St. John's-worts (*Hypericum* spp.) in the Indiana Dunes, with the most similar being spotted St. John's-wort (*H. punctatum*). The latter is less branched, has smaller flowers (usually much less than 1" in diameter), and has black spots covering the petals.

Spotted St. John's-wort. Courtesy Michael Huft.

LITHOSPERMUM CAROLINIENSE VAR. CROCEUM
(HAIRY PUCCOON)

BORAGINACEAE—borage family

Description A native perennial that grows up to 2' tall. The alternate leaves are sessile, toothless, and covered in short, stiff spreading hairs that have swollen, pustular bases. Orangish-yellow flowers form at the top of the bristly hairy stems. The corollas are fused over half their length, separating into 5 spreading lobes. The fruit is a shiny, bone-white nutlet.

Bloom Period April–July

Plant Communities Secondary dune, savanna complex

Notes The common name puccoon comes from the Algonquian tribe's word *poughkone*, which means "a plant that is used as a dye" (note that bloodroot, *Sanguinaria canadensis*, was once called red puccoon). Native Americans would use the roots as a dye for face paint and ornamentation.

Etymology *Lithospermum* means "stone seed," referencing the extremely hard white nutlets, and *caroliniense* means "of Carolina." The varietal name *croceum* means "saffron," referring to the color of the flowers.

Look-alikes Hoary puccoon (*Lithospermum canescens*) looks very similar to hairy puccoon but has longer, soft, appressed hairs lacking pustular bases and more round-tipped leaves, and it blooms slightly earlier.

Hoary puccoon.

Ludwigia alternifolia (SEEDBOX)

ONAGRACEAE—evening primrose family

Description A native perennial that typically grows to 2–3' tall. The smooth stem is often red to reddish green. The alternately arranged, deep-green, hairless leaves have distinctive "fishbone-like" venation and are sessile or subsessile with a light-colored midrib. Each stalked flower has 4 (rarely 5) dainty yellow petals that look as though they were lightly glued on. The pointed green sepals are often about the same length as the petals. Fruit are capsules that are in the shape of a box and rattle when shaken.

Bloom Period June–September

Plant Communities Bog, marsh, sedge meadow / wet prairie

Notes This is one of our easiest and funnest plants to identify in the depths of winter, as the unique box-shaped capsules remain long after the seeds have escaped through the small, central, terminal pore.

Etymology The genus was named by Linnaeus to honor his colleague, botanist Christian Gottlieb Ludwig, who shared correspondence with Linnaeus for his taxonomic classification system. *Alternifolia* means "alternate leaves."

Look-alikes Many-fruited water primrose (*Ludwigia polycarpa*), sometimes referred to as false loosestrife, is somewhat similar but often shorter. Its stalkless (or nearly so) flowers lack petals (or have tiny ones much shorter than the sepals), and the ovary and fruit are more cup-shaped and clearly longer than broad.

Many-fruited water primrose.

LYSIMACHIA CILIATA (FRINGED LOOSESTRIFE)

PRIMULACEAE—primrose family

Courtesy Michael Huft.

Description A shade-tolerant, colony-forming native perennial that typically grows to 1–4' tall. The thin-textured, hairless, oppositely arranged leaves are ovate-lanceolate to lanceolate with long, fine hairs restricted to the length of the margins of the conspicuous, slightly winged, 0.6"-long or longer petioles. Individual 5-parted flowers are produced on long, often nodding stalks from leaf axils. The spreading petals

Courtesy Michael Huft.

possess a pointed apical tip and typically have a reddish base that appears to surround the 5 yellow stamens. Fruit are round capsules that are surrounded by the 5 green star-shaped calyx lobes.

Bloom Period June–August

Plant Communities Sedge meadow / wet prairie, bottomland, hydromesophytic forest, conifer swamp, pin oak flatwoods

Notes Unlike most flowers, those of *Lysimachia* produce floral fatty oils instead of just sweet nectar. Many of the species of the solitary bee genus *Macropis* rely specifically on *Lysimachia* for these oils for nest building and as a food source. Fringed loosestrife has been said to be a natural repellent for gnats and flies, both used from live plants and as a fire smudge; however, the authors have found no scientific evidence defending these claims.

Etymology *Lysimachia* is derived from the Greek words *lysis* and *mache*, meaning "loose from strife." The genus was named in honor of the Greek king Lysimachus, who, when attacked by a raging bull, waved a loosestrife plant in front of the bull to soothe it. It was then thought that placing a loosestrife plant on the yokes of a grumpy oxen would relax it; however, the authors have found no scientific evidence defending these claims. *Ciliata* means "fringed hairs," referencing the fringe of hairs along the petiole margins.

Look-alikes Prairie loosestrife (*Lysimachia lanceolata*), a shorter plant of generally drier ground in disturbed areas as well as in the prairie complex and savanna complex, has shorter petioles that taper into lanceolate to elliptic or oblanceolate leaves. It also has ciliate margins to the petioles and sometimes into the base of the leaf blades.

Lysimachia terrestris (swamp candles)

PRIMULACEAE—primrose family

Courtesy Michael Huft.

Description An erect native perennial that typically grows to 1–3' tall. The oppositely arranged leaves are toothless, sessile to subsessile, tapering to both ends, and dotted with glands on the undersides. Flowers are borne loosely in a terminal raceme. Each flower is 5-parted with the base of the yellow petals showcasing a red stripe that surrounds the 5 yellow stamens. Fruit are dotted dark capsules. Oftentimes strange elongated red bulblets are formed in the axils of the leaves.

Swamp candle bulblets.

Bloom Period June–August

Plant Communities Bog, marsh, prairie fen, sedge meadow / wet prairie

Notes Tufted loosestrife (*Lysimachia thyrsiflora*) and swamp candles have been known to hybridize (*L. × commixta*). The flowers of swamp candles produce a specialized floral fatty oil that coevolved with some species of *Macropis* bees (see *Lysimachia ciliata* notes). When Linnaeus received a specimen of swamp candles from botanist Pehr Kalm, it had the odd axillary bulblets, so Linnaeus put it in the mistletoe genus *Viscum* (*V. terrestre*), naming it such because the bulblets grow after falling to the ground (see etymology). It wasn't until over 100 years later that botanists Britton, Stearns, and Poggenburg described it in its proper sense, placing it in the genus *Lysimachia*.

Etymology For genus, see *Lysimachia ciliata*. *Terrestris* means "terrestrial" or "growing on ground" (see notes).

Look-alikes Tufted loosestrife looks similar, but only when flowers or fruit aren't present. Tufted loosestrife has 6–7 petals (unusual for *Lysimachia*) on flowers borne in short, dense racemes in the leaf axils.

Tufted loosestrife.

Monarda punctata (HORSEMINT)

LAMIACEAE—mint family

Description A short-lived native perennial (sometimes annual) that typically grows to 1–2.5' tall. The oppositely arranged leaves are often shallowly toothed toward their tips; soft pubescent on the underside, giving them a lighter color than the top surface; and tapering to a winged petiole that attaches to the hairy stem that is square in cross-section. The bruised stem and leaves are strongly fragrant. The inflorescence is positioned in what appears to be whorls between whorls of leaflike, purplish-pink to cream-colored bracts; the flowers are actually in stalked, axillary cymes. Each flower is tubular and creamy-yellow-speckled with purple spots, and has an arching upper lip. The outside of the flower is covered in long, scraggly hairs.

Bloom Period July–October

Plant Communities Disturbed areas, foredune, secondary dune, prairie complex, savanna complex

Notes Horsemint's fragrance has been greatly praised for its pleasing, calming aroma. The most abundant compounds are thymol and carvacrol, which have been

shown to repel mosquitos. The spotted floral guides on the petals are important "open" signs for bumblebees and other pollinators. In a classic study by Scora (1964) titled "Dependency of Pollination on Patterns of *Monarda*," mutant horsemints with no spots also saw no pollinators. This is something to consider when planting "nativars" that have been chosen and bred based on "desirable" characteristics such as larger or different-colored flowers, flowers with mutant multiple whorls of petals, interesting leaf colors or patterns, and so on.

Etymology *Monarda* is named in honor of sixteenth-century botanist Nicolás Bautista Monardes, and *punctata* means "dotted," referencing the spotted flowers.

Look-alikes None.

Nuphar advena (YELLOW POND-LILY)

NYMPHAEACEAE—water lily family

Description An aquatic native perennial. The leaves are large and broadly ovate to nearly circular, often standing above the water (they can be floating when water levels are high). There is a deep sinus that runs one-third to one-half the leaf length. The leaf stalk is oval in cross-section. Flowers project out of the water with usually 6 yellow, rounded sepals typically with a basal green patch (rarely maroon). The inconspicuous, rounded petals are yellow, small, and numerous, often hidden by the large sepals and towering table-like column in the center. The fruit is a purplish green ribbed capsule that is slightly contracted beneath the stigmatic disc (tabletop). Plants oftentimes spread through monstrously large, knobby rhizomes that look like a sea-dragon's legs.

Bloom Period May–September

Plant Communities Submerged aquatic, bog, marsh

Notes The rare water-lily bee (*Lasioglossum nelumbonis*) prefers plants in the water lily family, such as yellow pond-lily in the Indiana Dunes. Many aquatic invertebrates and algae rely on pond-lily leaves for habitat. The fruit floats due to built-in air sacs, which makes

them an easy and important food source for ducks, bitterns, and many other birds. Yellow pond-lily can slowly change an aquatic system through its massive rhizomes by reducing water flow, which can increase sediment buildup. Yellow pond-lily is also known as spatterdock.

Etymology *Nuphar* is an ancient word that has evolved from a Persian word meaning "water-lily." It also means "keep dry" or "out of the rain," a reference to the leaves and flowers that are often emergent from the water in which the plant is growing. *Advena* means "guest" or "alien," which refers to the adventive nature of this American plant in Europe.

Look-alikes Variegated pond-lily (*Nuphar variegata*) has petals that are flat in cross-section (not rounded, as in yellow pond-lily), and the sepals have a maroon basal patch (rarely green). The leaves float flat on the surface of water, and the leaf stalks are triangular in cross-section (often winged).

Oenothera biennis
(COMMON EVENING PRIMROSE)

ONAGRACEAE—evening primrose family

Courtesy Michael Huft.

Description A native, sometimes weedy biennial that can grow up to 6–7' tall. The stout stem is covered in hair, light green or sometimes greenish red, and can be branched, giving the plant a large bushy appearance. The alternately arranged leaves are broadly lance-shaped, sessile, and usually toothless or with few small teeth; they often fold slightly along the whitish to pinkish midrib. The flowers are fairly large, reaching up to 2" across, with 4 yellow, notched petals subtended by 4 long, hairy sepals draped downward. The sepals have glandular hairs mixed with non-glandular hairs, and pairs of sepals are often connected with their tips free. The fruit is a capsule that is rounded in cross-section to obscurely 4-sided and tapers upward from the base.

Bloom Period June–November

Plant Communities Disturbed areas, prairie complex, savanna complex

Notes The common name comes from the plant's tendency to fully open its flowers in the evening or morning. The gorgeous primrose moth (*Schinia florida*) relies on species within the primrose family.

Etymology The derivation of *Oenothera* is uncertain. One possible explanation is that it is derived from the Greek words *oinos*, meaning "wine," and *thera*, which can be interpreted to mean many things, such as "seeker," "to imbibe," and "smelling." The lore surrounding this name is that if you eat evening primrose roots, you will want to drink wine, or that the root was a possible additive in wine. Another explanation is that it is derived from the Greek words *oeno*, meaning "ass" or "donkey," and *thera*, which can also mean "to hunt" or "chase." So, quite literally, an ass-chaser due to some unknown association of the plant with a donkey. *Biennis* simply means "biennial."

Look-alikes There are three species in the Indiana Dunes that can easily be confused with common evening primrose by amateur and professional botanists alike. Both Oakes' evening primrose (*O. oakesiana*) and small flower evening primrose (*O. parviflora*) differ in that their 4 sepals are usually separated (rarely connected in pairs) with a visible protrusion at the end. Hairy evening primrose (*O. villosa*) differs in that it doesn't have any glandular hairs.

Opuntia cespitosa (eastern prickly pear)

CACTACEAE—cactus family

Description A native, sprawling perennial cactus that grows up to 1.5' tall. The flattened, round paddlelike photosynthetic stem has 0–2 spines on each areole. Flowers are 2–3" wide and vividly yellow with an orangish-red base. The yellow anthers on the many stamens make the large flower an explosion of color. The fruit are sessile, green turning dark red to purple to brown, and look like colorful toes on a flat foot.

Bloom Period June–July

Plant Communities Disturbed areas, secondary dune, prairie complex, savanna complex

Notes Until recently our prickly pear was known as *Opuntia humifusa*, but recent taxonomic work has shown that it is different in flower color and geographical range and should be called *O. cespitosa*. *Opuntia humifusa* has strictly yellow flowers (lacking red centers). Eastern prickly pear is present in the Indiana Dunes, which seems out of range for a cactus, because of the receding glaciers, which allowed two separate prickly pear species from the southwest and the southeast to meet. As the temperatures warmed, the species slowly migrated north. This meeting led to a fling between the two once geographically isolated species. Those flings produced a hybrid that later became the distinct species that we have here today.

Eastern prickly pear needs well-drained, dry, often slightly disturbed habitat for its survival, preferring sandy soil. Rank vegetation can heavily impact its ability to succeed.

Etymology *Opuntia* comes from Opus, a Greek city, where an unrelated cactus-like plant grew. *Cespitosa* means "clumped," referring to the growth form of this species.

Look-alikes None.

Oxalis stricta (COMMON YELLOW WOOD SORREL)

OXALIDACEAE—wood sorrel family

Courtesy Michael Huft.

Description A somewhat weedy native perennial that grows up to 2' tall (usually much shorter). There is usually a single stem with long spreading hairs mixed with short spreading hairs, or the stem can be hairless. The alternately or whorled trifoliate leaves are hairless to sparsely hairy. Each leaf looks as though three hearts have joined together at their points. No stipules are present. Flowers are on long, ascending pedicels in an often branched inflorescence. Each flower has 5 yellow petals that are almost twice as long as the 5 green sepals beneath them. The petals are often slightly notched at the rounded tip. The fruit is an erect, columnar capsule that can have spreading hairs or be hairless. Seeds are transversely ridged and uniformly brown.

Bloom Period June–November

Plant Communities Disturbed areas, prairie complex, savanna complex

Notes Historically, common yellow wood sorrel has gone by common names such as sourgrass, lemon clover, upright yellow wood sorrel, and sheep sorrel. At night, the leaves curl up, opening back up in the morning sun. The taxonomy of wood sorrels has been laced with confusion. For more information and keys to the wood sorrels, see "Again: Taxonomy of Yellow-Flowered Caulescent *Oxalis* (Oxalidaceae) in Eastern North America" (Nesom 2009).

Etymology *Oxalis* comes from the Greek word meaning "sour, sharp," in reference to the tart flavor of the fruits and leaves. *Stricta* is Latin for "erect, upright," in reference to the upright growth form of the plant.

Look-alikes Southern yellow wood sorrel (*Oxalis dillenii*) differs in that it has short, appressed hairs on the stem, and its seeds have white to gray stripes on the transverse ridges. In fruit, although the capsules are upright, they are on deflexed stalks (stalks are ascending in common yellow wood sorrel).

PACKERA AUREA (GOLDEN RAGWORT)

ASTERACEAE—sunflower family

Description A colony-forming native perennial that typically grows up to 2' tall. Basal leaves are oval, usually large, with rounded teeth and a heart-shaped base. The alternately arranged stem leaves have 2–4 lobes and are lyrate to lance-shaped, becoming smaller up the stem. The flowerheads are made up of over 60 fertile disc flowers surrounded by 8–13 fertile petallike ray flowers and are in a flattish terminal array. There are 13–21 green phyllaries accented with purples and black beneath each flowerhead. The fruit is a seedlike achene with a fluff of white hair (pappus) attached at its tip.

Bloom Period May–July

Plant Communities Disturbed areas, marsh, prairie fen, bottomland, hydromesophytic forest, conifer swamp

Notes Golden ragwort, which has gone by names such as life weed and cough root, was used medicinally in a variety of ways. However, it includes pyrrolizidine alkaloids that can cause liver disease if used too frequently.

Etymology *Packera* is named after twentieth-century Canadian botanist John G. Packer, and *aurea* is Latin for "golden." A previously used name is *Senecio aureus*, *Senecio* meaning "old man," referring to the seed heads looking like an old man's poofy white hair.

Look-alikes Butterweed (*Packera glabella*) is an annual with pinnately compound lower and basal leaves and thick, ridged stems. Balsam ragwort (*P. paupercula*) has basal leaves that taper to the stalk; it occurs in prairie fens and pannes.

Butterweed.

Pedicularis canadensis (WOOD BETONY)

OROBANCHACEAE—broomrape family

Description A hemiparasitic native perennial that can grow a little over 1' tall. The basal leaves occur in a rosette and are almost fernlike; they can grow to around 6" long and are deeply lobed and hairy. The sparse, alternately to suboppositely arranged stem leaves are attached to a stem covered in long white hairs. The inflorescence is a spike of tubular flowers, each with an upper hoodlike lip that curves and surpasses the 3 fused corolla lobes that make up the lower lip. Flowers more commonly are yellow; however, many are bicolored with red on the upper lip or covering the entire corolla. The fruit are large, hairy, angular capsules.

Bloom Period May–June

Plant Communities Sedge meadow / wet prairie, prairie complex, savanna complex

Notes As a hemiparasite, wood betony steals nutrients from fellow plant neighbors (especially as it is becoming established) but also photosynthesizes. It parasitizes big bluestem (*Andropogon gerardii*) and Canada

Swamp betony.

goldenrod (*Solidago canadensis*), among many other species. It has been shown to negatively impact Canada goldenrod's shoot mass, allowing for less competitive species to succeed. When in tallgrass prairies, there appears to be a correlation between wood betony's abundance and biodiversity, due to its hemiparasitic nature. If being hemiparasitic isn't cool enough, wood betony (as well as others in the genus) requires a specific frequency of vibration for the pollen to be released. Bumblebees find flowers that they fit within and are rewarded by nectar, and as they buzz their wings, pollen is released, and the bumblebee unknowingly transports it to the next flower it visits.

Etymology *Pedicularis* in Latin means "louse," because it was thought that when cattle or livestock would ingest betony, they would get lice. *Canadensis* means "of Canada."

Look-alikes Swamp betony (*Pedicularis lanceolata*) typically is taller, has opposite stem leaves, and has corollas that are creamy white; it also grows in wetter habitats such as prairie fen and conifer swamp.

RANUNCULUS HISPIDUS VAR. NITIDUS
(BRISTLY BUTTERCUP)

RANUNCULACEAE—buttercup family

Description A sprawling native perennial that grows to 1' tall. As it sprawls, it can root into the ground from nodes along the lax stem. Alternately arranged leaves are trifoliate, dark green, and hairless. Leaflets are oftentimes deeply lobed; the side leaflets are sessile, and the terminal leaflet is stalked. A single flower is at the end of each stalk, with 5 bright-yellow petals (fading with age) above 5 pale-green sepals. Yellow stamens crowd around the receptacle. Fruit are dry, beaked, flat achenes.

Bloom Period April–June

Plant Communities Sedge meadow / wet prairie, bottomland, hydromesophytic forest

Notes Contrary to popular belief, if your chin reflects a yellow color when you put a buttercup underneath it, you don't necessarily like butter. But most people do.

Etymology *Ranunculus* comes from the Latin words *rana* and *unculus*, which combine to mean "little frog," in reference to the wet habitat where many species within this genus reside. *Hispidus* means "bristly," referring to the stiff, spreading hairs of *R. hispidus* var. *hispidus* (and var. *caricetorum*), and *nitidus* is Latin for "shine," likely a reference to the bright-yellow flowers.

Look-alikes Early buttercup (*Ranunculus fascicularis*) differs in that it grows in calcareous dry habitats such as the savanna complex, it has rounded leaflet lobes (more acute in bristly buttercup), and its petals are widest at or below the middle (petals widest above the middle in bristly buttercup). Yellow water crowfoot (*R. flabellaris*) has similar-looking flowers, but its leaves are deeply dissected. It also grows in areas that are inundated early in the year but that often dry to mudflat later in the season, especially in the savanna complex.

Yellow water crowfoot.

Rudbeckia hirta (BLACK-EYED SUSAN)

ASTERACEAE—sunflower family

Description An annual, biennial, or perennial native that grows up to 2–3' tall. The alternately arranged leaves are incredibly variable in toothiness, shape, and leaf stalk. The basal leaves are usually long stalked, and the upper stem leaves can be clasping. Leaves are always covered in short, stiff hairs. Flowerheads are typically borne singly on a long stalk (rarely with 2–5 stalks on a plant). Each flowerhead is made up of 8–20 yellow petallike ray flowers (that only contain pistils) surrounding oftentimes >300 bisexual brownish disc flowers. The fruit are seedlike achenes that lack a pappus.

Bloom Period June–October

Plant Communities Disturbed areas, sedge meadow / wet prairie, secondary dune, prairie complex, savanna complex

Notes There are many varieties and cultivars of black-eyed Susan, with two varieties known in the Indiana Dunes. In *Rudbeckia hirta* var. *hirta*, the leaves are coarsely toothed with basal leaves mostly two times as long as wide. *Rudbeckia hirta* var. *pulcherrima* has basal leaves that are 3–5 times as long as wide and leaves with no teeth or that are serrulate.

Etymology *Rudbeckia* is named in honor of the Swedish botany father-and-son team O. J. and O. O. Rudbeck, and *hirta* means "hairy."

Sweet coneflower.

Look-alikes Two similar species, sweet coneflower (*Rudbeckia subtomentosa*) and thin-leaved coneflower (*R. triloba*), both differ in having deep lobes on at least some of their leaves. Another species that is often sold at native plant nurseries but that is not native in the Indiana Dunes is orange coneflower (*R. fulgida*). It differs in that its stems and leaves have sparse, soft pubescence.

Thin-leaved coneflower.

Rudbeckia laciniata (CUTLEAF CONEFLOWER)

ASTERACEAE—sunflower family

Description A tall native perennial that reaches up to 10' tall. The stem is hollow, hairless, and glaucous. The alternately arranged leaves are hairless and pinnately lobed and toothed, typically with 5–9 lobes on the lower leaves and fewer on the upper. Leaves near the inflorescence are sometimes entire and unlobed. The corymbiform array consists of flowerheads with 8–12+ drooping, sterile petallike ray flowers surrounding 150–300+ fertile disc flowers that form a dome-shaped disc. The fruit is a ribbed seedlike achene that lacks a pappus.

Bloom Period July–October

Plant Communities Prairie fen, bottomland

Notes Cutleaf coneflower is a favorite of foragers that enjoy eating the fresh, young leaves. If collected later, the flavor may be a little much (unless you're a fan of eating turpentine). There is a cultivar called "golden-glow" that has more ray flowers and fewer disc flowers.

Etymology See *Rudbeckia hirta* for genus etymology. *Laciniata* is from the Latin word *lacer*, meaning "torn," in reference to the deeply lobed leaves.

Look-alikes Because of the dome-shaped disc, cutleaf coneflower may be confused for gray-headed coneflower (*Ratibida pinnata*), which is shorter (<4'), has compound leaves, and has dark-brown disc flowers. Gray-headed coneflower also occurs in drier habitats of the prairie complex and the savanna complex.

Gray-headed coneflower. Courtesy Michael Huft.

ASTERACEAE—sunflower family

Description A native perennial that grows up to 6.5' tall. The stems may be slightly squared in cross-section or angled and are either pubescent or glabrous. The oppositely arranged, stalkless leaves are tightly attached but do not clasp. The flowerheads are up to 3" wide with 12–36 petallike ray flowers surrounding up to 225 disc flowers. Both ray flowers and disc flowers are fertile. The phyllaries are in 2–3 rows and, depending on variety, are smooth, hairy, or glandular hairy. The fruit is a seedlike achene lacking a hairlike pappus.

July–September

Prairie fen, sedge meadow / wet prairie, prairie complex, savanna complex

We recognize three varieties of rosinweed in the Indiana Dunes; var. *integrifolium* has rough or hairy phyllaries; var. *deamii* has glandular hairs on the phyllaries and soft hair on the undersides of the leaves; and var. *neglectum* has glandular hairs on the phyllaries and short, rough hairs scattered on the undersides of the leaves. Rosinweed was once commonly called gum plant, due to Native American children chewing the fragrant resin. The rare Silphium borer moth (*Tebenna silphiella*) relies on these plants for its survival.

Cup plant.

Compass plant.

Prairie dock.

Etymology *Silphium* was named after the ancient plant called *Silphion* that was common in Roman culture, but that was driven to extinction by farmers who saw more profit in cattle than in the plant. The original *Silphion* plant was in the carrot family (Apiaceae). *Integrifolium* means "entire leaf" (the leaves are entire or nearly so).

Look-alikes There are three other species of *Silphium* in the Indiana Dunes. Compass plant (*S. laciniatum*) has large basal leaves and alternate, deeply lobed, hairy leaves that become smaller up the stem. Cup plant (*S. perfoliatum*) has larger, clasping leaves that often form a cup around the sharply 4-angled stem. Prairie dock (*S. terebinthinaceum*) has strictly basal leaves that are elephant-ear-sized and triangular to shallowly heart-shaped.

Solidago altissima (TALL GOLDENROD)

ASTERACEAE—sunflower family

Description A freely spreading and colony-forming native perennial that grows up to 6.5' tall. Stems are hairy (becoming glabrous below). The alternately arranged leaves taper to each end with 3 deeply impressed veins. They are often shallowly toothed, but upper leaves can be entire. The top surface of the leaves is rough hairy, and the underside is short hairy. Lower leaves usually wither by flowering time. Each flowerhead has up to 15 ray flowers surrounding usually up to 6 disc flowers. The involucre is over 0.12" long. The flowerheads are in a pyramidal array that is quite robust, with the potential of having over 1,200 flowerheads on a single plant! The fruit is a seedlike achene with a fluff of hair (pappus) attached to the tip.

Bloom Period August–October

Plant Communities Disturbed areas, prairie complex, savanna complex

Notes Despite the seemingly aggressive nature of this beautiful plant, it plays an important ecological role for a variety of insects. A swollen, ball-like lump called an "apple gall" is often found on the stems; this is caused by the goldenrod gall fly (*Eurosta solidaginis*).

Another gall fly called the goldenrod bunch gall (*Rhopalomyia solidaginis*) causes the plant to create a tight lettuce-like cluster of leaves called a "rosette gall" at or near the top of the plant. The Solidago gall moth (*Gnorimoschema gallaesolidaginis*; don't ever complain about a plant's scientific name again!) creates a gall similar to that of the goldenrod gall fly; however, the gall is more spindle-shaped than ball-shaped. In addition to these common insect uses, the leaves are often infected with the orangish fungal rust *Puccinia dioicae*.

Etymology *Solidago* comes from the Latin word meaning "to make whole," referring to the ancient medicinal usage of the plant by Native Americans for stomach aches, colds, fevers, and burns. *Altissima* means "tall."

Look-alikes There are many species of goldenrods in the Indiana Dunes, with the two most similar being Canada goldenrod (*Solidago canadensis*) and giant goldenrod (*S. gigantea*). Tall goldenrod was once thought to be a subspecies of Canada goldenrod, but the latter begins blooming a week or two earlier and has more coarsely toothed leaves, involucres that are always under 0.12" long, and more secund array branches (especially in var. *hargeri*); it is rarely infected by the goldenrod gall fly. Giant goldenrod has a hairless, often glaucous stem and usually grows in wetter places than tall goldenrod; however, they often overlap in habitat.

Giant goldenrod's hairless to glaucous stem.

Solidago caesia (BLUE-STEMMED GOLDENROD)

ASTERACEAE—sunflower family

Description A native perennial that grows up to 2.5' tall. Stems often arch and are usually a light yellowish-green to blue to purplish-blue color with a glaucous coating. The alternately arranged, elliptic leaves are sessile with one strongly impressed vein, often toothed, and mostly hairless but sometimes sparsely hairy. Inflorescences form in the axils of the upper leaves in clusters of 1 to 12 flowerheads, with a small, terminal panicle-like array forming as well. One plant can have a few to over 350 flowerheads. Each flowerhead has 4–5 ray flowers surrounding 4–5 disc flowers. The fruit is a seedlike achene with a fluff of hair (pappus) attached to the tip.

Bloom Period August–October

Plant Communities Savanna complex, mesophytic forest

Notes Unlike most of the goldenrods that occur in the Indiana Dunes, blue-stemmed goldenrod is a shade-loving plant. When not in flower, it could be confused for an aster (*Symphyotrichum* sp.).

Etymology See *Solidago altissima* for genus etymology. *Caesia* is derived from the Latin word meaning "bluish gray," referencing the stem color.

Look-alikes Blue-stemmed goldenrod can be confused with zigzag goldenrod (*Solidago flexicaulis*), which often grows in the same woodland habitats. The leaves of the latter are broader (ovate-elliptic) and have a winged petiole. In addition, the stem of zigzag goldenrod angles between nodes in a way that makes it look somewhat zigzaggy.

Zigzag goldenrod.

Solidago rigidiuscula (SHOWY GOLDENROD)

ASTERACEAE—sunflower family

Courtesy Michael Huft.

Description A native perennial that grows to 5' tall. The stem is unbranched, erect, smooth, and red to green. The alternately arranged leaves are toothless to shallowly toothed, often scabrous on the margins, and hairless. They are stalkless above and usually taper to a winged petiole below. Sometimes the upper leaves will have bundles of small leaves at their base. Basal leaves usually do not persist at flowering time. One plant can have over 300 flowerheads in a dense pyramidal array. Each yellow flowerhead has 3–7 ray flowers surrounding 6–16 disc flowers. The fruit is a hairless seedlike achene with a fluff of hair (pappus) at the tip.

Bloom Period August–October

Plant Communities Secondary dune, prairie complex, savanna complex

Notes Another botanical name for this plant is *Solidago speciosa* var. *rigidiuscula*. One of the authors considers this the most charismatic of all goldenrods in northwest Indiana, the other . . . does not.

Etymology See *Solidago altissima* for genus etymology. *Rigidiuscula* means "a little stiff," referencing the stiffish leaves.

Look-alikes Dune goldenrod (*Solidago racemosa* var. *gillmanii*) is a smaller plant with larger flowerheads and resinous, shiny, and often somewhat sticky leaves. Seaside goldenrod (*S. sempervirens*) has leathery, smooth, toothless leaves and grows in more wet, disturbed habitats (often near roads and highways). Gray goldenrod (*Solidago nemoralis*) is usually a shorter plant covered in gray hairs with an inflorescence that often leans to one side. Early goldenrod (*Solidago juncea*) is mostly smooth with flowerheads usually secund within the terminal arrays; at least the basal leaves are toothed. Early goldenrod is our earliest-flowering species in the genus, often beginning to bloom in late June or early July.

Tragopogon dubius (Western Goat's Beard)

ASTERACEAE—sunflower family

Description A nonnative annual, biennial, or monocarpic perennial that grows to 2.5' tall. The alternately arranged leaves are sessile and linear. First-year growth is often a rosette of grasslike leaves. Milky latex exudes from the stem and leaves if broken. Flowerheads are borne singly at the top of the stem, which is slightly swollen and hollow directly under the flowerhead. Flowerheads are made up of fertile pale-yellow ray flowers, with the outer ray flowers longer than the inner. No disc flowers are present. Narrow, long, green phyllaries extend beyond the ray flowers, giving the flowerhead an edgy look. Fruit have a large white to brownish pappus attached at the tip, and the cluster collectively forms a large spherical puff-ball, like a giant dandelion fruiting head.

Bloom Period May–August

Plant Communities Disturbed areas, foredune, secondary dune, prairie complex, savanna complex

Notes Native to Eurasia, western goat's beard has naturalized throughout the United States. It has commonly been called go-to-bed-at-noon because the flowerheads open at sunrise and often are closed by lunchtime (your lunchtime, that is . . . the authors don't stop botanizing for lunch). Another common name for western goat's beard is salsify, which has French origins; however, the origin of this common name is unknown.

Etymology *Tragopogon* is derived from the Greek words *tragos*, meaning "goat," and *pogon*, meaning "beard." This is in reference to the beard-like pappus. *Dubius* means "doubtful." So, what is doubtful with regard to this species? The answer is not clear. Maybe it's doubtful that its seed head actually looks like a goat's beard, or that it is a distinct species at all.

Look-alikes Common goat's beard (*Tragopogon pratensis*) has brighter-yellow ray flowers, flower stalks that are not inflated below the flowerhead, and phyllaries that are shorter than or equal to the length of the outer ray flowers.

Common goat's beard.

Utricularia vulgaris (common bladderwort)

LENTIBULARIACEAE—bladderwort family

Description An aquatic, submergent or free-floating carnivorous native perennial. The alternately arranged leaves are irregularly divided, forked 6–17+ times. On the leaves near the bases of the forked divisions are small bladders. The yellow flowers are arranged 1 to many in a raceme above the water. They have an inflated lower lobe that has orangish-red venation on the hump and a duck-like bill with a narrow spur that slightly curls up under the lower lobe. The upper lip is shorter and sits like a little flat hat on the duck face. The fruit is a small rounded capsule.

Bloom Period June–August

Plant Communities Submerged aquatic, bog, marsh, panne

Notes Bladderworts are an evolutionary wonder. Relative to other carnivorous genera, bladderworts evolved most recently with a surprisingly small genome crammed with a lot of different genes (what!?!). In short, these bladderworts have cut a lot of the noncoding parts of their genome.

The underwater bladders use reverse osmosis (suction) to suck up the unexpecting passerby. They actually do a really bad job of sucking up small invertebrates but a good job of sucking up any passing algae, protists, and bacteria, which collectively form a whole tiny ecological community within their bladders similar to that of our gut. The bladders have a literal hair trigger that when touched creates a rapid suction. A whole book could be written on just how many cool features these plants have.

Etymology *Utricularia* is derived from the Latin word for "bladder," referring to the bladders on the leaves. *Vulgaris* means "common."

Look-alikes Of the at least eight species of *Utricularia* in the Indiana Dunes, common bladderwort is by far the most common. Common bladderwort differs from

Horned bladderwort (*Utricularia cornuta*).

the others by the collection of the following traits: (1) leaves are alternately arranged (not whorled as in purple bladderwort, *U. purpurea*), (2) leaves are forked >6 times, and (3) often has >4 flowers on 1 long stalk.

Humped bladderwort (*Utricularia gibba*).

Verbascum thapsus (GREAT MULLEIN)

SCROPHULARIACEAE—figwort family

Description A soft, woolly, nonnative biennial that grows up to 7' tall. The leaves are in basal rosettes for the first year. The alternately arranged stem leaves are stalkless and taper to a wing that runs down the stem. Flowers are borne on a long, dense, terminal spike. The 5-parted flowers individually only open for one day, usually closing by the early afternoon. When the spike gets clipped it may branch. Flowers can self-pollinate if cross-pollination does not occur. The fruit are large, hairy capsules.

Bloom Period June–October

Plant Communities Disturbed areas, prairie complex, savanna complex

Notes Great mullein has vulgarly been called "cowboy toilet paper," but the soft hairs on the leaves are barbed, so it can cause serious irritation if used in this way.

Moth mullein.

Other common names include Aaron's rod (get your head out of the gutter!) in allusion to Moses's brother's staff in the biblical story. The leaves and seeds contain rotenone and coumarin, both of which have been used as a fish poison and insecticide. Fish poison was one of the reasons great mullein was introduced to North America in the 1700s. It was also historically used by Romans and US miners as a torch, lit after dipping it in tallow.

Etymology *Verbascum* is from the goofed-up Latin word *barbascum*, which means "bearded," referring to the hairy leaves. *Thapsus* was a name for what is now Tunisia, or is from the Sicilian Isle of Thapsos, where it was found.

Look-alikes Moth mullein (*Verbascum blattaria*) has flowers that are stalked and less dense in the inflorescence; it also has nearly hairless stem leaves. Moth mullein's flowers are white or yellow with purple hairs in the center.

Verbesina alternifolia (WINGSTEM)

ASTERACEAE—sunflower family

Courtesy Michael Huft.

Description A native perennial that reaches from 3.5'
to 8'+ tall. The leaves are alternately arranged (rarely
few opposite) along the conspicuously winged stem.
They taper to a winged stalk appearing to be a continuation of the leaf and are shallowly and coarsely toothed
with a rough upper surface. Three to over 50 flowerheads occur at the top of the plant in a panicle-like or
corymbiform array. Each flowerhead has 6–8 sterile
petallike ray flowers that open prior to the disc flowers
that they surround. Disc flowers are fertile and numerous (20–60+), each having its stamens maturing first,
being replaced later by the maturing pistil. The fruit are
flat, seedlike achenes that are often winged (although
this is variable).

Bloom Period July–October

Notes Wingstem is the host plant to the spectacular gold moth (*Basilodes pepita*).

Etymology *Verbesina* means "Verbena-like," referring to the shape of the leaves being somewhat like those of a vervain (*Verbena* sp.). *Alternifolia* means "alternate leaves."

Look-alikes Without flowerheads, common sneeze-weed (*Helenium autumnale*) can appear similar, as it also has winged stems and alternately arranged, coarsely toothed leaves. They differ in that common sneeze-weed's leaves are sessile and narrower, its disc flowers are tightly arranged in a globular disc, and its ray flowers are lobed at their tips. Common sneezeweed also grows in various other wet habitats.

Common sneezeweed.

Viola pubescens var. scabriuscula
(DOWNY YELLOW VIOLET)

VIOLACEAE—violet family

Description A common woodland perennial that reaches 4–11" tall. There are typically 3 or more stems with 0–4 basal, coarsely toothed heart-shaped leaves. Along the stems are 1–4 heart-shaped leaves with stipules that are usually toothless. Leaf surfaces are usually glabrous. The flowers are 5-parted with yellow petals with purplish veins toward the base. The 2 lateral petals are bearded near the base. Later in the year, cleistogamous flowers are borne in the leaf axils and resemble unopened flower buds. The fruit is a glabrous or hairy capsule containing pale, shiny brown seeds.

Bloom Period April–June

Plant Communities Disturbed areas, hydromesophytic forest, savanna complex, mesophytic forest

Notes Violets are an important larval host plant for many lepidopterans, including the great spangled fritillary (*Speyeria cybele*).

Etymology *Viola* is the Latin name for "violet." *Pubescens* means "fuzzy with short hairs," and *scabriuscula* means "slightly rough."

Look-alikes Hairy yellow violet (*Viola pubescens* var. *pubescens*) is a variety that differs in that it has hair on its leaf undersides, hairier stems, 1–2 stems per plant, and usually no basal leaves. Canada violet (*Viola canadensis*) can look similar, with leafy stems and toothless stipules, differing in that it has white petals with a yellow spot at the base and a bluish-purple blush on the backside.

Canada violet.

ZIZIA AUREA (GOLDEN ALEXANDERS)

APIACEAE—carrot family

Description A native, short-lived perennial that can grow up to 2.5' tall. The alternately arranged leaves are twice to thrice compound with 3–5 leaflets. Leaflets are hairless, toothed, and shiny. The tiny yellow 5-parted flowers are arranged in an umbel with 10–18 umbellets, with the central flower of each umbellet being stalkless and all other flowers being stalked. The fruit are flattened, dry schizocarps with prominent ribs.

Bloom Period April–June

Plant Communities Prairie fen, sedge meadow / wet prairie, prairie complex, savanna complex

Notes The flowers smell somewhat like old socks. The common name comes from the resemblance to a European medicinal herb called alexanders (*Smyrnium olusatrum*), which was named for the city of Alexandria (named after Alexander the Great), where it was first found.

Etymology *Zizia* is named in honor of German botanist Johann Baptist Ziz, and *aurea* in Latin means "golden yellow," a reference to the flower color.

Look-alikes Both golden alexanders and hairy Hairy meadow parsnip (*Thaspium chapmanii*) have compound umbels and toothed, compound leaves; however, hairy meadow parsnip has all of the creamy-yellow flowers in the umbels stalked. Hairy meadow parsnip also has winged fruit.

Hairy meadow parsnip.

7. ORANGE FLOWERS

Asclepias tuberosa, butterflyweed
Impatiens capensis, touch-me-not
Lilium michiganense, Michigan lily
Platanthera ciliaris, orange-fringed orchid

Description A native perennial that grows from 1' to 3.5' tall. The usually alternately arranged (sometimes some opposite or whorled), toothless, linear to elliptic leaves are deep green and deeply veined. Leaves are sub-sessile along the hairy stem, which is green to reddish colored. The undersides of the leaves are hairy, and the top surfaces are variable. The 5-parted orange flowers (rarely yellow) have upright hoods that have small hornlike structures and petals that drape down like a skirt. The fruit is a follicle that contains scaly seeds with a tuft of silky hair attached to the tip; this allows them to blow with the wind.

Bloom Period July–September

Plant Communities Disturbed areas, secondary dune, prairie complex, savanna complex

Notes Butterflyweed does not bleed a milky latex like its sister milkweed species do but rather a clear latex, thus the reason why it isn't commonly called butterfly milkweed. It has also been called pleurisy root, due to its toxins causing one to vomit, and it has been used as a diuretic. Butterflyweed is mostly self-incompatible and is pollinated predominately by large bees and wasps.

Green milkweed.

Etymology *Asclepias* is named after the Greek god of medicine and healing. *Tuberosa* means "tuberous," as the roots end in a thickened tuber.

Look-alikes Of the ten milkweeds found in the Indiana Dunes, none have the bright-orange flowers and clear latex of butterflyweed. The most similar vegetatively is green milkweed (*Asclepias hirtella*), due to both having alternate to subopposite linear leaves (unlike the other eight species that have opposite leaves). Green milkweed differs from butterflyweed by its greenish flowers, no horns on the hoods, and milky sap.

IMPATIENS CAPENSIS (TOUCH-ME-NOT)

BALSAMINACEAE—balsam family

Description A native annual that grows to 5' tall and that is ubiquitous in many wet habitats. The stem is hollow, light green (often with some reddish coloration), and somewhat translucent. The stalked, mostly alternate leaves (lower leaves can be opposite) have round-toothed margins and are hairless. The orange flowers are somewhat tubular and look a little like a fish, with modified sepals that possess a curved, tail-like nectar spur and a stomach-like pouch. Five petals form the face of the flower with a large, usually 2-lobed lower lip, 2 smaller upper petals, and 2 even smaller and inconspicuous lateral petals. The petals are often speckled with red spots. Rarely the flowers are yellowish, reddish, or white. The fruit is an elongated capsule that is highly pressurized so that any bump will cause it to burst open, rapidly ejecting the seeds.

Bloom Period June–September

Plant Communities Disturbed areas, bog, marsh, prairie fen, sedge meadow / wet prairie, bottomland, hydromesophytic forest, conifer swamp, pin oak flatwoods

Notes The common name touch-me-not comes from the seed dispersal mechanism, as when the fruit is "touched," it explodes. Another common name is jewelweed, which refers to the way water droplets form into beads, or "jewels," on the leaves. Leaves that are submerged in water also display a silvery, jewellike reflection. Touch-me-nots have two flower types—the open, orange, speckled form and a self-fertilizing closed flower that never opens (cleistogamous). The clear, watery, soothing sap from this plant has been used topically by Native Americans for poison ivy rashes, insect bites, nettle stings, and other skin irritants.

Pale touch-me-not.

Etymology *Impatiens* comes from the word *impatient* because the seed capsules impatiently explode when touched. *Capensis* means "of the cape," as when it was named, the origin was thought to be from South Africa. Someone messed up there.

Look-alikes Touch-me-not is often called orange touch-me-not or orange jewelweed because its sister species, pale touch-me-not (*Impatiens pallida*), has larger, yellow flowers (often called yellow touch-me-not or yellow jewelweed). The latter looks very similar but has more teeth per leaf margin (usually >9 teeth per side, whereas orange touch-me-not usually has <9 teeth per side) and often has a glaucous stem. Pale touch-me-not is sometimes found in similar habitats, especially where there is disturbance, but is usually found in slightly drier areas.

Lilium michiganense (Michigan lily)

LILIACEAE—lily family

Description A native perennial that grows up to 6.5' tall. The lanceolate to linear leaves are in several whorls of 3–14 and taper to a point. Near the top of the plant, reduced leaves may be alternate. At the top of the plant are 1–11 long-stalked drooping flowers, reminiscent of an exquisite chandelier. The flowers have 6 deep-orange, reddish-orange, or orangish-yellow tepals that are mottled with brownish-purple spots and curl back, immodestly exposing the 6 long stamens and single, oftentimes red style. The fruit are 3-valved capsules that are held erect.

Bloom Period June–August

Plant Communities Prairie fen, sedge meadow / wet prairie, bottomland, hydromesophytic forest

Notes The spectacular flowers are often visited by large charismatic butterflies and moths such as the great spangled fritillary (*Speyeria cybele*), swallowtails (*Papilio* spp.), and hummingbird moths (*Hemaris* spp.). The nonnative invasive scarlet lily beetle (*Lilioceris lilii*) has been found to prey on the leaves of Michigan lily and is expanding its range throughout North America.

Etymology *Lilium* means "lily," and *michiganense* means "from Michigan."

Look-alikes Although orange flowers are at a premium in nature, there are a few similar species often found in the Indiana Dunes. The nonnative ornamental tiger lily (*Lilium lancifolium*) is planted throughout the Indiana Dunes landscape, escaping into drier disturbed areas, differing in having alternate leaves, a hairy stem, and dark bulblets that form in the upper leaf axils. The less-common native wood lily (*L. philadelphicum*) differs

Wood lily.

in having flowers that are erect (not drooping), tepals that abruptly narrow to a stalklike "claw," and only a few whorls of leaves along the stem. The weedy, nonnative tiger daylily (*Hemerocallis fulva*) also has orange, spotted tepals, but unlike Michigan lily, it has much larger flowers that are more or less erect, and the leaves are basal and grasslike; it is often found in ditches, at old homesites, and in other disturbed areas.

Tiger daylily.

PLATANTHERA CILIARIS (ORANGE-FRINGED ORCHID)

ORCHIDACEAE—orchid family

Courtesy Michael Huft.

Description A showy native perennial that reaches 1.5–3' tall. The erect, hairless stem arises from a thickened tuberoid. The 2–5 alternately arranged, sessile and sheathing, hairless, toothless, lance-shaped leaves are up to a little over 1' long, reduced in size dramatically up the stem. The orange, stalked flowers are numerous, with 20 to over 100 flowers in a terminal raceme, opening from the bottom of the inflorescence up. The lip petal is dramatically fringed, and the side petals end in a slight fringe and are somewhat hidden by the sepals. The lateral sepals are reflexed or spreading, and the top sepal is hoodlike. The fruit are stalked, ellipsoid capsules.

Bloom Period July–August

Plant Communities Bog (historically also found in wet sand prairies and swales)

Notes The flowers on orange-fringed orchids (and in nearly all of our orchids) are resupinate, meaning that they are actually flipped upside down so that what appears to be the lower lip petal is actually an upper petal. Because of the gorgeous orange flowers, this species has been threatened by orchid poachers. Orange-fringed orchids rely on pollinators for seed set, with swallowtails (*Papilio* spp.) being the most important pollinators. Pollination of this orchid is an amazing evolutionary example of different populations having different-sized flowers due to different pollinators. For example, in mountainous populations where a different species of swallowtail with a shorter tongue pollinates the flowers, the flowers are shorter due to selection pressure.

Etymology *Platanthera* is derived from the Greek words *platys* and *anthera*, meaning "flat or broad anther," referring to the genus's broad anther. *Ciliaris* is derived from the Latin word *cilium*, meaning "eyelashes," referencing the fringed petals.

Look-alikes The Indiana Dunes are home to seven *Platanthera* species, with one thought to be extirpated from the region. The more common green-fringed orchid (*P. lacera*) has a lip that is fringed and also 3-parted, differing in its flowers, which are yellowish to cream colored. Club-spurred orchid (*P. clavellata*) grows on hummocks in swampy woods or on wet margins, differing from orange-fringed orchid by its unfringed lip, whitish flowers, shorter stature, and lack of stem leaves.

Green-fringed orchid.

Club-spurred orchid.

8. RED FLOWERS

Apios americana, groundnut
Aquilegia canadensis, red columbine
Asarum canadense, American wild ginger
Epifagus virginiana, beechdrops
Lobelia cardinalis, cardinal flower
Sarracenia purpurea, northern purple pitcher plant
Symplocarpus foetidus, skunk cabbage
Trillium recurvatum, bloody-butcher

APIOS AMERICANA (GROUNDNUT)

FABACEAE—legume family

Description An herbaceous, twining perennial vine that grows up to 5–10' in length. The alternately arranged leaves are pinnately compound, with 3–7 (always an odd number) toothless leaflets. Leaflets are egg-shaped to a pointed tip. When torn, the leaves exude a milky latex. At the base of each leaf there is a pair of tiny linear stipules. The flowers are reddish pink to purplish pink and look like a conquistador helmet. They are 5-parted and pea-shaped, with a large banner (upper petal), side wings that are a deeper brownish red and curve downward, and a keel that protrudes in between the bottom side lobes and is a creamy white to

brownish red. Flowers are borne in clusters from the leaf axils. The fruit is a legume that is relatively straight or sometimes slightly curved, reaching up to 4" long with a dark-brown, wrinkled surface.

Bloom Period July–August

Plant Communities Disturbed areas, marsh, prairie fen, sedge meadow / wet prairie

Notes Groundnut has numerous common names such as wild potato, Indian potato, and wild bean. It has tubers that have been eaten, usually picked in the late fall through early spring. Native Americans used groundnut as a staple food source, boiling or drying the tubers like potatoes. It also quickly became a food source for the early colonists of New England. The eccentric botanist Constantine Rafinesque mentioned that the Creek Indians cultivated groundnuts. Native American cultivation of groundnut was not restricted to Creek Indians.

Etymology *Apios* comes from the Greek word for "pear," referencing the tuber shape, and *americana* means "from America."

Look-alikes The leaves and twining habit can sometimes look like hog-peanut (*Amphicarpaea bracteata*) when flowers are not present. Hog-peanut always has 3 leaflets and has pairs of tiny stipels at the base of the leaflets, whereas groundnut usually has 5–7 leaflets (but can sometimes have 3 leaflets on some leaves) and lacks stipels.

Aquilegia canadensis (RED COLUMBINE)

RANUNCULACEAE—buttercup family

Description A short-lived native perennial that grows up to 3' tall. The alternately arranged leaves are 2–3 times compound into shallowly lobed leaflets. The leaves are usually long stalked below with upper leaves often exhibiting shorter stalks. First-year plants produce basal leaves only. The leaflets often have a grayish blush and can be somewhat sticky. The dangling flowers are borne singly on long stalks, with numerous flowers in the upper portion of a single plant. Flowers are 5-parted with red sepals and long, straight corolla tubes (spurs) complemented by yellow petals. Collectively, each flower looks like a spectacularly colored lantern. The fruit are 5-chambered, erect, beaked follicles.

Bloom Period April–June

Plant Communities Secondary dune, prairie complex, savanna complex, mesophytic forest

Notes The name columbine is derived from the Latin word for "dove" or "pigeon" because the flowers look somewhat like five doves huddled together around a dish to eat.

Etymology *Aquilegia* is derived from the Latin word *aquilam*, which means "eagle," in reference to the flowers, which are shaped like the feet of an eagle (yeah, that's right . . . the flowers look like lanterns, a quintet of doves, and eagle talons . . . botanists have good imaginations). *Canadensis* simply means "of Canada."

Look-alikes The nonnative garden columbine (*Aquilegia vulgaris*) looks similar but has flowers that lack yellow and red and that are instead purple, pink, and white with inwardly curved spurs. It rarely escapes from homesites.

Asarum canadense (American wild ginger)

ARISTOLOCHIACEAE—birthwort family

Description A colony-forming native perennial groundcover that can grow up to 8" tall. The 2 basal, kidney-shaped, hairy leaves are stalked from a short, densely white, hairy horizontal stem. A single flower forms under the leaves at the intersection of the 2 leaf stalks. Each flower is hairy, tubular, and bell-shaped with a 3-parted calyx that is fused for much of its length, spreading and recurving as horned lobes. The inside of the flower is white with a deep-purplish-red

pattern, with 12 stamens and 6 styles. The fruit is a fleshy capsule that contains many dark-brown seeds.

Bloom Period April–June

Plant Communities Bottomland, mesophytic forest

Notes There are a couple of varieties of this species, with the one in the Indiana Dunes being var. *reflexum* (with sepal lobes recurved). Seed dispersal is aided by ants (see *Dicentra cucullaria* for more on myrmecochory). Pollination is mostly conducted by ants, beetles, and flies. When hiking in the spring, make sure to lift up the leaves to see if there are flowers. If found, make sure to smell them, as they have a very unique aroma like that of rotten flesh. The bruised rhizomes smell distinctly like ginger (*Zingiber officinale*). The name *American wild ginger* is a result of its history in being used as a ginger replacement; however, eating too much of the rhizomes can cause kidney failure, due to the aristolochic acid.

Etymology *Asarum* is the ancient Greek name for a European species, and *canadense* means "of Canada."

Look-alikes Somewhat similar is Virginia snakeroot (*Endodeca serpentaria*), which has more arrowhead-shaped leaves arranged alternately along an arching stem; it also has a solitary reddish-brown flower hidden at the base of the plant (often in leaf litter), but the flower is pipe-shaped and somewhat snakelike.

EPIFAGUS VIRGINIANA (BEECHDROPS)

OROBANCHACEAE—broomrape family

Description A parasitic native annual growing on the roots of American beech (*Fagus grandifolia*) that is usually about 1' tall but that can reach 1.5'. The branched stems range from pink to tan and are often marked with purplish-red stripes. The leaves are reduced to inconspicuous, alternate scales the same color as the stem. Stalkless or very short-stalked flowers sit just above the leaves along the length of most of the stem. The flowers lower on the stem are self-fertilizing and remain closed (cleistogamous), appearing as teardrop-shaped buds, whereas those above are chasmogamous with tubular creamy white and purplish-red striped corollas to about 0.5" long with 4 small lobes at the tip, enclosing a style and 4 stamens, though they are often sterile. The fruit is a brown capsule.

Bloom Period August–October

Plant Communities Hydromesophytic forest, mesophytic forest

Notes Beechdrops, an easily overlooked forest wildflower, is the only species worldwide in the genus *Epifagus*. It is parasitic but does not harm the beech tree on which it grows. Because it is completely parasitic,

Note the branching form and cleistogamous flowers below the chasmogamous flowers.

it does not need to produce any chlorophyll, and the resulting stem color could lead one to assume it was a fungus or even a fallen branch! Although the gorgeous and intriguing chasmogamous flowers are often present (especially at ends of branches), plants sometimes produce all cleistogamous flowers, making them even more inconspicuous. Recent research has shown that ants may be the primary pollinators of the chasmogamous flowers.

Etymology *Epifagus* is derived from the Greek *epi-* and *Fagus*, meaning "upon beech," aptly describing the only place that the plant can be found, around beech trees, growing on their roots.

Look-alikes None in the Indiana Dunes.

Lobelia cardinalis (Cardinal Flower)

CAMPANULACEAE—bellflower family

Description An unbranched perennial that grows from 2' to 4' tall. The basal leaves are in a rosette. The stem leaves are sharply toothed, lanceolate-shaped, sessile, and alternately arranged. Torn leaves emit a white sap. Flowers are resupinate (turned upside down), growing in a terminal raceme that can reach 2' long. They are tubular with 3 "lower" lobes and 2 spreading "upper" lobes. The 5 sepals are fused at the base to form a cup-like calyx.

Bloom Period July–September

Plant Communities Disturbed areas, sedge meadow / wet prairie, bottomland, hydromesophytic forest, pin oak flatwoods

Notes The brilliant flowers of cardinal flower are pollinated predominantly by hummingbirds. It has historically been used as a love charm when the root is rubbed on, well, the important love parts. It is a favorite for native landscaping, especially in wet areas. Cardinal flower is commonly planted in wetland restoration areas such as marshes and prairie fens, where it may not naturally occur.

Etymology The genus name *Lobelia* is in honor of sixteenth-century botanist Mathias de Lobel, and *cardinalis* references the fact that the flowers look like the robes worn by Catholic cardinals.

Look-alikes None.

Sarracenia purpurea
(Northern Purple Pitcher Plant)

SARRACENIACEAE—pitcher plant family

Description A carnivorous native perennial that grows in a spreading rosette up to 1.5' tall. The leaves have evolved into inflated "pitchers" that are widest at or above the middle and that persist through the winter. The pitchers are pubescent to hairless on the outer surface, often with distinct red to purple veins, and overall reddish, purplish, or green, sometimes with mottling of all three colors. The pitcher lacks a lid (operculum). Inside the mouth of the pitcher are downward-pointing hairs that make it nearly impossible for insects that have made their way into the pitcher to escape from it. Solitary flowers to 2.5" wide nod atop naked stems. The flower has 5 spreading yellowish to reddish or purplish sepals surrounding 5 drooping, soon deciduous red petals. The petals wrap loosely around a large stigmatic disc that looks like an umbrella covering the many stamens.

Bloom Period May–June

Plant Communities Bog

Notes The operculum of pitcher plant leaves is thought to be an evolutionary structure to keep the water concoction that accumulates in the pitchers from evaporating in the southern heat. Northern purple pitcher plant lacks the lid due to the northern climate but still holds rainwater. Within the water is an ecosystem of mycobacteria, protozoans, and arthropods that all evolved closely with the plant. With the exception of adolescent young leaves, northern purple pitcher plant, unlike many other pitcher plants around the world, does not produce its own digestive enzymes. It relies on the work of the pitcher ecosystem to break down the plant's victims. The pitcher plant mosquito (*Wyeomyia smithii*) is one example of a species that coevolved with the northern purple pitcher plant. The carnivorous nature of the plant is clear; however, a recent Canadian study found that young spotted salamanders were often found to be victims to the pitcher's deadly game.

Etymology *Sarracenia* was named by Linnaeus to honor Canadian botanist and physician Michael Sarrazin.

Sarrazin discovered the northern purple pitcher plant and argued that it "ate" insects, a theory that was scoffed at by academics; however, it was a young Charles Darwin that proved Sarrazin to be correct. *Purpurea* means "purple," referencing the color of various parts of the plant.

Look-alikes None.

Symplocarpus foetidus (skunk cabbage)

ARACEAE—arum family

Description A native perennial that grows up to 2' tall. The large (to 2' long and over 1' wide) basal leaves are hairless and toothless, unfurling after flowering. The inconspicuous yellowish flowers lack petals and are attached to a fleshy, ovoid spadix that is reddish, dark purple, or yellow and surrounded by a hoodlike spathe. The spathe is maroon to dark reddish purple to green and mottled with yellows, maroons, and greens,

resembling the hood of a warlock rising through the winter's snow. The fruit is a packed cluster of dark chocolate-colored berries that looks like an egg of some strange, foreign creature.

Bloom Period February–May

Plant Communities Prairie fen, sedge meadow / wet prairie, hydromesophytic forest, conifer swamp, pin oak flatwoods

Notes One of the earliest-blooming native wildflowers in the Indiana Dunes. Throughout the year, skunk cabbage stores up food reserves in its thick underground stems. When late winter and early spring arrive, these food stores move to the spadix and create heat through a process called thermogenesis. This heat can melt the snow or ice, reaching up to 77°F. The flowers have an awful stench, like rotting flesh, attracting flies and carrion beetles that then pollinate the flowers. What a perfect set of adaptations for a plant that flowers when there's snow on the ground, as early-season insects need both food and warm shelter. At the time of writing, while in quarantine, the shape and structure of the spadix is a reminder of the COVID-19 virus.

Water arum.

Etymology *Symplocarpus* is derived from the Greek words *symploce*, meaning "interweaving," and *carpus*, meaning "fruit," referencing the dense cluster of berries. *Foetidus* means "fetid," referring to the foul smell of the flowers and bruised foliage.

Look-alikes Species within the arum family have a unique spathe and spadix structure, with the true flowers on the spadix. Water arum (*Calla palustris*) could be confused for skunk cabbage; however, water arum has smaller leaves and a pure-white spathe similar to the peace lilies (*Spathiphyllum* spp.) popular around Easter. In the Indiana Dunes, water arum is restricted to bogs.

Trillium recurvatum (BLOODY-BUTCHER)

MELANTHIACEAE—bunchflower family

Description A native woodland perennial that grows up to 1.5' tall. The true leaves are actually reduced to subterranean, dry scalelike structures arranged alternately along the rhizomes. The 3 aboveground "leaves" are actually bracts (modified leaves associated with a flower) at the end of an upright branch from the horizontal stem. The hairless bracts are borne on short stalks and are medium green mottled with dark purple to brown to light green. The solitary flower is stalkless and erect with 3 dark-maroon petals often huddling together above 3 smaller green sepals that are recurved and hang below the plane of the bracts. The fruit is a berry-like capsule.

Bloom Period April–June

Plant Communities Disturbed areas, mesophytic forest

Notes A rare form with yellow petals and yellow anthers (forma *shayi*) is sometimes seen in northwest Indiana; more common is a form with yellow petals and purple anthers (forma *luteum*). Occasionally one may find a bloody-butcher with 4 bracts, which is a sign of good luck. Rarely you may find an individual with

forma *luteum.*

5 bracts, which is a sign of bad luck. Other common names include prairie trillium (even though it doesn't grow in prairies), toadshade, wood lily, and red trillium.

Etymology For *Trillium* etymology, see *T. grandiflorum*. *Recurvatum* means "recurved," referring to the recurved sepals.

Look-alikes Bloody-butcher is often confused with sessile toadshade (*Trillium sessile*), which isn't known to grow in the Indiana Dunes. It has sessile leaflike bracts and sepals that spread but do not recurve (they remain in the same plane as the bracts).

9. PINK, LAVENDER, AND MAGENTA FLOWERS

Agalinis purpurea, purple false foxglove
Amphicarpaea bracteata var. *comosa*, lowland hog-peanut
Asclepias incarnata, swamp milkweed
Asclepias syriaca, common milkweed
Calystegia sepium, hedge bindweed
Centaurea stoebe subsp. *micranthos*, spotted knapweed
Cirsium discolor, pasture thistle
Cirsium pitcheri, Pitcher's thistle
Claytonia virginica, spring beauty
Cypripedium acaule, pink lady slipper
Desmodium canadense, showy tick trefoil
Dipsacus fullonum, fuller's teasel
Eutrochium maculatum, spotted Joe-Pye-weed
Geranium maculatum, spotted geranium
Hesperis matronalis, dame's rocket
Hylodesmum glutinosum, pointed leaf tick trefoil
Leonurus cardiaca, motherwort
Liatris aspera, rough blazingstar
Lythrum salicaria, purple loosestrife
Mimulus ringens, Allegheny monkeyflower
Monarda fistulosa, wild bergamot
Nabalus albus, white rattlesnake root
Persicaria amphibia var. *stipulacea*, water smartweed
Phlox pilosa, downy phlox
Prunella vulgaris subsp. *lanceolata*, common selfheal
Sabatia angularis, rose pink
Tephrosia virginiana, goat's-rue
Teucrium canadense, American germander
Triadenum virginicum, Virginia marsh St. John's-wort

AGALINIS PURPUREA (PURPLE FALSE FOXGLOVE)

OROBANCHACEAE—broomrape family

Description A native annual that grows to a little over 2' tall. Stems are quadrangular and can be much-branched. The oppositely arranged leaves are linear, usually hairless, have a prominent midrib, and are no wider than 0.12". Relatively large purplish-pink flowers form at the ends of very short stalks in leaf axils. The corolla is tubular with 2 upper lobes and 3 lower lobes around a spotted white throat, with yellow lines directing pollinators to their reward. The fruit is a round capsule.

Bloom Period August–October

Plant Communities Prairie fen, sedge meadow / wet prairie, panne

Notes The glamorous flowers of false foxgloves open in the morning and often wilt by the end of the day. Purple false foxglove can self-pollinate but predominantly outcrosses. Furthermore, it is a facultative parasite, meaning that it can survive to seed without parasitizing anything; however, if there are host plants nearby, it develops haustoria (modified projections from the roots that allow it to parasitize the host) on its roots. Curiously, if there are no host plants (i.e., bushclovers [*Lespedeza* spp.]), no haustoria will develop.

Etymology *Agalinis* is derived from *aga-* and *-linis*, meaning "great or remarkable flax." It was taxonomically split from the genus *Gerardia* by the truly mad genius and botanist Constantine Rafinesque, who placed all of the species that had narrow leaves and purplish flowers similar to true flax species (*Linum* spp.) into *Agalinis*. *Purpurea* means "of purple," referring to the purplish-pink flowers.

Look-alikes There are two false foxgloves in the Indiana Dunes that can commonly be mistaken for purple false foxglove. Pauper false foxglove (*Agalinis purpurea* var. *parviflora*; sometimes called *A. paupercula*) has flowers that are <0.75" long (>0.75" long in purple false foxglove). Slender false foxglove (*Agalinis tenuifolia*) differs in having flatter flowers on stalks over 0.25" long.

Slender false foxglove; notice the long flower stalk.

AMPHICARPAEA BRACTEATA VAR. COMOSA
(LOWLAND HOG-PEANUT)

FABACEAE—legume family

Description A twining annual native vine that can blanket areas with its overarching presence. It has trifoliate leaves alternately arranged along the abundantly spreading hairy, thin, green to red stem. At the base of each leaf there is a pair of tiny linear stipules, and at the base of each leaflet there is a pair of tiny linear stipels. The flowers are pink to lavender. These flowers are tightly clustered at the end of long flowering stalks coming from the leaf axils. For fruit, see notes.

Bloom Period August–September

Plant Communities Prairie fen, sedge meadow / wet prairie, bottomland, hydromesophytic forest

Notes Lowland hog-peanut twines left to right. If that isn't cool enough, it produces a flower on stolons near to the ground that never opens because it self-pollinates. This cleistogamous flower turns into a round, single-seeded, edible fruit that is sometimes subterranean. The cross-pollinating pealike chasmogamous flowers each mature into a hairy legume that contains 2–4 small seeds. Native Americans frequently

used these edible fruits as a part of their diet. Dakota Nation women also harvested the small seeds from the terrestrial legume.

Amphi- means "two," and *carpaea* means "seed," a reference to the two types of fruit that the plant produces (one underground, or nearly so, and one aerial). *Bracteata* means "bracted" in reference to the small oval bracts that are opposite the flowers. The varietal name *comosa* is Latin for "having hairs."

There are two varieties of hog-peanut in our flora. Upland hog-peanut (*Amphicarpaea bracteata* var. *bracteata*) has little to no hair on the stems (when present they are often appressed to the stem), smaller terminal leaflets (2.5" or less long, whereas those of lowland hog-peanut are up to 4" long), and glabrous fruit; the former also often has white flowers and tends to grow in drier conditions, such as the savanna complex and mesophytic forest. Carl Linnaeus originally split these into *Glycine bracteata* and *Glycine comosa*.

See *Apios americana* for a detailed comparison with that species.

Asclepias incarnata (SWAMP MILKWEED)

APOCYNACEAE—dogbane family

Description A native perennial that grows up to 6' tall. The oppositely arranged leaves are toothless, short-stalked, hairless, and taper to the tip. The 5-parted flowers are light to dark pink (rarely white and sometimes reddish pink) and have upright hoods that have small hornlike structures, petals that drape down like a skirt, and a white column that is between the hoods and the petals; they are arranged in umbels. The fruit is a smooth follicle up to 4" long that turns tan, splitting open to expose the scalelike seeds, each with a tuft of silky hair at the tip, allowing them to blow in the wind.

Bloom Period June–September

Plant Communities Disturbed areas, bog, marsh, prairie fen, sedge meadow / wet prairie, panne, bottomland

Notes Swamp milkweed flowers are very fragrant when fresh, smelling like bubblegum. Little orange oleander aphids (*Aphis nerii*) can be frequent on swamp milkweed stems, creating an eyesore. All oleander aphids are females! These aphids create a honeydew that is toxic to many creatures; however, some ants enjoy the tasty treat and hang out with the many aphids. Another dogbane family obligate insect is the swamp milkweed beetle (*Labidomera clivicollis*), which prefers swamp milkweed. For more on milkweed herbivores, see the notes section of common milkweed (*Asclepias syriaca*).

Etymology *Asclepias* was named after the Greek god of medicine, Asclepius, and *incarnata* means "to make flesh, real; with human form" (think of the incarnation of Christ). The specific epithet more than likely refers to the color incarnate, which is a fleshy pink color (not so much the actual color of a Caucasian's skin).

Look-alikes See the accounts for common milkweed (*Asclepias syriaca*) and butterflyweed (*A. tuberosa*).

Asclepias syriaca (COMMON MILKWEED)

APOCYNACEAE—dogbane family

Description A common native perennial that grows up to 7' tall. The oppositely arranged leaves are stalked, thick textured, toothless, and with a conspicuous midrib that is white to pink. The underside of the leaf is softly hairy, and the top is covered with tiny, appressed gray hairs. The 5-parted flowers are light to dark pink to purplish-white (rarely completely white or cream colored) and have upright hoods that have small hornlike structures, petals that drape down like a skirt, and a short column that is between the hoods and the petals; they are arranged in spherical umbels. The fruit is a large, hairy, warty follicle that turns grayish brown, splitting open to expose the scalelike seeds that each have a tuft of silky hair at the tip, allowing them to blow in the wind.

Bloom Period June–August

Plant Communities Disturbed areas, secondary dune, prairie complex, savanna complex

Notes Milkweeds are the host plants to not only the monarch butterfly (*Danaus plexippus*) but also the unexpected cycnia (*Cycnia collaris*) and the milkweed tussock moth (*Euchaetes egle*). Other insects that are dependent on milkweeds include longhorn milkweed beetles (*Tetraopes tetrophthalmus*), small milkweed bugs (*Lygaeus kalmii*), and the milkweed stem weevil (*Rhyssomatus lineaticollis*), among others. Milkweed isn't just for monarchs!

Etymology See *Asclepias incarnata* for genus etymology. *Syriaca* means "of Syria," due to the thought that it originated from Syria . . . it didn't.

Look-alikes Sullivant's milkweed (*Asclepias sullivantii*) looks very much like common milkweed but has sessile leaves that are hairless on the undersides and that usually ascend upward, and it produces fewer flowers per dome-shaped umbel. It is restricted to the transitional zone between the sedge meadow / wet prairie and the prairie complex. Another similar milkweed is the divine purple milkweed (*Asclepias purpurascens*), which differs in having consistently deeper-purple-colored flowers that usually occur in terminal umbels (terminal and axillary in common milkweed) and smooth follicles.

Purple milkweed.

Calystegia sepium (HEDGE BINDWEED)

CONVOLVULACEAE—bindweed family

Description A native, twining, perennial herbaceous vine that can grow over 10' in one growing season, making a visual mess of things. The alternately arranged leaves have no teeth, are usually hairless, and are shaped like an arrowhead with a V-shaped sinus between the basal lobes. The flowers are relatively large, attached to the stem via long stalks. They are usually white with strong flushes of pink or lavender but can

be pure white. The flowers have shallowly 5-lobed corollas that form a funnel shape, like the bell of a tuba. In addition to the small 5-lobed calyx under the corolla, there are 2 large sepal-like bracts. The fruit is a small, round, single-chambered capsule.

Bloom Period June–September

Plant Communities Disturbed areas, marsh, prairie fen, sedge meadow / wet prairie, bottomland, secondary dune, prairie complex, savanna complex

Notes All bindweeds (*Calystegia* spp.) twine counterclockwise. Because of the large flowers and aggressive habit, this is one native plant that you either love or hate.

Etymology *Calystegia* means "covered calyx," referencing the large bracts that hide the calyx, and *sepium* is derived from the Latin word meaning "hedge," referring to its occurrence oftentimes on fences or hedges.

Look-alikes Hedge bindweed can be confused with field bindweed (*Convolvulus arvensis*), with the latter having smaller flowers and an exposed calyx. Hedge bindweed's sister species large-bracted bindweed (*Calystegia silvatica*) differs in having completely white flowers, larger and seemingly inflated bracts, and a square sinus between the leaf basal lobes.

CENTAUREA STOEBE SUBSP. MICRANTHOS
(SPOTTED KNAPWEED)

ASTERACEAE—sunflower family

Courtesy Michael Huft.

Description A nonnative, invasive, branched biennial or perennial that can grow up to 4' tall. Basal leaves are arranged in a rosette. The alternately arranged, deeply divided stem leaves are gray-green and are covered in rough hairs. It can take up to 4 years before flowering occurs. The flowerheads are numerous at the ends of branches in the upper part of the plant and are composed of elongated, showy but sterile petallike ray flowers surrounding the shorter, fertile disc flowers. The flowerhead is usually pink to lavender (rarely white). The involucre is made up of stiff phyllaries that are fringed and black tipped. There can be up to 1,000 small fruit produced by each plant.

Bloom Period July–October

Plant Communities Disturbed areas, foredune, secondary dune, blowout, prairie complex

Notes Spotted knapweed is native to eastern Europe and is thought to have arrived in North America on the ballast of ships during the late nineteenth century. The roots of spotted knapweed exude allelopathic chemicals, which inhibit the growth of competing plants.

Etymology *Centaurea* comes from the Greek word *kentaurin*, which means "knapweed," and *stoebe* is Greek for "stuffing" or "to stuff"; the foliage of spotted knapweed is similar, at least in color, to plants in the genus *Stoebe*. *Micranthos* means "small flower," referring to the flower size relative to the other subspecies (which is not known to occur in the United States).

Look-alikes See Pitcher's thistle (*Cirsium pitcheri*), which has similar-colored foliage.

Cirsium discolor (PASTURE THISTLE)

ASTERACEAE—sunflower family

Description A native biennial to short-lived perennial that grows up to 10' tall. The stem is oftentimes hairy and branched. The alternately arranged leaves (sometimes opposite below) are deeply lobed (rarely some unlobed, especially in basal rosettes), each lobe ending in a long spine tip. The top surface of the leaf is green with long hairs or almost hairless, and the underside is covered in a white feltlike mat of hair. The flowerheads are often composed of over 100 disc flowers that are pink to lavender pink (rarely white). The phyllaries have a white stripe down the middle and a small spine tip that abruptly spreads outward. The fruit is a seedlike achene with a fluff of hair (pappus) at the tip.

Bloom Period August–October

Plant Communities Disturbed areas, prairie complex

Notes Thistles are the larval host plant for the painted lady butterfly (*Vanessa cardui*). Finches commonly feast on the seeds of thistles. Although it often grows in disturbed habitats, pasture thistle is not invasive.

Cirsium comes from the Greek word for "swollen vein," from the ancient thought that it cured swollen veins, and *discolor* is Latin for "two-colored," referencing the distinctly different colors on the top and underside of the leaves.

Canada thistle. Courtesy Michael Huft.

Look-alikes There are a half dozen or so thistle species in the Indiana Dunes. Swamp thistle (*Cirsium muticum*) differs in that it lacks the spine tips on the phyllaries, grows in wetlands (i.e., marsh, prairie fen, sedge meadow / wet prairie), and has leaves that are not as tomentose beneath as in pasture thistle. The nonnative bull thistle (*C. vulgare*) differs in that it has spiny wings on the stem, green leaf undersides, and gnarly spine-tipped phyllaries that ascend upward. Canada thistle (*C. arvense*), which has a misapplied common name, is native to Eurasia (not Canada!) and is invasive. It has smaller flowerheads, is rhizomatous (forming colonies), and usually has green leaf undersides (though young leaves can be covered in white hairs).

Swamp thistle.

Bull thistle.

CIRSIUM PITCHERI (PITCHER'S THISTLE)

ASTERACEAE—sunflower family

Description A federally threatened, monocarpic native perennial that grows to 1.5–4' tall. For most of its life, Pitcher's thistle consists of a basal rosette. These leaves are grayish green, deeply pinnately lobed almost to the midvein, and completely covered in matted, soft white hairs. In the final year of its life, a grayish-green stem with scattered spines is produced with alternately arranged leaves that decrease in size upward. The stem leaves are similar in color and pubescence to the basal leaves, and there are usually spines on the tips of the lobes. Flowerheads are large, showy, fragrant collections of 100–150 pinkish-white to creamy-white (rarely deep-pinkish-purple) disc flowers. The phyllaries are in 6–8 rows, have short spines on the tips of the outer series that ascend to spread, and are green. The fruit is a small seedlike achene with a fluff of hair (pappus) at the tip.

Bloom Period May–September (has been seen blooming in late November)

Plant Communities Blowout

Notes Pitcher's thistle is endemic to the beach and dunes along Lake Huron, Lake Michigan, and Lake Superior, once occurring more commonly in these areas. It is federally threatened with populations decreasing throughout its range, due to development pressures, human disturbance, dune/beach stabilization, and invasive species such as the introduced thistle-head weevil (*Rhinocyllus conicus*), which was introduced as a biological agent to control nonnative, invasive thistles (whoops). Pitcher's thistle usually takes 5–7 years to flower; however, in garden experiments it can bloom in its second to third year. The matted, white hairs help protect the plant from the heat by reflecting the sun. The hairiness also helps prevent herbivory and desiccation.

Etymology See *Cirsium discolor* for genus etymology. *Pitcheri* is in honor of Zina Pitcher, who discovered the plant in the late 1820s.

Look-alikes See spotted knapweed (*Centaurea stoebe* subsp. *micranthos*), which has similar-colored foliage.

Claytonia virginica (SPRING BEAUTY)

MONTIACEAE—miner's lettuce family

Description A small native perennial that grows from 2" to 10" tall. The basal leaves can be up to 8" long. There are usually 2 opposite stem leaves that can be 4–5" long and strap-like. Each plant has approximately 5–10 flowers that can showcase whites, pinks, lavenders, and candy stripes on their 5 petals. Each flower has 5 stamens and a pistil. To keep from self-pollinating, the stamens mature prior to the pistil. Flowers close when it is cloudy. The roots possess spherical tubers. The fruit is a small capsule.

Bloom Period March–May

Plant Communities Disturbed areas, bottomland, hydromesophytic forest, mesophytic forest

Notes The common name spring beauty comes from the sparkle of color displayed by the plant in early spring. Another, more fantastical, common name for this plant, fairy spuds, comes from their delicious tiny tubers that were historically an important food source for Native Americans. The flowers, which smell lovely, show up before the leaves of the trees to capture the sun before the canopy closes.

Etymology *Claytonia* is in honor of Virginia botanist John Clayton, and *virginica* simply means "of Virginia."

Look-alikes None.

CYPRIPEDIUM ACAULE (**PINK LADY SLIPPER**)

ORCHIDACEAE—orchid family

Description A native perennial that grows up to 17" tall. The true stem is short and underground, covered by 2–3 hairless sheaths. There are 2 large, oval, glossy, entire-margined basal leaves covered in short hairs that grow up to 12" long and 6" wide. Nonflowering plants have a solitary leaf. A scape holds up a large solitary flower (rarely 2), which slightly nods. The flower has 3 yellowish-green to maroon sepals and 2 petals that look similar. The 2 linear-lanceolate, hairy side petals twist and reach past the swollen labellum (lip petal). The labellum is a hot pink (rarely white) sac with a vertical slit in the front (an entrance for pollinators) and darker veins running around the sides. The fruit is an erect, hairy capsule.

Bloom Period May–June

Plant Communities Bog, hydromesophytic forest

Notes When a pollinator such as a bumblebee enters the small slit opening into the flower, it cannot leave the same way it came in because of the folded structure of the pouch. It is through the floral maze that the bumblebee finds the exit, inadvertently running into the stigma. When the bumblebee enters looking for nectar, it gets frustrated not only because there is no reward but also because it is a trap. Quick learning bumblebees do not return to pink lady slipper flowers, but naïve ones do. With fewer naïve bumblebees, there is low fruit set in this species.

Etymology *Cypripedium* is derived from the Greek words *Kypris* and *pedion*. *Kypris* is an ancient name for the goddess of love, Aphrodite, and *pedion* means "shoe" or "slipper." One of the legends behind the name goes as such. One day Aphrodite was hunting with the beautiful mortal man Adonis. During the hunt, a storm hit, forcing the two into a cave for shelter. Alone in the cave, they made love. After the storm cleared, the two left with haste so as to not get caught in such a precarious situation, and in a Cinderella-esque fashion, Aphrodite left one of her shoes in the cave. When a mortal passerby found and picked up the shoe, it turned into a beautiful flower (a yellow lady slipper, *C. parviflorum*). Ironically, the flower of pink lady slipper also looks suspiciously like a portion of Adonis's nether region. *Acaule* means "stemless," referring to the lack of a true stem.

Look-alikes None.

DESMODIUM CANADENSE (SHOWY TICK TREFOIL)

FABACEAE—legume family

Description A native perennial that typically grows up to 3–5' tall. The alternately arranged, dusty-green leaves are trifoliate, with each leaflet slightly widest near its base. The undersides of the leaves have straight hairs with denser, longer hairs on the veins. The leaflets are less than half as wide as long and are attached to the hairy stem by a hairy petiole that is usually under 1" long. A pair of small, thin mustache-like stipules are present where the petioles meet the stem. The flowers are clustered in a branched terminal panicle. They are pink to pinkish purple with two yellowish-cream-colored spots bordered by a darker pinkish purple on the large banner petal. A curved tube that contains the pistil and stamens protrudes with 2 lateral petals positioned right below it. The fruit is a flat, hairy legume called a loment, which has 3–5 rounded sections that each contains a single seed. The hairs on the loments are short-hooked, allowing them to attach to passing animals or clothes.

Bloom Period July–August

Plant Communities Prairie fen, sedge meadow / wet prairie, prairie complex, savanna complex

Notes Regardless of the annoyance of pulling the loments off of your pants or out of your dog's fur, showy tick trefoil is an important larval host plant for many species, including the gray hairstreak (*Strymon melinus*), eastern tailed-blue (*Cupido comyntas*), and silver-spotted skipper (*Epargyreus clarus*).

Etymology *Desmodium* comes from the Greek word *desmos*, meaning "chain" or "bond," referring to the loments. *Canadense* means "of Canada."

Look-alikes There are many tick trefoils in the Indiana Dunes. Hoary tick trefoil (*Desmodium canescens*) differs in that it has tiny, hooked hairs as well as long straight hairs on the leaves. Smooth tick trefoil (*D. glabellum*), panicled tick trefoil (*D. paniculatum*), and perplexed tick trefoil (*D. perplexum*) differ in all three having uniform hairs along the undersides of the leaves. Short-stalked tick trefoil (*D. sessilifolium*) has trifoliate leaves that are sessile or nearly so.

DIPSACUS FULLONUM (FULLER'S TEASEL)

DIPSACACEAE—teasel family

Description A colony-forming, nonnative, invasive, monocarpic biennial to short-lived perennial that grows up to 5'–7' tall. Only basal leaves are present for the first year or two. The prickly, oppositely arranged, oblong stem leaves are unlobed and entire or with roundish-tipped teeth, hairless, and clasp the stem, forming a cup at their intersection around the stem. The flowerheads are made up of 200–1,000 small, purplish-pink flowers clustered in a dense egg-shaped head. Extending beneath and beyond each flower is a small, linear, stiff, spiny bractlet, and the entire head is subtended by long, irregular, spiny bracts. The fruits are hairy achenes.

Bloom Period June–September

Plant Communities Disturbed areas, sedge meadow / wet prairie, prairie complex

Notes Introduced from Eurasia, fuller's teasel has rapidly expanded along roadsides and in prairies, savannas, and wet meadows. Water captured in the cup created by the clasping leaves has been thought to contain magical properties, including the ability to ease eye inflammation. The spiny flowerheads have been and still are used as a comb to full wool.

Etymology *Dipsacus* is from the Greek *dipsa-*, meaning "thirst," due to the clasping leaves that form cups that hold water. *Fullonum* is derived from its use in fulling or pleating fabric.

Look-alikes Cutleaf teasel (*Dipsacus laciniatus*) is another nonnative, invasive teasel that differs from fuller's teasel in that it has deeply lobed leaves and white flowers. Cup plant (*Silphium perfoliatum*) also has opposite leaves that clasp and connect across the stem to form a cup that holds water. It differs in that it has a square stem and is in the sunflower family (Asteraceae) with flowerheads made up of yellow ray and disc flowers.

Cutleaf teasel. Courtesy Michael Huft.

EUTROCHIUM MACULATUM
(SPOTTED JOE-PYE-WEED)

ASTERACEAE—sunflower family

Description A native perennial that can grow to over 6' tall. The mostly hairless stem is often green or light purple with darker-purple spots or small vertical dashes. The short-stalked leaves are in numerous whorls of 4–5 (sometimes 3 or 6). The inflorescence is a somewhat flat corymbiform array with flowerheads each having 8–22 purplish-pink disc flowers. Each disc flower has 2 long, white, protruding styles. Four to 6 rows or series of oblong phyllaries surround each flowerhead, with the inner phyllaries longer than the outer ones. The fruit is a seedlike achene with a brownish tuft of hair attached to the tip, allowing it to be dispersed by wind.

Courtesy Michael Huft.

Bloom Period July–October

Plant Communities Disturbed areas, marsh, prairie fen, sedge meadow / wet prairie, bottomland

Notes Until the turn of the twenty-first century, the genus *Eutrochium* was taxonomically included in the genus *Eupatorium*. Morphologically, *Eutrochium* differs from *Eupatorium* in having whorled leaves and phyllaries that are unequal. The leaves are often mottled by the paths of the Joe-Pye leaf miner beetle (*Liriomyza eupatorii*). There are numerous stories about the origin of the common name Joe-Pye-weed; however, Richard Pearce and James S. Pringle went on a search to discover who Joe Pye was. They found that "Joe Pye" was Joseph Shauquethqueat, a Mohican sachem from Massachusetts and New York. See Pearce and Pringle's 2017

Hollow-stemmed Joe-Pye-weed.

article from the journal *The Great Lakes Botanist*, "The History and Eponymy of the Common Name, Joe-Pye-Weed for Eutrochium Species" to read the whole exciting story.

Etymology *Eutrochium* comes from *eu-* and *trochus*, meaning "true" and "wheel," in reference to the whorled leaves. *Maculatum* means "spotted," in reference to the purple-spotted stem.

Look-alikes Two similar species that grow frequently in the Indiana Dunes are hollow-stemmed Joe-Pye-weed (*Eutrochium fistulosum*) and purple Joe-Pye-weed (*E. purpureum*), both of which have up to 7 disc flowers per tiny flowerhead and arrays that are more dome-shaped than flat-topped. As the name suggests, hollow-stemmed Joe-Pye-weed has a thin-walled hollow stem with usually over 6 leaves in a whorl. Purple Joe-Pye-weed, which commonly has purple coloration at the nodes, is typically found in more shaded habitats, such as mesophytic forest.

Purple Joe-Pye-weed.

Geranium maculatum (spotted geranium)

GERANIACEAE—geranium family

Description A native perennial that can grow up to 2.5' tall. Other than a couple of pairs of small leaves along the hairy stem, most of the leaves are basal. The leaves are hairy, palmately 3–7-lobed, toothed, and deeply veined. Flowers are 5-parted, about 1–1.5" wide, and form in clusters at the top of the plant. The 10 stamens contrast their yellow anthers against the pinkish-lavender petals. Each flower matures into an erect, elongated, hairy columnar fruit. The column has

5 chambers that attach to each of the 5 sections of the ovary. The column dries and the sides rapidly curl up, shooting the seeds up to 30' away.

Bloom Period April–July

Plant Communities Disturbed areas, savanna complex, mesophytic forest

Notes One may often find the little geranium metallic wood-boring beetle (*Pachyschelus purpureus*) copulating on the flowers. Sometimes the leaves have orangish spots on them—that is the rust *Puccinia polygoni-amphibii*. Spotted geranium serves as the aecial host, whereas *Persicaria amphibia* as well as other species in the family Polygonaceae are the uredinial host plants.

Etymology *Geranium* comes from the Greek word *geranos*, meaning "crane," referencing the "cranesbill"-like fruit, and *maculatum* means "spotted," referencing the lighter-colored splotches sometimes seen on the leaves.

Look-alikes There are no other geraniums with such large, showy flowers that grow outside of plantings in the Indiana Dunes.

Hesperis matronalis (DAME'S ROCKET)

BRASSICACEAE—mustard family

Description A nonnative, invasive biennial to short-lived perennial that typically grows from 2' to 4' tall. Both the stem and leaves are softly pubescent. The alternately arranged leaves are sessile to subsessile with sharp teeth on the margins. The flowers are arranged in a loose terminal raceme with the bottom flowers opening first. Each flower has 4 hairy, pinkish-purple-and-green-tipped sepals and 4 showy petals that can

Basal leaves.

be pink, lavender, purple, or white. The fruit is a long, narrow silique.

Bloom Period May–August

Plant Communities Disturbed areas, savanna complex, mesophytic forest

Notes Each gaudy flower has a brilliant sweet, spicy perfume-like fragrance, especially when the day is waning. It was introduced from Europe in the 1600s as a garden ornamental. Because of its voracity at invading natural areas, it is illegal in the state of Indiana to sell, buy, or trade. Other common names include dames' violet and fragrant rocket. The French call it, beautifully, *julienne*. M. A. Karr wrote in his massive volume that it was a favorite flower of the "unfortunate Queen Marie Antoinette."

Etymology *Hesperis* is derived from the word *evening*, in reference to the evening scent of the flowers. *Matronalis* comes from the Roman Festival of Matrons, in which this flower is an important ornament.

Look-alikes Often confused for *Phlox* species (especially garden phlox, *P. paniculata*), differing in that phlox have 5 petals (usually) and opposite leaves. Money plant (*Lunaria annua*) differs in that it has large coin-like silicles (fruit) and shorter, wider leaves.

Hylodesmum glutinosum
(POINTED LEAF TICK TREFOIL)

FABACEAE—legume family

Courtesy Michael Huft.

Description A native perennial that typically grows to 2–4' tall. The long-stalked, alternately attached leaves are so closely clustered that they appear whorled. Each leaf is trifoliate with broad, roundish-to-oval leaflets that end in a long, abrupt tip. The terminal leaflet is larger than the 2 lateral leaflets. From the top of the stem, just above the leaves, arises an open panicle of 5-parted pink to whitish-pink flowers. The flowers have a typical pea family shape, with the pistil and stamens in the protruding keel, 2 lateral petals, and a larger banner petal above. The fruit is a flat, segmented legume called a loment. The loment has up to 3 bell curve–shaped segments, with each segment breaking off individually and including a single seed. The loments are covered with short-hooked hairs that readily attach to passing animals or clothes.

Bloom Period July–August

Plant Communities Savanna complex, mesophytic forest

Notes *Hylodesmum* was formerly included in the genus *Desmodium*. Although bees find the flowers of pointed leaf tick trefoil desirable, the flowers contain no nectar.

Etymology *Hylodesmum* is from the Greek words *hyle*, meaning "forest," and *desmos*, an abbreviated version of *Desmodium*, meaning a "chain" and referencing the chain of segments making up the loment; thus, *Hylodesmum* is essentially a forest *Desmodium*. *Glutinosum* means "sticky," a reference to the hooked hairs covering the inflorescence, making it feel sticky.

Look-alikes Naked leaf tick trefoil (*Hylodesmum nudiflorum*) has the flowering stem lacking leaves and arising from the ground separate from the leafy stem; its leaflets are not as abruptly sharp pointed.

LEONURUS CARDIACA (MOTHERWORT)

LAMIACEAE—mint family

Courtesy Michael Huft.

Description A weedy, nonnative perennial that grows up to 4' tall. The stalked, oppositely arranged leaves are reduced in size up the quadrangular stem, with the lower leaves palmately 3-lobed (rarely 5-lobed) (more maplelike) with irregular teeth. The upper leaves have smaller lobes relative to the lower leaves. Veins on the leaves are deeply impressed. The flowers are arranged 1 to many in whorls within the upper leaf axils. They are bilaterally symmetrical, with a hairy, pink to white, 2-lobed upper lip and a 3-lobed, purple-spotted, pink to white lower lip. The whole corolla is covered in fuzzy white hair and sits in a hairy calyx that has long teeth. These teeth are especially apparent after the flower falls away, appearing as quite spiny clusters. The calyx turns brown, holding four 3-sided nutlets that are tucked within.

Bloom Period May–September

Plant Communities Disturbed areas, savanna complex, mesophytic forest

Notes Native to southeast Europe and Asia, motherwort was introduced to North America for its medicinal properties and has naturalized throughout its range. If crushed, the leaves give off an unpleasant odor. The common name and the specific epithet are from its historic usage medicinally. In the 1653 book *Complete Herbal*, botanist Nicholas Culpepper writes:

> Venus owns the herb, and it is under Leo. There is no better herb to take melancholy vapours from the heart, to strengthen it, and make a merry, chearful, blithe soul than this herb. It may be kept in a syrup or conserve; therefore, the Latins called it Cardiaca. Besides, it makes women joyful mothers of children, and settles their wombs as they should be, therefore, we call it Motherwort. It is held to be of much use for the trembling of the heart, and faintings and swoonings; from whence it took the name Cardiaca. The powder thereof, to the quantity of a spoonful, drank in wine, is a wonderful help to women in their sore travail, as also for the suffocating or risings of the mother, and for these effects, it is likely it took the name of Motherwort with us. It also provokes urine and women's courses, cleanses the chest of cold phlegm, oppressing it, kills worms in the belly.

Etymology *Leonurus* is derived from the Greek words *leon* and *oura*, meaning "lion's tail," in reference to the hairy inflorescence looking like a lion's tail. *Cardiaca* in Latin means "pertaining to the heart" (see notes).

Look-alikes Horehound (*Marrubium vulgare*) is similar to motherwort, differing in having densely white tomentose stems and leaves (motherwort's stems and leaves are sparsely hairy), unlobed leaves, and 10 lobes on the calyx, with spine tips recurved (motherwort has 5 calyx lobes with straight spine tips).

LIATRIS ASPERA (ROUGH BLAZINGSTAR)

ASTERACEAE—sunflower family

Description A native perennial that typically grows to 3–5' tall. The alternately arranged leaves diminish in size up the stem. Basal leaves can be up to 1' long in a rosette. Each leaf has a strong midvein and often is complemented by stiff, short hairs; sometimes the stem is covered by short hairs as well. The inflorescence is a long, tall raceme-like array that can grow up to 1.5' tall with 5 to over 75 button-esque purplish-pink, usually short-stalked flowerheads. Each flowerhead is made up of 15–35+ small 5-lobed disc flowers, each with a long, divided, exserted style. Five stamens hide within the small corolla. The bullate (puckered) phyllaries are usually in 4–5 series. The fruit is a seedlike achene with a fluff of brown hair attached at the tip.

Bloom Period August–October

Plant Communities Secondary dune, prairie complex, savanna complex

Notes Rough blazingstar has been known to hybridize with Cylindrical blazingstar (*Liatris spicata*). Even though the two species can share the same habitat, their flowering time (phenology) is different, as marsh blazingstar blooms from July to August, oftentimes already in seed when rough blazingstar starts opening its flowers; this makes hybridization between the two rare. Blazingstar flowerheads open from the top of the array downward. Blazingstars are the host plant for the gorgeous blazingstar borer (*Carmenta anthracipennis*).

Cylindrical blazingstar.

Etymology The genus name *Liatris* is an ancient name whose origin has been lost in history. *Aspera* means "rough," referring to the hairy stem.

Look-alikes Marsh blazingstar differs in that its involucres are cylindrical, its array axis is hairless, and the array is made up of densely arranged, sessile flowerheads. It also is most frequent in wetter habitats, growing in prairie fen and sedge meadow / wet prairie, though it also occurs in the prairie complex. Marsh blazingstar (*Liatris cylindracea*) differs in that it is usually a shorter plant with phyllaries that are sharp pointed and flat.

Marsh blazingstar.

Lythrum salicaria (PURPLE LOOSESTRIFE)

LYTHRACEAE—loosestrife family

Description An extremely aggressive, nonnative, invasive perennial that grows up to 8' tall. The often branched stems are 4–6-sided and somewhat woody, covered with downy hair. The oppositely arranged leaves (rarely whorled or some alternate) are often slightly hairy, entire, and lance-shaped; the pairs alternate at 90-degree angles along the stem. The flowers are bright magenta to purplish pink, with 5–6 petals in often dense spikes terminating branches. The fruit are small capsules. One plant can produce 2 million or more seeds that remain viable for up to 20 years.

Bloom Period June–October

Plant Communities Disturbed areas, marsh, prairie fen, sedge meadow / wet prairie, panne, bottomland

Notes Because of its stunning summer explosion of purplish-pink color, purple loosestrife was introduced from Europe as a landscape plant for wetter areas. However, it spread prolifically through wetlands, outcompeting important native plants. To control purple loosestrife, loosestrife beetles (*Galerucella calmariensis* and *G. pusilla*) have been released as biological control agents. These small beetles, native in the native range of purple loosestrife, devour the leaves of the plant, which eventually reduces its vitality. Over time, populations produce fewer flowers and eventually decrease in density, allowing other plants to thrive. The loosestrife beetles will never completely eliminate purple loosestrife (you wouldn't want to eat all of your food because you couldn't persist as a species if you did!), but the goal is to keep this aggressive plant in check. It is now illegal to sell, buy, or trade purple loosestrife in Indiana.

Etymology *Lythrum* is derived from the Greek word meaning "bloody," a reference to either the flower color or the use of some plants in the genus to stop bleeding. *Salicaria* is derived from the Latin words meaning "willowlike," in reference to the leaf shape.

Look-alikes The native winged loosestrife (*Lythrum alatum*) is similar but has smaller, usually lighter-colored flowers that are solitary in upper leaf axils; it has very slightly winged stems.

Winged loosestrife. Courtesy Michael Huft.

Mimulus ringens (Allegheny monkeyflower)

PHRYMACEAE—lopseed family

Description A native wetland perennial that grows up to 4' tall. The oppositely arranged leaves are sessile and clasping the squared, sometimes slightly winged, erect stem. The leaves taper to the tip and have sharp teeth on the margins, at least toward the tips. The flowers are in the leaf axils in the upper part of the plant, on relatively long stalks that are over half the length of the leaves beneath them. The lavender to bluish-pink to purplish-blue corollas have 2 lips, with the upper lip split into 2 erect lobes, and the lower lip divided into 3 wide-spreading lobes with wavy edges. The middle lobe of the lower lip arches at the base into the throat of the flower and has a yellow to white spot that is covered in yellow hairs. Beneath the corolla is a long green calyx tube with 5 pointed lobes. The fruit is an oblong capsule containing many seeds.

Bloom Period June–September

Plant Communities Disturbed areas, marsh, prairie fen, sedge meadow / wet prairie, bottomland

Notes Allegheny monkeyflower is the first and only species of *Mimulus* described in the first edition of Linnaeus's 1753 *Species Plantarum* and is the type specimen for the genus. Monkeyflower gets its name from the flower looking somewhat like a monkey's head (use your imagination). Although the flowers can self-pollinate, worker bumblebees are the main pollinator for this plant.

Etymology *Mimulus* is derived from the Latin words for "little or small mime," in allusion to the flowers mimicking faces. *Ringens* comes from the Latin words meaning "to have an open mouth," referring to the corolla looking as though it has a gaping mouth.

Look-alikes Winged monkeyflower (*Mimulus alatus*) also has square stems but differs in that it has petioled leaves and flower stalks that are less than half the length of their subtending leaves. It usually occurs in more shaded bottomland systems.

Monarda fistulosa (WILD BERGAMOT)

LAMIACEAE—mint family

Description A colony-forming native perennial that grows up to 4' tall. The stem is square in cross-section and often red to reddish green. The oppositely arranged, stalked lance-shaped leaves are toothed and hairy. The tubular flowers are tightly arranged in round flower-heads that terminate branching stems. Each flower is pink to lavender with an arching upper lip that has a tiny white tuft of hair at the tip. Extending out of the upper lip are 2 stamens and a long style. The lower lip is shorter and wider than the upper lip, with undulating edges. After the flowers fall away, the calyces remain, persisting throughout the winter collectively as a grayish-brown round ball.

Bloom Period June–September

Plant Communities Disturbed areas, prairie fen, prairie complex, savanna complex

Notes The common name wild bergamot comes from the odor of the crushed foliage, which is similar to the Italian bergamot orange (*Citrus bergamia*), a common ingredient in Earl Grey tea. Wild bergamot smells like . . . well, bergamot, which is somewhat like oregano. It is a very common plant in native plantings and prairie restorations. Another common name is bee balm.

Etymology *Monarda* is named in honor of sixteenth-century botanist Nicolás Bautista Monardes, and *fistulosa* means "tubular," describing the flowers.

Look-alikes Oswego tea (*Monarda didyma*), introduced from farther east and often used in landscaping, differs in that it has brilliant-red corollas and larger, darker-green leaves that smell like marijuana when crushed. Keep in mind that wild bergamot is sometimes also called Oswego tea . . . this illustrates the problem with using common names.

Oswego tea.

Nabalus albus (WHITE RATTLESNAKE ROOT)

ASTERACEAE—sunflower family

Description An often overlooked native perennial that typically grows to 1–5' tall. The stem is purple to purple splotched. The alternately arranged, stalked leaves are variable in shape, often 3-lobed like a lion's paw, heart-shaped, or triangular to oval; regardless of shape, they exude a white latex when torn. The top surfaces of the leaves are hairless. A loose panicle-like array of 3–8 clustered, short-stalked, drooping bell-shaped flowerheads terminates the stem. Each flowerhead has 7 to 13 pinkish-cream to white fertile petallike ray flowers peeking out of the 6–9 purplish-pink phyllaries. Out of each flower protrudes a long style that splits and curls at the tip like a shepherd's hook. White rattlesnake root lacks disc florets. The fruit is an achene with a tuft of rusty-brown hair (pappus) attached to the tip.

Bloom Period August–September

Plant Communities Sedge meadow / wet prairie, savanna complex

Notes The pretentious, wealthy aristocrat William Byrd chronicled his adventures of the 1728 boundary

expedition, which formed the line between North Carolina and Virginia. He published two books outlining this expedition in a serious and often satirical tone. It was here that he wrote absurdly that he smeared root-powder of a *Nabalus* all over the nose of his dog, then forced his dog to trample venomous snakes. In a comedy of sorts, as he forced his dog to trample the snakes, they would not bite due to the horridity of the dog's scent. Thus the common name. It is unknown whether Byrd was mocking an old folktale or making up something new.

Our *Nabalus* are sometimes treated in the genus *Prenanthes*.

Etymology *Nabalus* is Latin for a Native American name for rattlesnake root, and *alba* means "white," which references the ray flower color.

Tall white rattlesnake root (*Nabalus altissimus*) differs in that it has 4–5 pale-green to green phyllaries surrounding creamy-yellowish ray flowers; it occurs in more mesophytic forest habitats.

Tall white rattlesnake root.

Persicaria amphibia var. stipulacea
(WATER SMARTWEED)

POLYGONACEAE—buckwheat family

var. *stipulacea*.

Description An emergent aquatic to terrestrial native perennial that grows in water to more than 6' deep and terrestrially (when stranded on land) up to 4' tall. The alternately arranged leaves float (when in water). When growing on land, stems are prostrate, ascending, or erect. The leaf blades are relatively large and

ovate-elliptic. The tops of the ocreae (sheathing stipules) flare out to form a collar perpendicular to the
stem. The flowers are bright pink with 5 tepals and are
crammed together on a thimble-shaped, short, cylindrical spikelike raceme that is typically broadest at the
base and tapering to the tip. The fruit are dark-brown
seedlike achenes.

Bloom Period June–September

Plant Communities Submerged aquatic, bog, marsh,
prairie fen

var. *emersa*.

Notes Sometimes the leaves have dark splotches on them, which is the rust *Puccinia polygoni-amphibii*. Water smartweed serves as the uredinial host, whereas spotted geranium (*Geranium maculatum*) is *P. polygoni-amphibii*'s aecial host plant.

Etymology See *Persicaria lapathifolia* for genus etymology. *Amphibia* is from the Greek word meaning "living a double life" (this is coincidentally the nickname of one of the authors). This is in reference to water smartweed growing in both submerged aquatic habitats and in more terrestrial habitats.

Look-alikes Scarlet smartweed, treated either as a separate species (*Persicaria coccinea*) or as a variety of water smartweed (as *P. amphibia* var. *emersa*), can grow in similar habitats but typically occurs in slightly drier conditions (i.e., sedge meadow / wet prairie and disturbed areas, including on edges of agricultural fields). It differs in that its inflorescence is narrower, longer, and cylindrical with generally parallel margins, and the ocreae lack flaring collars; the leaves also have a tendency to be broader.

Phlox pilosa (DOWNY PHLOX)

POLEMONIACEAE—phlox family

Description A native perennial that grows up to 2' tall. The oppositely arranged leaves are linear to lance-linear (less than 0.5" wide) tapering to a sharp pointed tip, toothless, and covered with short hairs. The fragrant flowers have a colorful explosion of pink to whitish-pink with 5 spreading corolla lobes, often with darker nectar guides on the corolla tube opening. It is not uncommon to find a white-flowered plant. The inflorescence is covered in glandular hairs and has 12 to 50 flowers in a loose panicle. The fruit is a capsule.

Bloom Period May–August

Plant Communities Prairie fen, prairie complex, savanna complex

Notes There are five to nine recognized subspecies. In the Indiana Dunes, besides *Phlox pilosa* subsp. *pilosa*, the only other subspecies that occurs is *Phlox pilosa* subsp. *fulgida*, which differs in having silky glandless hairs in the inflorescence.

Etymology *Phlox* is derived from the Greek word meaning "flame." This name was attributed to a plant by Theophrastus, a student of Aristotle, and given to the genus by Carl Linnaeus, who called the flowers "the color of glowing flame." *Pilosa* means "softly pubescent," describing the stems and leaves.

Look-alikes Wild blue phlox (*Phlox divaricata*) differs in that it has blue corollas and leaves that are more ovate-lanceolate (less than five times as long as wide). Smooth phlox (*P. glaberrima*) is generally taller than downy phlox and hairless (as the common name implies). In addition, smooth phlox usually grows in sedge meadow / wet prairie habitats.

Smooth phlox.

Prunella vulgaris subsp. lanceolata
(common selfheal)

LAMIACEAE—mint family

Courtesy Michael Huft.

Description A ubiquitous, native perennial that typically grows 0.5–1.5' tall. The stems are square in cross-section and usually erect. The oppositely arranged, stalked leaves are lance-oblong with shallow, rounded teeth on their margins; mid-stem leaves are about three times or more as long as wide. The short tubular flowers are crammed into a cylindrical, terminal spike. They are often bicolored, with a lavender to pinkish-purple upper hoodlike lip and a whitish-lavender to white lower lip with 2 fringeless side lobes and a larger fringed center lobe. The fruit are smooth nutlets.

Bloom Period June–November

Plant Communities Disturbed areas, prairie fen, sedge meadow / wet prairie, bottomland, hydromesophytic forest, conifer swamp, pin oak flatwoods, prairie complex

Notes The individual flowers look like sock puppets. Common selfheal has a long history in herbal medicine, thus the common name. It is also sometimes called heal-all. Even though it is still used as a natural medicine for things like high blood pressure, common selfheal takes up pollutants that may actually be detrimental to health, so don't use plants that were picked from an urban area or roadside for this purpose.

Etymology *Prunella* is Latin and a diminutive form of *prunum*, which means "plum," the color of the flowers, but this might be nothing more than a coincidence. Some sources refer to *Prunella* as a German modification of *Brunella*, which came from the German common name of the plant now known as *Prunella grandiflora* (*Die Großblütige Braunelle*), which was used to treat quincy (*Bräune*). *Vulgaris* means "common," and *lanceolata* means "lance-shaped."

Look-alikes Lawn prunella (*Prunella vulgaris* subsp. *vulgaris*) is a European introduction that is predominantly restricted to disturbed areas. It differs from the native subspecies by its more sprawling habit, often rooting at the nodes, and by its stubbier egg-shaped stem leaves (two times or less as long as wide).

Sabatia angularis (rose pink)

GENTIANACEAE—gentian family

Description A native biennial that typically grows from 6" to 2' tall. The oppositely arranged egg-shaped leaves have 3–7 prominent veins and clasp the square and often wing-angled stem. Basal leaves are in a tight rosette and usually are absent by flowering time. The fragrant 5-parted flowers have pink petals (rarely white) that are 0.3–0.8" long with a yellow or greenish-yellow base collectively forming a star near the stigma and 5 stamens. Oftentimes there is a thin red border around the yellow basal patch on the petals. The fruit is a many-seeded cylindrical capsule.

Bloom Period July–October

Plant Communities Sedge meadow / wet prairie, panne, savanna complex

Notes Possibly one of the most beautiful wildflowers in the Indiana Dunes, the attractiveness of the pink flowers is rivaled only by their sweet and subtle fragrance.

Etymology *Sabatia* is in honor of eighteenth-century Italian botanist Liberato Sabbati. *Angularis* means "angular," in reference to the wing-angled stems.

Look-alikes The nonnative branching centaury (*Centaurium pulchellum*) differs in that it has much smaller flowers (petals <0.25" long) that sit atop a long tube. Branching centaury is restricted to disturbed areas, often adding color to barren industrial sites.

Branching centaury.

TEPHROSIA VIRGINIANA (GOAT'S-RUE)

FABACEAE—legume family

Courtesy Michael Huft.

Description A native perennial that grows up to 2' tall. The stem and leaf stalks are silvery hairy. The alternately arranged leaves are odd-pinnately compound with 9–31 leaflets that are densely covered with hairs on the underside and hairy to hairless on the top surface. The flowers are almost 1" long with hot-pink lateral lower petals, a pale-pink hidden keel, and a cream to yellowish-white upper banner petal. They are borne in a terminal raceme. The fruit is a legume that is covered in white to silvery hairs.

Bloom Period June–July

Plant Communities Secondary dune, savanna complex

Notes The common name came from the belief that if goat's-rue was fed to goats, it would help their milk production. In some areas of its range, mostly in the southeastern United States, goat's-rue's roots contain a compound called rotenone, which is a fish poison and pesticide. It has been documented to have been used by southeastern Native Americans as a fish poison. However, the presence of the toxin in the roots is more than likely absent in the Indiana Dunes populations.

On a hike led by one of the authors, after showing off the beautiful blooms of goat's-rue, one of the trip participants excitedly lifted up her shirt to show the small crowd a tattoo of the flower on her back . . . this all to the joy (or shock) of the participants.

Etymology *Tephrosia* is from the Greek word *tephros*, which means "ashy-color," in allusion to its ashy-colored leaves from the dense pubescence. *Virginiana* means "from Virginia."

Look-alikes Lead plant (*Amorpha canescens*) differs in its shrubbier habit, dense spike of tiny purple flowers, and clusters of small single-seeded pods. It looks similar to goat's-rue when not in flower but has more numerous leaves, each with smaller and more numerous leaflets (up to 50).

Teucrium canadense (American germander)

LAMIACEAE—mint family

Description A colony-forming native perennial that can grow up to 4' tall. The stem is square in cross-section. The oppositely arranged leaves are toothed, short-stalked (often stalkless above), and taper to the tip. The undersides of the leaves are short hairy, and the top surface can be hairy or hairless. The flowers are arranged in a terminal spikelike raceme. The upper lip of the pink to pinkish-purple to whitish-pink flower is reduced to 2 stubby incurved lobes, and the lower lip is pronounced and purple spotted, appearing somewhat violin-shaped. Four stamens arch over the diminutive upper lip, causing the flower to appear as though the upper lip is missing. Fruit are nutlets that are in clusters of four.

July–August

Disturbed areas, marsh, prairie fen, sedge meadow / wet prairie, bottomland, prairie complex, savanna complex

In Homer's *Iliad*, some gods party and end up promising a young man, Paris, a woman who is already married. Paris takes the woman, Helen, to Troy, and the Greek husband, Menelaus, wages war. Teucer was the king of Teucria and a great Achaean (pre-Greek) archer. He fought with the Greek army to retrieve Helen. In the story, he aimed his bow to kill Hector of Troy to end the fighting and retrieve Helen. In the myth (read the book), Zeus favored Hector and broke Teucer's bowstring (probably because the whole war was pretty much Zeus's fault to begin with). Anyway, the Greek pharmacologist and botanist Dioscorides often named herbs after gods and heroes, so he named a plant after Teucer. Linnaeus figured that Dioscorides's description

Hairy hedge nettle (*Stachys pilosa*).

was regarding the germander (*Teucrium chamaedrys*). In many other wildflower books, it is mentioned that Linnaeus actually named the genus after medicinal botanist Dr. Teucer, whom history would have nearly forgotten (no one even mentions a first name for him!) if it weren't for these pesky wildflower guides regurgitating the story.

Etymology *Teucrium* is thought to have been named for *Teucer* (see notes). *Canadense* means "of Canada."

Look-alikes Hedge nettles (*Stachys* spp.) are similar but differ in their upper corolla lip not being reduced and split into 2 distinct lobes.

Triadenum virginicum
(Virginia marsh St. John's-wort)

HYPERICACEAE—St. John's-wort family

Description A native perennial that grows to 1–2' tall. The stems are often pigmented with pink or red. The oppositely arranged, gray-green (often with some pink coloration), egg-shaped to elliptic, toothless leaves are sessile and clasping the stem, terminating in a rounded or very shallowly notched tip. The flowers, in tight, branched clusters in the upper part of the plant, have 5 reddish-green sepals alternating with 5 pink petals. In the center of the flower is a pistil that terminates in 3 styles tipped by yellow stigmas. The pistil is surrounded by three distinct clusters of 3 stamens, each tipped by yellow anthers, with conspicuous knobby orange glands separating the clusters. Unfortunately, the flowers are rarely seen open! A contrasting red capsule replaces each flower at maturity.

Bloom Period July–September

Plant Communities Bog, marsh, sedge meadow / wet prairie, hydromesophytic forest

Virginia marsh St. John's-wort is somewhat disjunct in the Great Lakes region, with the core of its range being along the Gulf of Mexico and Atlantic Ocean coastal plains, most abundantly in the New England region. Our pink-flowered St. John's-worts are sometimes included in the genus *Hypericum*.

Triadenum is derived from the Greek *tri-* and *aden*, meaning "three glands," referring to the 3 glands that separate the 3 clusters of stamens in the flower (see description). *Virginica* means "from Virginia."

Fraser's marsh St. John's-wort (*Triadenum fraseri*) is very similar, differing primarily in the length of the 3 styles (most easily measured when in fruit). In Fraser's marsh St. John's-wort, the styles are up to 0.06" long, whereas they are longer in Virginia marsh St. John's-wort (you might need at least a hand lens and a ruler!). The sepals are slightly longer in Virginia marsh St. John's-wort as well, with those in Fraser's marsh St. John's-wort reaching only 0.2" long. Fraser's marsh St. John's-wort has open flowers even less frequently than Virginia marsh St. John's-wort, and when they are open, they rarely (if ever) appear fully open (the petals are more erect to ascending and incurved, as compared to the spreading petals of Virginia marsh St. John's-wort).

10. VIOLET AND BLUE FLOWERS

Anemone acutiloba, sharp-lobed hepatica
Campanulastrum americanum, American bellflower
Cichorium intybus, chicory
Commelina erecta, erect dayflower
Gentiana andrewsii, Andrews's closed gentian
Gentianopsis crinita, fringed gentian
Ionactis linariifolia, flax-leaved aster
Iris virginica, blue-flag iris
Lobelia siphilitica, great blue lobelia
Lupinus perennis, wild lupine
Phlox divaricata, wild blue phlox
Pontederia cordata, pickerelweed
Symphyotrichum cordifolium, heart-leaved blue aster
Symphyotrichum novae-angliae, New England aster
Symphyotrichum oolentangiense, sky blue aster
Tradescantia ohiensis, Ohio spiderwort
Verbena hastata, blue vervain
Vernonia missurica, Missouri ironweed
Viola pedata, bird's foot violet
Viola sororia, common blue violet

ANEMONE ACUTILOBA (SHARP-LOBED HEPATICA)

RANUNCULACEAE—buttercup family

Description An early-spring blooming native perennial that grows up to 6" tall. The basal leaves are often brilliantly mottled on the top surface and are 3-lobed with each lobe ending in a point. In the fall they turn a red to reddish-purple color and overwinter until the flowers welcome the new year and the old leaves fade away. Flowers are solitary at the ends of erect, conspicuously hairy stalks and range from blue to pink to white, with 5–12 petallike sepals. The colored sepals are accented by the 10–30 white stamens and are subtended by 3 green hairy bracts. The fruit is a narrow, hairy, tapering, slightly winged achene.

Bloom Period March–May

Plant Communities Mesophytic forest

Notes The old genus name (which some botanists still use) is *Hepatica*. Thank goodness, hepatica is also the common name, so we all can agree to keep calling it that. *Hepatica* is derived from the Greek word for "liver" because the leaf shape is similar to that of the human liver. Due to the archaic "Doctrine of Signatures," it was thought to be good for liver health.

Leaves of sharp-lobed hepatica.

Once in a while you find a flower that smells as pleasant as the spring awakening.

Etymology *Anemone* means "wind" in Greek, alluding to the flowers waving in the slightest breeze (see also *Anemone cylindrica* for more on the genus). *Acutiloba* means "sharp-lobed," referencing the tips of the leaf lobes.

Look-alikes The very similar round-lobed hepatica (*Anemone americana*) has leaf lobes that are rounded rather than pointed; the lobes are also cut less than halfway into the leaf (halfway or more in sharp-lobed hepatica). Round-lobed hepatica also thrives in more acidic soil, whereas sharp-lobed hepatica grows in more alkaline soil.

Leaf of round-lobed hepatica.

Campanulastrum americanum
(American bellflower)

CAMPANULACEAE—bellflower family

Description A native annual or biennial that can reach 3–6' tall. The large, thin, toothed leaves are alternately arranged on the erect, hairy stem. The upper surface of the leaf is usually somewhat rough, with hairs along the veins on the underside. Leaves taper both to the leaf stalk and to a long pointed tip. The blue star-shaped 5-parted flowers are up to 1" wide with a contrasting white ring in the center from which a long blue style protrudes. The 5 corolla lobes connect at the base into a short tube. Fruit are capsules.

July–October

Disturbed areas, bottomland, mesophytic forest

Most bellflowers have flowers that are shaped like bells, whereas American bellflower differs in that its corolla lobes are wide spreading. It is primarily pollinated by long-tongued bees. American bellflower can be found on riverbanks and in somewhat shaded wet woodlands, surprising the passerby with a subtle burst of blue.

Campanula is from the Latin word meaning "little bells," and *astrum* means "with the likeness of," referring to the similarity of the genus to the genus *Campanula*, which has bell-shaped flowers. *Americanum* refers to it being from America.

European bellflower (*Campanula rapunculoides*) can be mistaken for American bellflower but has bell-shaped flowers that occur on only one side of the stem; it is mostly restricted to disturbed areas.

Cichorium intybus (CHICORY)

ASTERACEAE—sunflower family

Description A nonnative biennial to perennial that can reach up to 4' tall. The alternately arranged stem leaves are clasping and linear, whereas the numerous basal leaves are more sharply lobed and generally spatulate-shaped, similar to those of dandelion (*Taraxacum officinale*). The 1–1.5" periwinkle-blue flowerheads are composed entirely of ray florets, usually with over a dozen. There is also a form with white flowerheads.

Courtesy Michael Huft.

Bloom Period June–October

Plant Communities Disturbed areas, secondary dune

Notes Chicory is invasive and very difficult to eradicate. It was once cultivated for its roots, which were used as a coffee substitute after being baked and ground. Indiana botanist Charles Deam mentioned that it was a garden escape, but more than likely it was put in pasture seed mixes. The leaves have been eaten cooked or raw. Author and poet John Updike once wrote a poem called "Chicory," in which he praised the plant's tenacity:

> Show me a piece of land that God forgot
> —a strip between an unused sidewalk,
> say, and a bulldozed lot, rich in broken glass
> —and there, July on, will be chicory,
> . . .
> It sends a deep taproot (delicious, boiled),
> is relished by all livestock, lends its leaves
> to salads and cooked greens, but will not thrive
> in cultivated soil: it must be free.

Etymology *Cichorium* comes from the Greek word "kichore," which is what the Greeks called this plant. The origin of the word *intybus* is unknown.

Look-alikes Superficially, some wild lettuce (*Lactuca*) species can be confused with chicory by their composite blue flowerheads, which are much smaller than those of chicory (compare to *Lactuca biennis*). Otherwise, there are no look-alikes in the Indiana Dunes.

Commelina erecta (ERECT DAYFLOWER)

COMMELINACEAE—spiderwort family

Description A native perennial that grows up to 3' tall (usually shorter). The few alternately arranged leaves are linear to lance-linear. The leaf bases sheath down the stem. The 3-parted flowers can be bisexual or staminate and emerge from a horizontal, often strongly veined crescent-shaped spathe that has its margins fused at the base (lower one-third). The petals are clawed. There are 2 large, round, earlike, brilliantly blue (rarely white) upper petals and a smaller 3-lobed white lower petal. Surrounded by the petals are 6 stamens, with 3 sterile with H-shaped yellow anthers, and 3 fertile with 1 having a yellow anther curled up and larger than the sterile anthers and the 2 lower with blue anthers. In between the lower 2 fertile stamens is the style. The fruit is a 3-chambered capsule that opens lengthwise.

Bloom Period June–September

Plant Communities Secondary dune, savanna complex

Notes Each flower is only open for one day, as the common name implies.

Etymology *Commelina* was named in honor of two accomplished botanists, Johannes Commelin and his nephew, Caspar Commelin. Carl Linnaeus noted that the third, smaller petal was in reference to Caspar Jr., who was *not* well accomplished as a botanist because he died before making it big. Linnaeus took the name from French botanist and monk Charles Plumier, who probably didn't even know at the time of naming it that there was a Caspar Jr. *Erecta* means "erect, upright," in reference to the growth habit.

Look-alikes The introduced and invasive common dayflower (*Commelina communis*) looks very similar, differing in that it is an annual that often roots at the nodes (erect dayflower is erect and does not root at nodes), and the large spathe under the flowers is open or free the entire length (united at the base in erect dayflower).

Common dayflower. Courtesy Michael Huft.

Gentiana andrewsii
(Andrews's closed gentian)

GENTIANACEAE—gentian family

Description A native perennial that grows up to 2–3' tall but is often shorter. The oppositely arranged leaves are toothless, glossy green, hairless on both surfaces but with hairy leaf margins, 3–7 veined, and sessile. Near the flowers, the leaves are often whorled. The flowers are blue (rarely pink or white) and stalkless. The corolla is fused and bottle-shaped, remaining closed at the top. At the top of the flower the corolla is folded and overlapping. The folded, hidden part is usually whitish and jagged across the top, very slightly sticking out of the top of the flower. The flowers are in clusters of 2 to over 20 at the top of the plant, often with smaller clusters in the leaf axils. The fruit is a capsule containing many small, flattened, smooth seeds.

Bloom Period August–October

Plant Communities Disturbed areas, prairie fen, sedge meadow / wet prairie, prairie complex, savanna complex

Notes Bumblebees pollinate closed gentians, as smaller insects fail to successfully enter or exit the flowers. Andrews's closed gentian is often called bottle gentian.

Andrews's closed gentian, as well as many other sister species, has been said to have great virtues from the roots with the addition of sugar and yeast when they are macerated in cold water. To this day, gentian root liqueur is still used and sold through names like *Avèze Gentiane*, *Salers gentiane*, and *Suze*. Gentian root is also an ingredient in the classic soft drink Moxie.

Etymology *Gentiana* is named after the last king of the Illyrian Kingdom, Gentius. Lore has it, according to Pliny, that Gentius originally discovered that the great yellow gentian (*G. lutea*) was a good bitter to make into a brew prior to the use of hops. *Andrewsii* is named in honor of the late eighteenth-century botanical artist Henry C. Andrews.

Look-alikes Soapwort gentian (*Gentiana saponaria*) is often confused for Andrews's closed gentian but differs in that its leaves are under 1" wide (over 1" wide in Andrews's closed gentian), and it has smooth-topped folds (not jagged) at the tip of the flower.

Soapwort gentian.

Gentianopsis crinita (FRINGED GENTIAN)

GENTIANACEAE—gentian family

Description A native annual or biennial that grows up to 2–3' tall. The oppositely arranged leaves are hairless, entire, sessile, yellowish green, and broader at the base, slightly tapering to a rounded tip. The corolla is fused into a tube with 4 bright blue, spreading lobes at the top, each terminating in a blunt tip, with fringes along the margins. Darker blue and white stripes track up the inside of the corolla tube. The corolla is set within 4 green to purplish-red tinged sepals that slightly spread.

The fruit is a large capsule that contains many small seeds.

Bloom Period August–October

Plant Communities Disturbed areas (in wet, sandy districts), prairie fen, panne

Notes Many poets and writers have lavished praise on the beauty of fringed gentians. Emily Dickinson eloquently wrote of the fringed gentian:

> God made a little gentian; it tried to be a rose
> And failed, and all the summer laughed, but just
>   before the snows
> There came a purple creature, that ravished all the hill;
> And summer hid her forehead, and mockery was
>   still . . .

Etymology *Gentianopsis* means "like a gentian," and *crinita* means "long hair," in reference to the long eyelash-like fringes on the corolla lobes.

Look-alikes Small-fringed gentian (*Gentianopsis virgata*) differs in that it has more linear leaves less than 0.4" wide (fringed gentian has ovate-lanceolate leaves usually over 0.4" wide).

IONACTIS LINARIIFOLIA (FLAX-LEAVED ASTER)

ASTERACEAE—sunflower family

Description A native perennial that grows up to 1.5' tall. The numerous alternately arranged leaves are stiff, linear, and sessile. The upper surface is dark green and hairless, and the underside is covered in dense gray-white hairs. Flowerheads are borne singly or more commonly in corymbiform arrays. Each flowerhead has 8–20 pale-blue (rarely white) pistillate ray flowers and up to 40 yellow bisexual disc flowers. Fruit are seedlike achenes with a tuft of hair attached at the tip for wind dispersal.

Bloom Period July–October

Plant Communities Savanna complex

Notes A previously used taxonomic name is *Aster linariifolius*. The common name comes from the similarity of the leaves to those of flax (*Linum* spp.). Although most of the plant species in the Indiana Dunes can also be found in the dunes in southwest Michigan, this is a species that is not known to occur in the state to our north.

Etymology *Ionactis* is derived from the Greek *ion-* and *aktis*, meaning "violet ray," referencing the flowers, and *linariifolia* means "linear leaves."

Look-alikes Although there are many asters in the Indiana Dunes in several genera (such as *Symphyotrichum*, *Eurybia*, and *Doellingeria*), and some species have pale-blue ray flowers surrounding yellow discs, none of the others have the combination of flat-topped arrays and linear leaves.

Iris virginica (BLUE-FLAG IRIS)

IRIDACEAE—iris family

Description A native perennial that grows up to 3' tall. The large, swordlike, gray-green leaves are basal, brown to purplish at the base, pointed at the tip, toothless, and hairless. Few similar-looking leaves occur on the flowering stem. Flowers are large and deep-to-light blue to violet with 3 drooping sepals that fade into a pale blue to white center and 3 shorter, often more erect blue petals. The sepals also have a large bright-yellow spot

in the center, with dark-purple veins erupting from the yellow. Beneath the flowers are papillose leaflike spathes that hug the stem. The fruit is an erect 3-angled capsule with flat, round hockey puck–like seeds stacked in two rows in each chamber.

Bloom Period May–July

Plant Communities Disturbed areas, marsh, prairie fen, sedge meadow / wet prairie, bottomland, hydromesophytic forest, conifer swamp, pin oak flatwoods

Notes Most animals do not eat the foliage of blue-flag iris, due to it producing glycosides and containing crystal inclusions, causing gastrointestinal issues.

Etymology *Iris* is the ancient Latin name for this plant, named after the virgin goddess that appeared in the personification of the rainbow; she was a messenger to the Olympians. *Virginica* means "from Virginia," as the species was described based on a specimen from colonial Virginia.

Look-alikes Nearly impossible to distinguish without flowers, the invasive yellow iris (*Iris pseudacorus*), a species restricted from being sold in Indiana, differs in that it has yellow flowers and a smooth outer spathe.

Yellow iris.

When in fruit, the capsules of yellow iris dangle. The blue-eyed grasses (*Sisyrinchium* spp.) are in the iris family but differ in having much smaller flowers (<0.55") and sepals that are indistinguishable from the petals.

Pale blue-eyed grass (*Sisyrinchium albidum*).

LOBELIA SIPHILITICA (GREAT BLUE LOBELIA)

CAMPANULACEAE—bellflower family

Description A native, short-lived perennial that grows to 4'+ tall. The stem is often hairless and somewhat angled. The alternately arranged leaves are sessile, shallowly toothed, and often with short hairs on the top surface. When broken, the leaves and stems exude a greenish-yellow sap. Flowers are resupinate, nearly 1" long, and borne in a spikelike terminal cluster that can be up to 2' long. The bright-blue to bluish-purple (rarely white) flowers are 2-lipped, with a 3-lobed "lower" lip and a 2-lobed "upper" lip. Some flowers are only functionally female and exhibit white, infertile anther tubes. Flowers that contain both functional anthers and pistils have bluish-purple anther tubes. Peculiarly, female-only populations are more common in the southern portion of the range of the species and not so much in the Indiana Dunes. The fruit is a 2-chambered capsule.

Bloom Period July–October

Plant Communities Disturbed areas, marsh, prairie fen, sedge meadow / wet prairie, bottomland, hydromesophytic forest, pin oak flatwoods

Great blue lobelia and cardinal flower (*Lobelia cardinalis*) rarely hybridize (*Lobelia × speciosa*). The reason for the rarity of the hybrid is that bumblebees are the main pollinators of great blue lobelia, and hummingbirds are the chief pollinators of cardinal flower. Curiously, the beautiful lobelia dagger moth (*Acronicta lobeliae*) does not, as the name implies, use lobelias as a host plant but is rather an oak (*Quercus*)-dependent species.

Lobelia is named in honor of sixteenth-century botanist Mathias de Lobel, and *siphilitica* is from the thought that it could cure syphilis . . . it doesn't.

Kalm's lobelia (*Lobelia kalmii*) is a calciphile (i.e., grows in prairie fen and panne), differing from great blue lobelia by having linear leaves with white sap and corollas that are up to 0.6" long and more pale in color.

Kalm's lobelia.

Lupinus perennis (WILD LUPINE)

FABACEAE—legume family

Description A colony-forming native perennial that grows up to 2' tall. The leaves are basal and alternately arranged along the stem with 7–11 palmately compound leaflets. Each leaflet narrows to the base and is more rounded at the end, often with a sharp point at the very tip. The pealike flowers are usually a deep blue to purple, ranging to light blue or (rarely) white or pink, arranged in a terminal raceme that can be up to 10" tall. The fruit is a fuzzy legume up to 2" long.

Bloom Period April–June

Plant Communities Disturbed areas, savanna complex

Wild lupine leaves with water droplets where leaflets attach.

Notes Henry David Thoreau poetically compared the blankets of blooming wild lupine on hillsides to a visual taste of heaven, writing, "such a profusion of the heavenly, the elysian color, as if these were the Elysian Fields." Wild lupine is the larval host of the federally endangered Karner Blue Butterfly (*Lycaeides melissa samuelis*), which was once common in parts of the Indiana Dunes (especially near Miller) but that are now thought to be extirpated from northwest Indiana. Wild lupine, often called "sundial lupine" because its leaves shift to face the sun, is the only native lupine in northwest Indiana.

Etymology *Lupinus* means "wolfish." It is unclear why. *Perennis* pertains to the perennial growth form.

Look-alikes Leafy lupine (*Lupinus polyphyllus*), a native to western North America that is considered invasive in parts of the Midwest, is introduced in northwest Indiana and is sometimes included in native seed mixes under the name *Lupinus perennis*. It is a much larger plant overall, and its leaves have at least 12 leaflets.

Phlox divaricata (WILD BLUE PHLOX)

POLEMONIACEAE—*phlox family*

Description A native perennial that typically grows to 1' or so tall. The oppositely arranged leaves are stalkless and round at the base. The leaves lower on the stem are often hairless with those higher on the stem pubescent to glandular pubescent. The inflorescence is covered in gland-tipped hairs and is made up of a cyme of 9–25+ light-blue to lavender (occasionally white) flowers. Flowers are about 1" wide with a narrowly tubular corolla that opens into 5 wide-spreading lobes. The fruit are round capsules.

Bloom Period April–June

Plant Communities Mesophytic forest

Notes There are two varieties of wild blue phlox in the Indiana Dunes—variety *divaricata*, with notched corolla lobes, and variety *laphamii*, with entire corolla lobes.

Etymology See *Phlox pilosa* for genus etymology. *Divaricata* means "strongly divergent," in reference to its spreading inflorescence.

Look-alikes Sand cleft phlox (*Phlox bifida*) blooms about the same time and has notched corolla lobes, but it differs in that it is not as erect (rather forming tufts), the notches at the tips of the corolla lobes are deeper, and it doesn't grow over 6" tall. Sand cleft phlox also occurs predominantly in the savanna complex.

Sand cleft phlox.

PONTEDERIA CORDATA (PICKERELWEED)

PONTEDERIACEAE—pickerelweed family

Description An emergent aquatic native perennial that grows up to 3.5' tall. The basal leaves when submerged are stalkless, linear, ribbonlike, and in a rosette. When not submerged, the waxy-looking leaves are heart-shaped with rounded tips and parallel venation and are attached to long air-filled stalks. The bluish-purple flowers are arranged in a terminal spike. Each spike can contain several hundred stalkless flowers. The tubular flower has a 3-lobed upper lip and 3-lobed lower lip, with the lower lobes more deeply cut. The fruit is a large achene.

June–September

Submerged aquatic, bog, marsh

Notes Pickerelweed is the host plant of the elusive pickerelweed borer moth (*Bellura densa*) as well as other *Bellura* species. The large fruits are an important source of food for many ducks.

Etymology *Pontederia* is in honor of eighteenth-century Italian botanist Giulio Pontedera. *Cordata* means "heart-shaped," referring to the heart-shaped leaves.

Look-alikes Arrow arum (*Peltandra virginica*) is quite similar vegetatively. It differs in that the leaves are more arrow-shaped with a pointed tip, and the veins run from the pronounced midrib out to the leaf margin (unlike pickerelweed, which has veins that run predominantly from above the sinus toward the tip).

Arrow arum.

Symphyotrichum cordifolium
(Heart-leaved Blue Aster)

ASTERACEAE—sunflower family

Description A native perennial that grows up to 4' tall. The alternately arranged leaves are deeply cordate and stalked. Leaves on the middle of the stem are sharply toothed, and their stalks are wingless to very slightly winged. The upper leaves are smaller and can lack the cordate base (especially within the floral array). The array is typically pyramidal and busy with flowerheads (sometimes with over 300 flowerheads). The flowerheads have 8–20 light-blue to lavender pistillate petallike ray flowers and about the same number of yellow to cream-colored bisexual disc flowers that turn purplish-red with age. The phyllaries have green diamond-shaped tips and are in 4–6 series. The fruit is a seedlike achene with a tuft of fluffy hair (pappus) attached to the top.

Bloom Period September–October

Plant Communities Mesophytic forest

Notes There are many moths that rely on asters as host plants, including the asteroid moth (*Cucullia asteroides*), which feeds on the flowers, the brown-hooded owlet (*C. convexipennis*), and the common pug moth (*Eupithecia miserulata*).

Etymology See *Symphyotrichum novae-angliae* for genus etymology. *Cordifolium* means "heart leaf," referring to the leaf shape.

Look-alikes Drummond's aster (*Symphyotrichum drummondii*) and arrow-leaf aster (*S. urophyllum*) are similar in that they have heart-shaped, stalked leaves with toothed edges along most of the blade. Both of these asters typically have wings on the petioles that are over 0.04" wide with the lower and basal leaves shallowly toothed; they also thrive under a more open canopy. Arrow-leaf aster also differs in having white ray flowers.

Symphyotrichum novae-angliae
(New England aster)

ASTERACEAE—sunflower family

Description A native perennial growing to 4' tall. The stem is covered in short grayish hairs. The alternately arranged gray hairy leaves clasp the stem. They are usually toothless and are reduced in size up the stem. The flowerheads are relatively large, with 50–75 petallike ray flowers that are usually deep purplish blue but that can range to pink. Each flowerhead is a bit larger than a half dollar with a diameter of 1.5". The 50–110 central disc flowers are yellow. The phyllaries are covered in gland-tipped hairs. The fruit is a seedlike achene with a fluff of hair (pappus) attached to the tip.

Bloom Period July–October

Plant Communities Disturbed areas, prairie fen, sedge meadow / wet prairie, prairie complex

Notes In the early nineteenth century, a prolific botanist and mycologist named Christian Nees von Esenbeck noticed that the New England aster pappus was arranged in a ring. He distinguished this from the European asters, giving it the genus name *Symphyotrichum* (see etymology). Ironically, this ring arrangement is not consistent or common in the genus. Until the work of Guy Nesom in 1994, taxonomists did not accept the genus name *Symphyotrichum*, instead referring to all related plants as *Aster*. Nesom's seminal work showed chromosomal and seed size differences between the European and American asters, leading to a segregation of nearly all American species in the genus into new genera, with only 2 American asters remaining within the genus *Aster*. Due to the rules of nomenclature, Nesom had to revive the old name established over 100 years previously by von Esenbeck.

Etymology *Symphyotrichum* is the combination of the Greek *sýmphysis*, meaning "growing together," and *-trichum*, meaning "hair." *Novae-angliae* refers to it being initially collected in what was then New England.

Look-alikes In the Indiana Dunes, only three other asters, smooth aster (*Symphyotrichum laeve*), shining aster (*S. firmum*), and bristly aster (*S. puniceum*), have leaves that clasp the stem. Shining and bristly aster both have more toothed leaves than New England aster and phyllaries that are hairless and eglandular. They grow in marsh and prairie fen systems. Smooth aster has toothless leaves and is completely glabrous. It also has stalked lower leaves and grows in the oak savanna and prairie complexes.

Bristly aster.

Shining aster.

Symphyotrichum oolentangiense
(SKY BLUE ASTER)

ASTERACEAE—sunflower family

Description A native perennial that grows up to 3' tall. The alternately arranged, stalked leaves have cordate bases (especially at the base of the plant); however, higher on the stem, where they are reduced in size and quantity, they can be sessile and simply tapering to the base. The leaves have a rough, short, hairy upper surface and are toothless on the margins (sometimes with few irregular teeth). The flowerheads are in a loose pyramidal panicle-like array and are made up of 10–25 pale-blue to lavender (rarely white) pistillate petal-like ray flowers surrounding approximately 20 yellow bisexual disc flowers. The phyllaries are hairless and in 4–6 series. The fruit is a seedlike achene with a tuft of fluffy hair (pappus) attached to the top.

August–October

Prairie complex, savanna complex

The mid-nineteenth-century botanist John L. Riddell named the species *Aster oolentangiensis* in the spring of 1835. In November of that year, another English botanist, John Lindley, published the species, calling it *Aster azureus*. Both names held until the genus *Aster* was restructured, which led to this species being placed in the genus *Symphyotrichum*. Per the rules of nomenclature, the older published specific epithet, *oolentangiense*, became the accepted name.

Notice the heart-shaped basal leaves. Courtesy Michael Huft.

stem is broken, looking like gobs of snot. When the clear sap dries it looks like strings of a spider web, thus the common name. The leaves and flowers have been eaten for centuries cooked and raw; however, within the plants are tiny calcium oxalate bundles that can irritate the skin and tongue.

Gardener Eloise Butler wrote in 1911 for the *Minneapolis Sunday Tribune*: "The stalks of the stamens are densely fringed with purple hairs, whose beauty has a depth 'that is deeper still' under the armed eye of the microscope. The hairs, when magnified, are seen as branching chains of exquisitely tinted spherical and cylindric, bead-like cells, within which pulsate circling streams of protoplasm—the living substance—endowed with the same properties in the humblest and in the highest forms of life." Go find your microscope!

Etymology *Tradescantia* is named in honor of the luxuriously bearded gardener John Tradescant, who collected and received plants from all over the world, including from the colonist and his friend John Smith, to exhibit in his gardens. He was also the gardener for King Charles I. *Ohiensis* means "of Ohio."

Look-alikes Zigzag spiderwort (*Tradescantia subaspera*) has been collected within the Indiana Dunes once, differing in having leaves wider than their sheaths (leaves at most as wide as sheaths in Ohio spiderwort) and a zigzag growth structure.

Verbena hastata (BLUE VERVAIN)

VERBENACEAE—vervain family

Description A native perennial that grows up to 5' tall. The oppositely arranged leaves are stalked, coarsely toothed, lance-shaped, and sometimes have 2 spreading to ascending lobes at the base, especially on those lower on the 4-angled stem. The leaf undersides are hairy with longer hairs on the midvein. The terminal inflorescence consists of several spikes of overlapping, tightly packed tiny flowers, somewhat like a candelabrum. Each small flower is purple to bluish white (or pink in forma *rosea*, or rarely white) with 5 ascending to spreading corolla lobes atop a short tube. The fruit are 4-sided nutlets.

Bloom Period June–September

Plant Communities Disturbed areas, marsh, prairie fen, sedge meadow / wet prairie, bottomland

Notes Blue vervain is a larval host plant for the common buckeye (*Junonia coenia*). It was once called *Herba veneris* in reference to Venus (Aphrodite), due to the ancient use of the plant as an aphrodisiac. The common

White vervain. Courtesy Michael Huft.

name, vervain, is from the Celtic word *ferfaen*, which means "to drive away a stone," as it was thought to help relieve kidney stones. This was also a name given to some species in the saxifrage family (*Saxifragaceae*).

Etymology *Verbena* is Latin for "sacred bough." A bough is a branch on a tree, so this name probably refers to a historical sacred use of the plant. *Hastata* means "spear-like," in reference to the sometimes halberd leaf shape.

Look-alikes White vervain (*Verbena urticifolia*) is similar vegetatively but differs in having flowers that are separate from each other on the spike, having white petals, and having leaves that are never lobed. White vervain often occurs in drier habitats.

Vernonia missurica (Missouri ironweed)

ASTERACEAE—sunflower family

Description A native perennial that typically grows to 3–5' tall. The stem is densely covered in short whitish hairs. The alternately arranged lance to lance-ovate leaves are dark green with tiny, sharp teeth on the margins. The leaf underside is densely hairy, but the upper surface is glabrous with deeply impressed veins. Flowerheads are arranged in a loose, flat-topped array. Each flowerhead has 32–50+ bright-purple (sometimes magenta) disc flowers with no ray flowers. The fruit is a seedlike achene with a brown tuft of hair attached to the top.

Bloom Period August–October

Plant Communities Disturbed areas, prairie fen, sedge meadow / wet prairie, prairie complex, savanna complex

Notes Ironweed is the host plant for the incredibly handsome ironweed borer moth (*Papaipema cerussata*).

Etymology *Vernonia* was named in honor of the British bryologist and entomologist from the late seventeenth and early eighteenth centuries, William Vernon. *Missurica* means "from Missouri."

Look-alikes Smooth ironweed (*Vernonia fasciculata*) differs in that it has hairless and glaucous stems, glabrous leaves, and fewer than 30 disc flowers per flowerhead. Tall ironweed (*V. gigantea*) differs in that it has up to 30 disc flowers per flowerhead (usually 22–27), leaves that are narrower, and thinly pubescent stems and leaf undersides. Illinois ironweed (*V. × illinoensis*), the hybrid between Missouri ironweed and tall ironweed, is fully intermediate between the two parents.

Smooth ironweed.

Viola pedata (bird's foot violet)

VIOLACEAE—violet family

Description A native perennial that grows up to 4" tall. The leaves are basal and deeply palmately 3–5-lobed, with the lobes often also lobed. Pale-blue to lavender flowers (rarely with 2 petals deep purple, or entirely white) are 1–1.5" wide with 5 spreading petals and a white blush toward the base of the lowest petal, which also has a short spur on the back. The 5 flattened orange stamens collectively look like the beak of a bird. The fruit is a green capsule containing copper-colored seeds.

Bloom Period April–June

Plant Communities Savanna complex

Notes Caroline Silver June wrote in *Bunny-Be-Glad and The Fifty Fairy Flower Legends*:

> A new bird visited the woods one day
> I heard him whistle and sing and say
> "Wherever I step when the woods are wet
> there blooms the Bird-foot violet".

The seeds have a fleshy, sugary structure (called an elaiosome), which ants love, attached to them. Ants take the seeds underground where they partake in the delicious elaiosomes (see Dutchman's breeches, *Dicentra cucullaria*, for more on elaiosomes). Unlike the other violets in the Indiana Dunes, bird's foot violet does not produce closed, self-pollinated (cleistogamous) flowers. Violets are the host plants for fritillary butterflies.

Etymology *Viola* is the Latin name for "violet," and *pedata* is Latin for "footlike," alluding to the bird's-foot shape of the leaves.

Look-alikes Prairie violet (*Viola pedatifida*), which has darker blue-violet flowers, also differs from bird's foot violet in that the stamens are not exserted from the flower and beak-like. It also has tufts of hair at the base of its lateral petals (petals glabrous in bird's foot violet). Prairie violet occurs only in the prairie complex.

Viola sororia (COMMON BLUE VIOLET)

VIOLACEAE—violet family

Description A native perennial that grows up to 6" tall. The long-stalked leaves to about 3" long and wide are in a basal rosette and are heart-shaped with blunt teeth on the margins. Hairiness is variable, with some botanists assigning separate names to hairy and hairless plants (see notes). The deep-blue to violet 0.75"-wide flowers are solitary at the tips of naked stalks from the base of the plant and have 5 spreading petals with a whitish throat that is marked with dark veins. The lowest petal is hairless or nearly so at the base, with a short spur on the back, and the lateral petals each have a dense patch of hair at the base. In summer, self-pollinating flowers that remain closed (cleistogamous) form on stalks near the base of the plant (sometimes underground). The fruit is a capsule.

Bloom Period April–June

Plant Communities Disturbed areas, bottomland, hydromesophytic swamp, pin oak flatwoods, prairie complex, savanna complex, mesophytic forest

Notes Plants occasionally bloom again in the fall. The *Viola sororia* complex is a tangled mess that has frustrated botanists for years. When growing in shade in natural areas, plants usually have hairy stems and leaves; these are *Viola sororia* in the strict sense. Similar plants with a dense patch of hair at the base of the spurred petal have been called *V. septentrionalis*, but recent work has shown that this species is not found in our area and that plants that have been called this are likely *V. sororia*. Plants growing in more weedy, treeless areas usually have hairless stems and leaves and have been called *V. communis* (which has also been called *V. papilionacea*) and *V. pratincola*. Also in weedy areas, watch for plants with white flowers that have purplish markings on the petals; these are sometimes referred to as *V. priceana*. This all goes to show how little we really know, even sometimes about seemingly common plants.

Etymology *Viola* is the Latin name for "violet," and *sororia* means "a sister," a reference to the similarities between this and related species.

Look-alikes There are a number of similar-looking violets that have only basal leaves with flowers on leafless stalks. Arrow-leaved violet (*Viola sagittata*) has arrowhead-shaped leaves at least 1.5 times as long as wide; it is frequent in the savanna complex. LeConte's violet (*V. affinis*) and Missouri violet (*V. missouriensis*)

Hooded violet.

are similar species of bottomlands that both usually have paler-blue flowers and heart-shaped leaves that are clearly longer than wide; the sepals have tiny hairs on their margins in the latter, these lacking in the former. Hooded violet (*V. cucullata*), a plant of wet areas, has very short, knob-tipped hairs making up the dense patch of pubescence on the lateral petals; it also has flower stalks that stick up well above the leaves. The introduced sweet violet (*V. odorata*), which occasionally has pure white flowers, blooms very early in the year and has sweet-smelling flowers with a conspicuously hooked style; it is found in disturbed areas.

GLOSSARY

achene a dry 1-seeded fruit that remains closed, relying on predation or decomposition to expose the seed.

acidophile acid-loving, in this case referring to plants that thrive in soils or water with pH below (often well below) 7.

actinomorphic of a flower that can be bisected along any plane and still result in mirror images. Also called radially symmetrical and regular. Compare with zygomorphic, bilaterally symmetrical, and irregular.

aecia the cuplike reproductive structures of rusts; singular aecium.

allelopathy the process by which one plant affects the growth of others nearby through the release of chemicals that serve as growth inhibitors.

annual a plant that completes its entire life cycle in 1 year.

anther the part of the stamen containing the pollen, usually at the end of the filament.

areole the small space created by the veinlets on a leaf or leaflet; also, on a cactus, the area where flowers or spines arise. Plural areolae.

berry a fruit with a thin outer skin, a fleshy middle, and a center of more than 1 seed (i.e., grape or banana). Compare with drupe.

biennial a plant that completes its entire life cycle in 2 years. Usually, in the first year, only leaves are produced, and the second year it flowers and dies.

bilaterally symmetrical of a flower that can be bisected along only 1 plane to result in mirror images. Also called zygomorphic and irregular. Compare with actinomorphic, radially symmetrical, and irregular.

bipinnatifid twice pinnately dissected.

bisexual of a flower, possessing both functional male and female reproductive organs (stamen and pistil, respectively); also called perfect.

bract a modified leaf that is most often associated with reproductive structures.

bullate puckered or blister-like.

calciphile lime-loving, in this case referring to plants that thrive in soils or water with high amounts of calcium and thus pH above (often well above) 7.

calyx the collective sepals of the flower, separate or fused. Plural calyces.

capsule a dry fruit that usually splits open along a seam and that contains numerous seeds.

carpel the collective female reproductive organ of the flower, including the stigma, style, and ovary; also called the pistil, and if there is more than 1 carpel, the group is called the pistil.

chasmogamous of a flower that opens before fertilization (compare to cleistogamous). Derived from Greek, meaning "open marriage."

ciliate with a fringe of hairs along the margin.

claw referring to the portion of the petal, sepal, or bract that narrows at its base almost like a stalk.

cleistogamous of a flower that self-fertilizes without opening (compare to chasmogamous). Derived from Greek, meaning "closed marriage."

column in orchid flowers, a modified reproductive structure composed of fused male and female reproductive parts, minus the ovary.

composite heads in the sunflower family (Asteraceae), a dense cluster of stalkless (or nearly so) flowers subtended by an involucre, made up of all disc flowers, all ray flowers, or ray flowers surrounding disc flowers; also referred to as flowerheads.

cordate heart-shaped.

corolla not just a car made by Toyota; the collective petals of the flower, separate or fused.

corymb a flat-topped, raceme-like inflorescence with the lower branches the longest.

corymbiform of an inflorescence, with the form of a corymb but without the true structure of one.

cyathium the inflorescence type in the genus *Euphorbia*, which has a cuplike structure made up of several fused bracts with free tips that alternate with nectar glands, these surrounding a single reduced female flower with 1 pistil and several reduced male flowers, each with 1 stamen. The cyathium often looks like a single flower. Plural cyathia.

cyme a flat or round-topped inflorescence formed by diverging branches with flowers at the tips and from their point of divergence, this sometimes repeating several times.

deciduous falling off after maturation, especially in reference to leaves of trees and shrubs, but also sometimes applied to other parts of herbaceous plants such as petals and fruit; compare with evergreen.

dioecious a plant with unisexual flowers, having the staminate and pistillate flowers present on separate plants.

disc flower in the sunflower family (Asteraceae), a regular (radially symmetrical), tubular flower making up the inner portion of, or the entire, composite flowerhead; also referred to as disc floret.

drupe a fleshy fruit with usually a single seed that is surrounded by a hardened layer (i.e., peach or cherry). Compare with berry.

elaiosome a fleshy structure attached to a seed that forms from seed or fruit tissue that is high in lipids and proteins. Often evolved closely with ants.

ephemeral persisting for a short period of time; with regard to plants, refers to those that come up early in spring, flower, and then wither away by summer.

evergreen with green leaves through the winter and lasting for more than one growing season; compare with deciduous.

filament stalklike structure of the stamen.

flower the reproductive portion of a plant, consisting of the essential reproductive parts (stamen and/or pistil) and often a perianth.

fruit the matured ovary.

glaucous possessing a powdery or waxy coating that often looks grayish, bluish, or purplish and can be wiped off.

hemiparasitic of a plant that acquires some of its nutrients by parasitizing another plant or organism but that also undergoes photosynthesis.

hypanthium the collectively fused base of the calyx and corolla that surrounds the ovary. Sometimes it is also fused with the receptacle. A common structure in the rose family (Rosaceae) and the gooseberry family (Grossulariaceae).

imperfect of a flower, possessing only functional male or female reproductive organs (stamen and pistil, respectively) but not both; also called unisexual.

inflorescence the floral axis, including the flower(s), peduncle(s), and their arrangement.

involucral bract a reduced leaflike structure that is in 1 or more whorls under the flowerhead(s) in the sunflower family (Asteraceae). Also called a phyllary. These collectively are called the involucre.

involucre a whorl of bracts beneath a flower or cluster of flowers, especially as present at the base of flowerheads in the sunflower family (Asteraceae); see also involucral bract and phyllary.

irregular of a flower that can be bisected along only 1 plane to result in mirror images. Also called zygomorphic and bilaterally symmetrical. Compare with actinomorphic, radially symmetrical, and irregular.

labellum a lip, especially used to describe the often larger and most spectacular petal in an orchid flower.

leaves the often flattened and expanded photosynthetic part of the plant. The broad portion is sometimes referred to as the blade, and the stalk is referred to as the petiole.

legume a fruit that matures from a folded carpel, usually splitting open lengthwise into 2 sections (in some species the legume does not open); the fruit of plants in the legume family (Fabaceae).

ligulate flowers in the sunflower family (Asteraceae), an irregular (bilaterally symmetrical), flattened strap-like flower making up the outer portion of, or the entire, composite flowerhead; also referred to as ray floret or ray flower.

loment a legume that is constricted between the seeds, thus appearing segmented.

lyrate shaped like a lyre, that being generally pinnately lobed with the terminal lobe the largest.

monocarpic a plant that, after it flowers one time, dies.

monoecious a plant with unisexual flowers, having the staminate and pistillate flowers present on the same plant.

myrmecochory seed dispersal by ants. See elaiosome.

ocrea a sheathing stipule, often appearing as a papery, tubular structure wrapping around the stem where the leaf attaches, found in many members of the buckwheat family (Polygonaceae). Plural ocreae.

operculum a small lid; in pitcher plants (*Sarracenia* spp.), the operculum is the lid of the pitcher.

ovary the lowest portion of the pistil that contains ovules; at maturity, the ovary becomes the fruit.

ovate egg-shaped.

palmate leaf a leaf that is lobed, with the lobes arising from a common point. A palmately compound leaf is composed of numerous leaflets that radiate from a central point like fingers on a hand. Compare to pinnate leaf.

papillose possessing tiny nipple-like bumps on the surface.

panicle an inflorescence type where the flowers are not directly attached (by stalk or otherwise) to the central axis; a raceme that is compound, with stalked flowers that are branched on the central axis.

pappus in the sunflower family (Asteraceae), the modified calyx, which manifests as bristles, hairs, or scales atop the ovary (and thus the achene at maturity), providing a means for seed dispersal.

pedicel the stalk of a single flower when in an inflorescence; see peduncle.

peduncle the stalk bearing a single flower (when not a part of an inflorescence) or bearing an inflorescence; see pedicel.

peltate shield-shaped, this occurring when a flat structure (such as a leaf) has a stalk attached directly into the tissue, rather than at the base or a margin.

perennial a plant with a life cycle that extends beyond 2 years, often with an indefinite life expectancy.

perfect of a flower, possessing both functional male and female reproductive organs (stamen and pistil, respectively); also called bisexual.

perfoliate a condition in which the leaf margins surround the stem, making it appear as though the stem is growing through the leaf.

perianth in a flower, the calyx and corolla collectively.

petal in a flower, an individual component of the corolla, often brightly colored or white and serving to attract pollinators and sometimes provide a landing pad for them during pollination.

petiole leaf stalk.

phenology broadly, the study of periodic events in life cycles of biological entities; with regard to plants, often refers to the blooming period.

phyllary reduced leaflike structure that is in 1 or more whorls under the flowerhead in the sunflower family (Asteraceae). Also called an involucral bract.

Pilla a fantastical, magical being full of pizzazz that can often be spotted in its habitat of remnant natural areas and that can be heard exclaiming "oof-da."

pinnate leaf a leaf that is lobed, with the lobes arising along an elongated axis. A pinnately compound leaf is composed of numerous leaflets arranged along either side of an elongated axis. Compare to palmate leaf.

pistil the female reproductive organ in a flower, consisting of the stigma, style, and ovary; see carpel.

pistillate a unisexual flower that is only functionally female (with a pistil), lacking functional stamens.

prickle a sharp appendage modified from a hairlike structure and containing no vascular tissue; compare with spine and thorn.

protandrous a condition in which the stamen is functional before the pistil becomes receptive.

puberulent minutely pubescent with straight, even-length hairs.

pubescent possessing hairs.

punctate covered in dots or minute glandular divots; dotted or studded.

raceme an inflorescence type where each flower is attached to the central stem by a stalk.

radially symmetrical of a flower that can be bisected along any plane and still result in mirror images. Also called actinomorphic and regular. Compare with zygomorphic, bilaterally symmetrical, and irregular.

ramet an individual stem within a colony-forming plant.

ray flower in the sunflower family (Asteraceae), an irregular (bilaterally symmetrical), flattened, strap-like flower making up the outer portion of, or the entire, composite flowerhead; also referred to as ray floret or ligulate flower.

receptacle the part of the flower stalk on which the flower parts are borne, or, in the sunflower family (Asteraceae), where the flowers of the composite flowerhead are borne.

regular of a flower that can be bisected along any plane and still result in mirror images. Also called actinomorphic and radially symmetrical. Compare with zygomorphic, bilaterally symmetrical, and irregular.

resin an organic, viscous substrate insoluble in water that is exuded by plants as a protective counter such as when injured.

resinous possessing resin, and therefore often sticky.

resupinate a floral or vegetation part that is upside down.

rhizome an underground stem that produces adventitious roots and lateral stems at nodes.

roots the underground portion of a plant that lacks leaves and provides stability.

rugose wrinkled, as in a leaf, caused by its venation.

sagittate arrowhead-shaped with 2 lobes spreading downward.

saprophytic of an organism that lives off of decomposing, dead organic matter.

scabrous rough or covered with scab-like scales, stiff and tiny broad-based hairs, or bumpy patches.

scape a leafless flower stalk that comes directly from the root or rhizome.

schizocarp a dry fruit that splits into 1-seeded segments when mature.

secund with parts along only one side of an axis.

sepal in a flower, an individual component of the calyx, often green.

serrate toothed with sharp, forward-pointing teeth.

serrulate toothed with very small, sharp, forward-pointing teeth.

sessile directly attached to the stem with no stalk.

silicle a short silique less than twice as long as wide; common in the mustard family (Brassicaceae).

silique a type of dry, elongated fruit that is usually more than twice as long as wide, formed from 2 fused carpels, and splitting open when mature; common in the mustard family (Brassicaceae).

spadix an inflorescence type that consists of a spike with a thickened and often fleshy axis.

spathe a large leaflike bract that surrounds or encloses an inflorescence.

spine a sharp appendage modified from a leaf or stipule and usually containing vascular tissue; compare with prickle and thorn.

stamen the collective male reproductive organ of the flower, including the anther and the filament.

staminate a unisexual flower that is only functionally male (with stamens), lacking a functional pistil.

staminode an undeveloped, sterile male organ of the flower.

stem the portion of the plant with leaves.

stigma the uppermost portion of the pistil that is often sticky and receives pollen.

stipel a stipule associated with a leaflet.

stipule a leaflike structure found where the leaf stalk attaches to the stem.

stolon a horizontal stem that runs along the ground, rooting at its nodes; sometimes called a runner.

style a tubelike stalk atop the ovary, connecting it to the stigma.

tepals petals and sepals collectively when they are indistinguishable.

thorn a sharp appendage modified from a branch or stem and usually containing vascular tissue; compare with prickle and spine.

tomentose densely covered with short, matted hairs.

trifoliate a leaf divided into 3 leaflets.

truncate squared or boxed off, often referring to a leaf or petal base or apex.

tuber a thickened portion of a rhizome with the purpose of food storage.

tuberoid a fleshy root that resembles a tuber.

umbel an inflorescence type with all of the stalks arising from a common point, resulting in a flat-topped, dome-shaped, or spherical structure; often compared to the form created by the spokes of an umbrella.

unisexual of a flower, possessing only functional male or female reproductive organs (stamen and pistil, respectively), but not both; also called imperfect. Also used to refer to plants with only male or female flowers.

uredinia the reddish-colored pustules that form on plants that are infected with rust fungi; singular uredinium.

zygomorphic of a flower that can be bisected along only 1 plane to result in mirror images. Also called bilaterally symmetrical and irregular. Compare with actinomorphic, radially symmetrical, and irregular.

RECOMMENDED READING AND REFERENCES

Deam, Charles C. *Flora of Indiana*. Indianapolis: Indiana Department of Conservation, 1940.

Fernald, Merritt Lyndon. *Gray's Manual of Botany: A Handbook of the Flowering Plants and Ferns of the Central and Northeastern United States and Adjacent Canada*. 8th ed. New York: American Book Company, 1950.

Flora of North America Editorial Committee, eds. *Flora of North America North of Mexico*. 21+ vols. New York and Oxford, 1993+.

Gleason, Henry A., and Arthur John Cronquist. *Manual of Vascular Plants of Northeastern United States and Adjacent Canada*. 2nd ed. Bronx: New York Botanical Garden, 1991.

Greenberg, Joel. *A Natural History of the Chicago Region*. Chicago: University of Chicago Press, 2004.

Harris, James G., and Melinda Woolf Harris. *Plant Identification and Terminology: An Illustrated Glossary*. Spring Lake, UT: Spring Lake, 1997.

Hedberg, Andrew M., Victoria A. Borowicz, and Joseph E. Armstrong. "Interactions between a Hemiparasitic Plant, *Pedicularis canadensis* L. (Orobanchaceae), and Members of a Tallgrass Prairie Community." *Journal of the Torrey Botanical Society* 132, no. 3 (2005): 401–410.

Holmgren, Noel H. *Illustrated Companion to Gleason and Cronquist's Manual: Illustrations of the Vascular Plants of Northeastern United States and Adjacent Canada*. New York: New York Botanical Garden, 2004.

Homoya, Michael A. *Orchids of Indiana*. Indianapolis: Indiana Academy of Science, 1993.

———. *Wildflowers and Ferns of Indiana Forests*. Bloomington: Indiana University Press, 2012.

Homoya, Michael A., D. Brian Abrell, Jim R. Aldrich, and Thomas W. Post. "The Natural Regions of Indiana." *Proceedings of the Indiana Academy of Science* 94 (1985): 245–268.

Jackson, Marion T., ed. *The Natural Heritage of Indiana*. Bloomington: Indiana University Press, 1997.

Nesom, Guy L. "Again: Taxonomy of Yellow-Flowered Caulescent Oxalis (Oxalidaceae) in Eastern North America." *Journal of the Botanical Research Institute of Texas* 3 (2009): 727–738.

Pavlovic, Noel B., Barbara Plampin, Gayle S. Tonkovich, and David R. Hamilla. "Special Flora and Vegetation of the Indiana

Dunes National Park." Natural Resource Report NPS/INDU/
NRR-2021/XXX. Fort Collins, CO: National Park Service,
2021.

Pearce, Richard B., and James S. Pringle. "Joe Pye, Joe Pye's
Law, and Joe-Pye-Weed: The History and Eponymy of the
Common Name Joe-Pye-Weed for *Eutrochium* Species (Aster-
aceae)." *The Great Lakes Botanist* 56 (2017): 177–200.

Peattie, Donald Culross. *Flora of the Indiana Dunes: A Handbook
of the Flowering Plants and Ferns of the Lake Michigan Coast of
Indiana and of the Calumet District*. Chicago: Field Museum of
Natural History, 1930.

Pepoon, Herman Silas. *An Annotated Flora of the Chicago Area:
With Maps and Many Illustrations from Photographs of Topo-
graphic and Plant Features (No. 8)*. Chicago: R. R. Donnelley &
Sons, 1927.

Voss, Edward G., and Anton A. Reznicek. *Field Manual of Michigan Flora*. Ann Arbor: University of Michigan Press, 2012.

Wilhelm, Gerould S. *Special Vegetation of the Indiana Dunes
National Lakeshore*. National Park Service: Midwest Region.
Indiana Dunes National Lakeshore Research Program, Re-
port 90–02, 1990.

Wilhelm, Gerould, and Laura Rericha. *Flora of the Chicago Region: A Floristic and Ecological Synthesis*. Indianapolis: Indiana
Academy of Science, 2017.

Yatskievych, Kay. *Field Guide to Indiana Wildflowers*. Bloomington: Indiana University Press, 2000.

Web Resources

Biota of North America Program: bonap.org
Consortium of Midwest Herbaria: midwestherbaria.org
Flora of North America: eFloras.org
Go Botany: gobotany.nativeplanttrust.org
Illinois Wildflowers: illinoiswildflowers.info
Michigan Flora: michiganflora.net
Minnesota Wildflowers: minnesotawildflowers.info

INDEX

Acer rubrum, 22; *saccharum*, 27
Achillea, 14; *millefolium*, 31–32, 73
Achilles, 32
Actaea pachypoda, 33–34; *rubra*, 34
Adonis, 42, 337
Agalinis paupercula, 315; *purpurea*,
    314–315; *purpurea* var.
    parviflora, 315; *tenuifolia*, 315
Ageratina, 14; *altissima*, 35–36
Alliaria petiolata, 11, 37–38
Allium, 38; *burdickii*, 40; *tricoccum*
    39–40, 121
Agrimonia gryposepala, 193;
    parviflora, 191–193;
    pubescens, 193
agrimony, soft,193; swamp,
    191–193; tall, 193
alumroot, prairie, 130
American beach grass, 24
Ammophila breviligulata, 24
Amorpha canescens, 375
Amphicarpaea bracteata, 294; var.
    bracteata, 318; var. *comosa*,
    316–318
Andrews, Henry C., 391
Andropogon gerardii, 25, 244
anemone (common name), false
    rue, 81–83; rue, 82–83; wood,
    82–83
Anemone (genus) *acutiloba*, 382–
    383; *americana*, 383; *cylindrica*,
    41–43, 383; *quinquefolia*,
    82–83; *virginiana*, 43
Angelica atropurpurea, 44–46
Antennaria, 14; *howellii*, 48;
    neglecta, 48; *parlinii*, 47–48;
    plantaginifolia, 48
Antoinette, Marie, 348
Aphrodite, 42, 337, 418. *See also*
    Venus
Apios americana, 292–294, 318
Apocynum androsaemifolium,
    50; *cannabinum*, 49–50;
    sibiricum, 50
Aquilegia canadensis, 295–296;
    vulgaris, 296
Arabidopsis lyrata, 51–52
Aralia nudicaulis, 53–54
Arisaema, 14; *dracontium*, 57;
    triphyllum, 55–57

arrow-grass, slender bog, 22
arrowhead, arum-leaved, 160
arum, arrow, 406
Asarum canadense, 297–298
Asclepias, 49; *exaltata*, 150;
    hirtella, 279, 280; *incarnata*,
    319–321; *purpurascens*, 324;
    sullivantii, 323; *syriaca*, 24, 320,
    321, 322–324; *tuberosa*, 25,
    278–280, 321
aster (common name), 258; arrow-
    leaf, 408; bigleaf, 101–102;
    bristly, 21, 410, 411; calico,
    181; Drummond's, 408; flat-
    topped, 76–77; flax-leaved,
    394–395; hairy frost, 179;
    heart-leaved blue, 407–408;
    New England, 178, 179, 408,
    409–410, 414; paniced,
    180–181; rice button, 179;
    shining, 410, 411; Short's, 414;
    sky blue, 412–414; smooth,
    410, 414; willow, 181
Aster (genus) *azureus*,
    413; *linariifolius*, 394;
    oolentangiensis, 413. *See also*
    Symphyotrichum
Aureolaria flava, 194–195;
    pedicularia, 194, 195; *virginica*,
    194, 195
avens, rough, 107, 108; white,
    106–108

baneberry, red, 34; white, 33–34
Baptisia alba, 58–59; *australis*, 59
bastard toadflax, 68–69, 100
bear corn, 70–71
beard-tongue, foxglove, 140–141;
    long-sepal, 141
beechdrops, 299–301
beggartick, nodding, 196–197
bellflower, American, 384–385;
    European, 385
bergamot, Italian, 361; wild,
    360–361
betony, swamp, 21, 63, 244, 245;
    wood, 63, 243–245
Betula alleghaniensis, 22, 23
Bidens, 14; *cernua*, 196–197

bindweed, field, 326; hedge, 325–326; large-bracted, 326
birch, yellow, 22, 23
bishop's cap, 128–130
black-eyed Susan, 248–249
black nightshade, 171
black snakeroot, Canadian, 164; clustered, 164; Maryland, 163–164
bladderwort, 20; common, 264–267; horned, 266; humped, 267
blazingstar, cylindrical, 354, 355; marsh, 21, 354, 355; rough, 353–355
bloodroot, 11, 27, 161–162, 222
bloody-butcher, 310–311
blue-joint grass, 22
bluestem, big, 25, 244; little, 24
blue cohosh, 200–201; giant, 201
blue-eyed grass, 398; pale, 398
Boehmeria cylindrica, 115
boneset, common, 95–96; false, 98; late, 97–98; tall, 98; upland, 96
Brasenia schreberi, 19, 135
Brickellia eupatorioides, 98
Buell, Dorothy, 4
bulrush, 21
bushclover, hairy, 119; round-headed, 25, 117–119; silky, 118, 119
Butler, Eloise, 416
buttercup, bristly, 246–247; early, 247; fig, 199; yellow water crowfoot, 247
butterflyweed, 278–280
butterweed, 242
Byrd, William, 362–363

Cakile edentula var. *lacustris*, 24
Calamagrostis canadensis, 22
Calamovilfa longifolia var. *magna*, 24
Calla palustris, 308, 309
Caltha palustris, 22, 198–199
Calystegia sepium, 325–326; *sylvatica*, 326
Campanula rapunculoides, 385
Campanulastrum americanum, 384–385
campion, bladder, 169; glaucous bladder, 168, 169; white, 167–169
Cardamine bulbosa, 61; *concatenata*, 60–61; *douglassii*, 61

cardinal flower, 302–303
Carex, 21; *aquatilis*, 22; *folliculata*, 22; *intumescens*, 22; *stricta*, 21, 22; *trisperma*, 20
Carpinus caroliniana, 22
Carya, 25
cattail, 21
Caulophyllum giganteum, 201; *thalictroides*, 200–201
cedar, northern white, 23
Centaurea, 14; *stoebe* subsp. *micranthos*, 327–328, 333
Centaurium pulchellum, 373
centaury, branching, 373
Ceratophyllum, 20
Chaddock, Diane, 1
Chamaedaphne, 127; *calyculata*, 20
Chelone glabra, 62–63
Cichorium intybus, 386–387
Cicuta bulbifera, 65; *maculata*, 64–65
Cinchona, 138
Cirsium, 14; *arvense*, 330; *discolor*, 329–331, 333; *muticum*, 330, 331; *pitcheri*, 25, 328, 332–333; *vulgare*, 330, 331
Citrus bergamia, 361
Cladium mariscoides, 22
Clayton, John, 45, 218, 335
Claytonia virginica, 27, 334–335
clearweed, 115
clematis (common name), autumn, 67
Clematis (genus) *terniflora*, 67; *virginiana*, 66–67
columbine, garden, 296; red, 295–296
Comandra umbellata, 68–69, 100
Commelina communis, 389; *erecta*, 388–389
compass plant, 254, 255
coneflower, cutleaf, 250–251; gray-headed, 204, 251; orange, 249; sweet, 249; thin-leaved, 249
Conium maculatum, 65
Conoclinium coelestinum, 36
Conopholis americana, 70–71
Convallaria majalis, 121
Convolvulus arvensis, 326
Conyza, 91
cordgrass, prairie, 22
Coreopsis, 14, 15; *lanceolata*, 204; *palmata*, 204; *tripteris*, 202–204

cottonwood, eastern, 24
Cowles Bog, 4, 23, 34
cowbane, 65
cow parsnip, 46
cranberry, large, 184–185;
    small, 185
culver's root, 186–187
cup plant, 253, 255, 341
Cypripedium acaule, 336–337;
    parviflorum, 337

dame's rocket, 9, 347–348
Darwin, Charles, 306
Dasistoma macrophylla, 195
Daucus carota, 32, 72–73
dayflower, common, 389; erect,
    388–389
daylily, tiger, 286
Deam, Charles, 387
Desmodium, 350; *canadense*,
    338–339; *canescens*, 339;
    glabellum, 339; *paniculatum*,
    339; *perplexum*, 339;
    sessilifolium, 339
Dicentra canadensis, 75; *cucullaria*,
    74–75, 298, 423
Dickinson, Emily, 393
Dioscorides, 61, 377
dock, curly, 158; prairie, 139, 254,
    255; swamp, 157–158
Doctrine of Signatures, 60, 95, 382
Doellingeria, 14, 395; *umbellata*,
    76–77
dogbane, 49–50; spreading, 50
doll's eyes, 33–34
Douglas, Paul, 4
Draba verna, 52
Drosera intermedia, 78–80;
    rotundifolia 80
Duchesne, Antoine Nicolas, 104
Duchesnea indica, 104, 105. *See also*
    Potentilla indica
duck-potato, 159–160
Dudley, Frank, 4
Dutchman's breeches, 74–75, 423

elderberry, 34
Elodea canadensis, 20
Endodeca serpentaria, 298
Enemion biternatum, 81–83
Epifagus virginiana, 299–301
Epipactis helleborine, 84–86
Equisetum variegatum, 22
Erica, 179

Erigenia bulbosa, 87–88
Erigeron, 14, 77; *annuus*, 89–91;
    philadelphicus, 90, 91; *pulchellus*,
    91; *strigosus*, 91
Eryngium yuccifolium, 92–94
Erythronium, 27; *albidum*, 206;
    americanum, 205–206
Eupatorium, 14, 343;
    altissimum, 98; *perfoliatum*,
    95–96; *serotinum*, 97–98;
    sessilifolium, 96
Euphorbia corollata, 69, 99–100;
    cyparissias, 207–208;
    polygonifolia, 24; *virgata*, 208; ×
    pseudoesula, 208
Eurybia, 14, 77, 395; *divaricata*,
    102; *furcata*, 102; *macrophylla*,
    101–102
Euthamia, 14; *caroliniana*, 210;
    graminifolia, 209–210;
    gymnospermoides, 210;
    nuttallii, 209
evening primrose, common,
    235–236; hairy evening, 236;
    Oakes', 236; small flower, 236

false foxglove, downy, 194; fern-
    leaf, 194; mullein, 195; pauper,
    315; purple, 314–315; slender,
    315; yellow, 194–195
false Solomon's seal, feathery, 86,
    122–123; starry, 122, 123
Fagus grandifolia, 27, 299
fern, bracken, 27; marsh, 21
Ficaria verna, 199
flax, 315, 394
fleabane, annual, 89–91;
    Philadelphia, 90, 91
Fragaria chiloensis, 104; *virginiana*,
    103–105; × *ananassa*, 104
Fraxinus pennsylvanica, 22

garlic mustard, 11, 37–38
gentian, Andrews's closed, 390–
    391; fringed, 392–393; great
    yellow, 391; small-fringed, 393;
    soapwort, 391
Gentiana andrewsii, 390–391;
    lutea, 391; *saponaria*, 391
Gentianopsis crinita, 392–393;
    virgata, 393
Gentius, 391
geranium (common name),
    spotted, 345–346, 367

Geranium (genus) *maculatum*, 345–346, 367
germander, American, 376–378
Geum canadense, 106–108; *laciniatum*, 107, 108
ghostpipe, 131–133
ginseng, dwarf 136–137; American 54, 137
goat's-rue, 27, 374–375
groundnut, 292–294
goat's beard, common, 263; western, 262–263
golden alexanders, 275–276
goldenrod, blue-stemmed, 258–259; Canada, 245, 257; dune, 261; early, 261; giant, 257; grass-leaved, 209; gray, 24, 26, 261; Ohio, 21; seaside, 261; showy, 260–261; tall, 256–257; zigzag, 259
golden-top, flat-topped, 209–210
great angelica, 44–46
green ash, 22
green dragon, 57
Gronovius, Jan Fredrik, 218

harbinger-of-spring, 87–88
hawkweed, northern, 218; prairie, 218; rough, 218
hedge nettle, 378; hairy, 377
Helenium autumnale, 272
Helianthus, 14, 25; *annuus*, 216; *decapetalus*, 212; *divaricatus*, 211–212, 214, 216; *giganteus*, 214; *grosseserratus*, 213–214; *hirsutus*, 212; *petiolaris*, 215–216; *strumosus*, 212
helleborine, 84–86
Hemerocallis fulva, 286
hemlock, poison, 65
hepatica, round-lobed, 383; sharp-lobed, 382–383
Heracleum maximum, 46
Heron Rookery, 5, 147
Hesperis matronalis, 9, 347–348
Heuchera richardsonii, 130
hickory, 25
Hieracium, 14, 15; *gronovii*, 217–218; *longipilum*, 218; *scabrum*, 218; *umbellatum*, 218
hog-peanut, 294
horehound, 352
hornwort, 20
horsenettle, Carolina, 170–171
horsetail, variegated, 22

Hydrophyllum appendiculatum, 111; *canadense*, 111; *virginianum*, 109–111
Hylodesmum glutinosum, 349–350; *nudiflorum*, 350
Hypericum, 380; *kalmianum*, 22; *perforatum*, 219–220; *punctatum*, 220
Hypopitys lanuginosa, 133, *monotropa*, 132, 133

Impatiens capensis, 281–283; *pallida*, 283
Indian grass, 25, 26, 27
Ionactis linariifolia, 394–395
iris (common name), blue-flag, 396–398; yellow, 397, 398
Iris (genus) *pseudacorus*, 397, 398; *virginica*, 396–398
ironweed, Illinois, 421; Missouri, 420–421; smooth, 421; tall, 421

Jack-in-the-pulpit, 55–57
Jeffersonia diphylla, 162
Jesus, 187
June grass, 25

Kalm, Pehr, 228
Koeleria macrantha, 25

Labovitz, Paul, 5
Lactuca, 14, 387; *biennis*, 112–113, 387; *canadensis*, 113; *serriola*, 113
ladies' tresses, Great Plains, 175, 176; nodding, 175; sphinx, 174–176
lady slipper, pink, 336–337; yellow, 337
lady's thumb, Oriental, 143; spotted, 143, 144
Laportea canadensis, 114–116
Larix laricina, 20, 23
lead plant, 375
leatherleaf, 20
Leonurus cardiaca, 351–352
Lespedeza, 314; *capitata*, 25, 117–119; *cuneata*, 118, 119; *hirta*, 119; × *longifolia*, 119
lettuce, tall blue, 112–113
Liatris, 14, 15; *aspera*, 26, 353–355; *cylindracea*, 354, 355; *spicata*, 21, 354, 355
Lieber, Richard, 3

Lilium lancifolium, 285;
    michiganense, 284–286;
    philadelphicum, 285, 286
lily, Michigan, 284–286; tiger,
    285; wood, 285, 286
Lincoln, Abraham, 36; Nancy, 36
Lindley, John, 413
Linnaeus, Carl, 46, 111, 127, 137,
    152, 218, 223, 228, 305, 318,
    359, 369, 377, 378, 389
Linum, 315, 394
Lithospermum canescens, 222;
    caroliniense var. *croceum*,
    221–222
lizard's tail, 165–166
Lobel, Mathias de, 303, 400
lobelia (common name), great blue,
    399–400; Kalm's 22, 400
Lobelia (genus) *cardinalis*, 302–303;
    kalmii, 22, 400; *siphilitica*,
    399–400; × *speciosa*, 400
loosestrife, fringed, 225–226;
    prairie, 226; purple, 356–357;
    winged, 357
Ludwig, Christian Gottlieb, 223
Ludwigia alternifolia, 223–224;
    polycarpa, 224
Lunaria annua, 348
lupine, leafy, 402; wild, 4, 25, 27,
    401–402
Lupinus perennis, 4, 25, 27,
    401–402; *polyphyllus*, 402
Lysimachia ciliata, 225–226;
    lanceolata, 226; *nummularia*,
    127; *terrestris*, 227–229;
    thyrsiflora, 228, 229; ×
    commixta, 228
Lythrum alatum, 357; *salicaria*,
    356–357

Maianthemum, 154; *canadense*,
    22, 120–121; *racemosum*, 86,
    122–123; *stellatum*, 122, 123
many-fruited water primrose, 224
maple, red, 22, 23; sugar, 27
Marrubium vulgare, 352
marsh marigold, 198–199
mayapple, 151–152
mayflower, Canada, 120–121
meadow parsnip, hairy, 276
meadowsweet, white, 172–173
Melilotus albus, 124–125;
    officinalis, 125
Michael the Archangel, 46
Michaux, André, 118, 119

milfoil, 20
milkweed, 49, 50; common, 24,
    322–324; green, 279, 280; poke,
    150; purple, 324; Sullivant's,
    323; swamp, 319–321
Mimulus alatus, 359; *ringens*,
    358–359
mistflower, blue, 36
Mitchell, John, 127
Mitchella repens, 126–127
Mitella diphylla, 128–130
Monarda didyma, 361; *fistulosa*,
    360–361; *punctata*, 230–231
Monardes, Nicolás Bautista,
    231, 361
money plant, 348
moneywort, 127
monkeyflower, Allegheny,
    358–359; winged, 359
Monotropa uniflora, 131–133
motherwort, 351–352
mountain-mint, slender, 156;
    Virginia, 155–156
mullein, great, 268–270; moth,
    269, 270
musclewood, 22
Myriophyllum, 20

Nabalus albus, 362–364
naiad, 20
Najas, 20
Nesom, Guy, 240, 410
nettle, false, 115; tall, 115, 116;
    wood, 114–116
Nuphar advena, 20, 232–234;
    variegata, 234
Nymphaea odorata, 19, 20,
    134–135
Nyssa sylvatica, 22

oak, 22, 70, 400; black, 25, 26,
    194; pin, 22, 23; white, 25, 194
Oenothera biennis, 235–236;
    oakesiana, 236; *parviflora*, 236;
    villosa, 236
Opuntia cespitosa, 237–238;
    humifusa, 238
orchid, club-spurred, 22, 288,
    289; green-fringed, 288, 289;
    orange-fringed, 287–289
Oswego tea, 361
Oxalis dillenii, 240; *stricta*,
    239–240
Oxypolis rigidior, 65

Packer, John G., 242
Packera, 14; *aurea*, 241–242;
    glabella, 242; *paupercula*, 242
Panax quinquefolius, 54, 137;
    trifolius, 136–137
Parietaria pensylvanica, 115, 116
Parlin, John Crawford, 48
Parthenium, 14; *integrifolium*,
    138–139
partridge berry, 126–127
Peattie, Donald, 1, 4
Pedicularis canadensis, 63,
    243–245; *lanceolata*, 21, 63,
    244, 245
Peltandra virginica, 406
Pennsylvania pellitory, 115, 116
Penstemon calycosus, 141; *digitalis*,
    140–141
Persicaria amphibia 346;
    amphibia var. *emersa*, 366,
    367; *amphibia* var. *stipulacea*,
    365–367; *coccinea*, 366, 367;
    lapathifolia, 142–144, 146,
    148, 367; *hydropiper*, 146, 147;
    hydropiperoides, 147; *longiseta*,
    143; *maculosa*, 143, 144;
    pensylvanica, 144; *punctata*,
    145–147; *robustior*, 147;
    virginiana, 148
phlox (common name), downy,
    368–369; garden, 348; sand
    cleft, 404; smooth, 369; wild
    blue, 369, 403–404
Phlox (genus), 348; *bifida*, 404;
    divaricata, 369, 403–404;
    glaberrima, 369; *paniculata*,
    348; *pilosa*, 368–369
Phytolacca americana, 149–150
pickerelweed, 11, 405–406
pine, jack, 25; white, 20
Pinus banksiana, 25; *strobus*, 20
pitcher plant, northern purple, 20,
    304–306
plantain, Robin's, 91
Platanthera ciliaris, 287–289;
    clavellata, 22, 288, 289; *lacera*,
    288, 289
Pliny the Elder (Plinius), 96, 108,
    171, 192, 218, 391
Plumier, Charles, 389
Podophyllum peltatum, 151–152
Pokeweed, American, 149–150
Polygonatum biflorum, 153–154;
    pubescens, 154

pond-lily, variegated, 234; yellow,
    20, 232–234
pondweed, 20
Pontedera, Giulio, 406
Pontederia cordata, 11, 405–406
Populus deltoides, 24
Potamogeton, 20
Potentilla indica, 104, 105. *See also
    Duchesnea indica*
Prenanthes alba, 362–364. *See also
    Nabalus albus*
prickly pear, eastern, 237–238
prunella (common name),
    lawn, 371
Prunella (genus) *vulgaris* subsp.
    lanceolata, 370–371; *vulgaris*
    subsp. *vulgaris*, 371
Pteridium aquilinum, 27
puccoon, hairy, 221–222; hoary,
    222; red, 222
pussytoes; field, 48; Howell's,
    48; Parlin's, 47–48; plantain-
    leaved, 48
Pycnanthemum virginianum,
    155–156; *tenuifolium*, 156

Queen Anne's lace, 32, 72–73
queendevil, 217–218
Quercus, 22, 70, 400; *alba*, 25, 194;
    palustris, 22, 23; *velutina*, 25,
    26, 194

Rafinesque, Constantine, 293, 315
ragwort, balsam, 242; golden,
    241–242
ramps, 39–40
Ranunculus fascicularis, 247;
    flabellaris, 247; *hispidus* var.
    caricetorum, 247; *hispidus* var.
    hispidus, 247; *hispidus* var.
    nitidus, 246–247
Ratibida pinnata, 204, 251
rattlesnake-master, 92–94
rattlesnake root, tall white, 364;
    white, 362–364
Riddell, John L., 413, 414
rose pink, 372–373
Rudbeckia, 14; *fulgida*, 249; *hirta*,
    8, 248–249, 251; *laciniata*,
    250–251; *subtomentosa*, 249;
    triloba, 249
Rumex, 143; *crispus*, 158;
    verticillatus, 157–158

Sabatia angularis, 372–373
Sabbati, Liberato, 373
Sagittaria cuneata, 160; *latifolia*, 159–160
Sambucus, 34
sandcress, 51–52
sand reed grass, 24
Sanguinaria canadensis, 11, 27, 161–162, 222
Sanicula canadensis, 164; *marilandica*, 163–164; *odorata*, 164
Saponaria officinalis, 168, 169
Sarracenia purpurea, 20, 304–306
Sarrazin, Michael, 305, 306
Saururus cernuus, 165–166
Schizachyrium scoparium, 24
Schoenoplectus, 21
sea rocket, American, 24
sedge, 21; greater bladder, 22; northern long, 22; three-seeded, 20; tussock, 21, 22; water, 22
seedbox, 223–224
selfheal, common, 370–371
Senecio aureus, 242
Silene csereii, 168, 169; *latifolia*, 167–169; *vulgaris*, 169
Silphium, 14; *integrifolium*, 252–255; *laciniatum*, 254, 255; *perfoliatum*, 253, 255, 341; *terebinthinaceum*, 139, 254, 255
Sisyrinchium, 398; *albidum*, 398
Sium suave, 65
skunk cabbage, 8, 22, 23, 307–309
smartweed, dotted, 145–147; pale, 142–144; Pennsylvania 144; scarlet, 366, 367; stout, 147; water, 365–367
Smilacina racemosa, 122–123. *See also Maianthemum racemosum*
Smilax ornata, 53
snakeroot, white, 35–36
sneezeweed, common, 272
soapwort, 168, 169
Solanum carolinense, 170–171; *ptychanthum*, 171
Solidago, 14; *altissima*, 256–257; 259, 261; *caesia*, 258–259; *canadensis*, 244, 245, 257; *flexicaulis*, 259; *gigantea*, 257; *juncea*, 261; *nemoralis*, 24, 26, 261; *ohioensis*, 21; *racemosa* var. *gillmanii*, 261; *rigidiuscula*, 260–

261; *sempervirens*, 261; *speciosa* var. *rigidiuscula*, 260–261
Solomon's seal, smooth, 153–154
Sorghastrum nutans, 25, 26, 27
Spartina pectinata, 22
Spathiphyllum, 309
spiderwort, Ohio, 415–416; zigzag, 416
spiraea (common name), Japanese, 173
Spiraea (genus) *alba*, 172–173; *japonicus*, 173; *tomentosa*, 173
Spiranthes cernua, 175; *incurva*, 174–176; *magnicamporum*, 175, 176
spring beauty, 334–335
spurge, cypress, 207–208; flowering, 69, 99–100; leafy, 208; seaside, 24
squirrel corn, 75
St. John's-wort, common, 219–220; Fraser's marsh, 380; Kalm's, 22; spotted, 220; Virginia marsh, 379–380
Stachys, 378; *pilosa*, 377
steeplebush, 173
strawberry, Indian-, 104, 105; Virginia, 103–105
sundew, round-leaf 80; spoonleaf 78–80
sunflower, 25; common, 216; giant, 214; pale-leaved, 212; prairie, 215–216; sawtooth, 213–214; ten-petaled, 212; woodland, 211–212
swamp candles, 227–229
sweet clover, white, 124–125; yellow, 125
sweet gum, 22
Symphyotrichum, 14, 77, 91, 258, 395; *cordifolium*, 407–408; *drummondii*, 408; *dumosum*, 179; *ericoides*, 177–179; *firmum*, 410, 411; *laeve*, 410, 414; *lanceolatum*, 180–181; *lateriflorum*, 181; *laeve*, 414; *novae-angliae*, 179, 181, 408, 409–410, 414; *oolentangiense*, 412–414; *pilosum*, 179; *praealtum*, 181; *puniceum*, 21, 410, 411; *shortii*, 414; *urophyllum*, 408; × *amethystinum*, 179
Symplocarpus, 14; *foetidus*, 8, 22, 23, 307–309

tamarack, 20, 23
Teale, Edwin, 4
Tephrosia virginiana, 27, 374–375
Teucer, 377, 378
Teucrium canadense, 376–378
Thalictrum thalictroides, 82, 83
Thaspium chapmanii, 276
Thelypteris palustris, 21
thimbleweed, 41–43; tall
    thimbleweed, 43
thistle, bull, 330, 331; Canada,
    330; Pitcher's, 25, 328,
    332–333; swamp, 330, 331
Thoreau, Henry David, 134, 196,
    197, 402
Thuja occidentalis, 23
tickseed, prairie, 204; sand, 203,
    204; tall, 202–204
tick trefoil, hoary, 339; naked leaf,
    350; panicled, 339; perplexed,
    339; pointed leaf, 349–350;
    short-stalked, 339; showy,
    338–339; smooth, 339
Tilia americana, 27
toadshade, sessile, 311
touch-me-not, 281–283; pale,
    282, 283
Tradescant, John, 416
Tradescantia ohiensis, 415–416;
    subaspera, 416
Tragopogon, 14; *dubius*, 262–263;
    pratensis, 263
Triadenum fraseri, 380; *virginicum*,
    379–380
Triglochin palustris, 22
trillium (common name),
    drooping, 183; great white, 27,
    182–183
Trillium (genus) 27; *flexipes*,
    183; *grandiflorum*, 27,
    182–183; *recurvatum*, 310–311;
    sessile, 311
trout-lily, American, 205–206;
    white, 206
turtlehead, white, 62–63
twig rush, 22
twinleaf, 162
Typha, 21

Updike, John, 387
Urtica dioica subsp. *gracilis*,
    115, 116
Utricularia, 20; *cornuta*, 266; *gibba*,
    267; *purpurea*, 267; *vulgaris*,
    264–267

Vaccinium corymbosum, 20;
    macrocarpon, 20, 184–185;
    oxycoccos, 185
Venus, 418. *See also* Aphrodite
Verbascum blattaria, 269, 270;
    thapsus, 268–270
Verbena, 272; *hastata*, 417–419;
    urticifolia, 418, 419
Verbesina, 14; *alternifolia*, 271–272
Vernonia fasciculata, 421; *gigantea*,
    421; *missurica*, 420–421; ×
    illinoensis, 421
Veronicastrum virginicum, 186–187
vervain, 272; blue, 417–419;
    white, 418, 419
Viola, 11; *affinis*, 425, 426;
    canadensis, 274; *communis*,
    425; *cucullata*, 425, 426;
    missouriensis, 425, 426; *odorata*,
    426; *papilionacea*, 425; *pedata*,
    25, 422–423; *pedatifida*, 423;
    pratincola, 425; *priceana*, 425;
    pubescens var. *pubescens*, 274;
    pubescens var. *scabriuscula*,
    273–274; *sagitatta*, 425;
    septentrionalis, 425; *sororia*,
    424–426
violet, 11; arrow-leaved, 425;
    bird's foot, 25, 422–423;
    Canada, 274; common blue,
    424–426; downy yellow,
    273–274; hairy yellow, 274;
    hooded, 425, 426; LeConte's,
    425, 426; Missouri, 425, 426;
    prairie, 423; sweet, 426
Virginia snakeroot, 298
virgin's bower, 66–67
Visclosky, Pete, 5
Viscum terrestre, 228

water-hemlock, 64–65; bulblet, 65
waterleaf, Canada, 111; great, 110,
    111; Virginia, 109–111
water parsnip, hemlock, 65
water-pepper, common, 146–147;
    mild, 147
watershield, 19, 135
waterweed, common, 20
white water lily, American, 19, 20,
    134–135
whitlow-grass, 52
wild ginger, American, 297–298
wild indigo, blue, 59; white, 58–59
wild leek, 39–40; narrow-
    leaved, 40

wild quinine, 138–139
wild sarsaparilla, 53–54
wingstem, 271–272
wood sorrel, common yellow, 239–240; southern yellow, 240

yarrow, common, 31–32, 73
yellow water crowfoot, 247

yucca (common name), weak-leaf, 94
Yucca (genus) *flaccida*, 94

Zeus, 62, 377
Zingiber officinale, 298
Zizia aurea, 275–276

Nathanael Pilla is a botanist and musician residing in northwest Indiana. He fell in love with plants while living in Minneapolis and moved to Indiana to pursue a path in botany. He received his master of science in biology from Purdue University Northwest. Nathanael is an active public speaker and nature enthusiast. His written work has appeared in peer-reviewed journals, including *Proceedings of the Indiana Academy of Science*.

Scott Namestnik has a degree in botany from Miami University and serves as the Natural Heritage Program Botanist at the Indiana Department of Natural Resources–Division of Nature Preserves, where he conducts botanical inventories, assesses sites for protection consideration, and documents and monitors endangered and threatened species. He is coauthor (with Michael Homoya) of *Wildflowers of the Midwest*.